THOMAS CARLYLE

THOMAS CARLYLE

The Life and Ideas of a Prophet

by

JULIAN SYMONS

In a century or less all Europe will be republican—democratic; nothing can stop that. And they are finding their old religions, too, to be mere putrid heaps of lies.

Thomas Carlyle to
William Allingham in 1878.

BOOKS FOR LIBRARIES PRESS
FREEPORT, NEW YORK

STANDARD BOOK NUMBER:
8369-5488-2

LIBRARY OF CONGRESS CATALOG CARD NUMBER:
76-126261

PRINTED IN THE UNITED STATES OF AMERICA

ACKNOWLEDGEMENTS

MY THANKS ARE due to the Keeper of the Manuscripts in the National Library of Scotland, Mr. W. Park, for permission to inspect and use the collection of Carlyle manuscripts in the Library. I am also indebted to the Marquess of Northampton for permission to make use of the Ashburton Papers; to Mr. Henry W. Allingham and Messrs. Macmillan for permission to reprint material from *William Allingham, A diary*, edited by H. Allingham and D. Radford; to Messrs. John Lane The Bodley Head for permission to reprint material from *Carlyle's First Love*, by R. C. Archibald, *New Letters and Memorials of Jane Welsh Carlyle*, edited by Alexander Carlyle, *New Letters of Thomas Carlyle*, edited by Alexander Carlyle, *Love Letters of Thomas Carlyle and Jane Welsh*, edited by Alexander Carlyle; to Messrs. John Murray for permission to reprint extracts from *Jane Welsh Carlyle: Letters to Her Family*, edited by Leonard Huxley; and to Messrs. Kegan Paul for permission to reprint material which appeared in David Alec Wilson's biography of Carlyle.

CONTENTS

CHAPTER ONE

THE IMPERFECT TRIUMPH

> It will be difficult for the future—judging by his books,
> personal dis-sympathies, etc.,—to account for the deep
> hold this author has taken on the present age, and the
> way he has color'd its method and thought. I am certainly
> at a loss to account for it all as affecting myself. But
> there could be no view, or even partial picture, of the
> middle and latter part of our Nineteenth century, that
> did not markedly include Thomas Carlyle.
>
> WALT WHITMAN: "Carlyle from
> American Points of View."

WHEN, IN NOVEMBER 1865, Thomas Carlyle was elected
Rector of Edinburgh University, leader-writers, literary critics
and personal friends all recognized that the event had something more than a local importance. It was notable enough
that this should be the first official recognition given by
Scotland to its most famous living man of letters; but the chief
interest of the election lay undoubtedly in its social, and even
political flavour. The retiring Rector was Gladstone, and
Carlyle's opponent was Disraeli: so that when the figures were
announced:

Thomas Carlyle   657
Benjamin Disraeli 310

the result seemed a symbolic triumph for some kind of political
idealism over the materialist machinations of Disraeli, who had
been called by Carlyle at various times in the past a man
almost professedly a son of Belial, a liar, a conscious humbug, a
pinchbeck Hebrew, and a vendor of old clothes. The new
Rector had been almost as hard upon Gladstone, whom he
regarded as a man of some faculty, but ponderous and wordy,
"gone irrecoverably into House of Commons shape" and thus
"possessed by the Prince, or many Princes, of the Power of the
Air".

The triumph, then, was for the Carlyle faction: but who
belonged to the Carlyle faction, and what were its views? It
was certain, at least, that they were separated from those of

Disraelian Conservatives and Gladstonian Liberals by what Carlyle himself called abysmal chasms and immeasurabilities. Carlyle had been concerned throughout his life with problems of social action and the means of creating a harmonious community; and yet he had persistently avoided linking himself with any political group or party. That this isolated figure should have succeeded the leader of the Liberal Party, and defeated so decisively the leader of the Conservatives, was a remarkable tribute to the vague but widespread feeling of his importance in Victorian society. His popularity was recent. When, eleven years earlier, some students had nominated Carlyle for the position of Rector of Glasgow University, he had been vilified in the press, the benches of the room in which his supporters met had been broken, and he had at last withdrawn his candidature.

Among all those involved and interested in the election the person apparently least affected was Carlyle himself. In the previous year he had refused to accept the nomination against Gladstone on the ground that he was still occupied with his book about Frederick the Great. Now, after more than thirteen years' labour, that book was finished: but still, as he told the student who came to see him, there were difficulties. He was nearly seventy years old, and suffering as always from what he called dyspepsia—"weak as a sparrow", he told his brother Dr. John Carlyle, "liver and nerves deeply *wrong*". And, most important, there was the customary installation speech which, Carlyle declared, he positively could not manage. With gallant rashness the young student said that they would dispense with the speech; and on this understanding Carlyle accepted the nomination.

It became plain after the election, none the less, that an address of some kind must be delivered; and Mrs. Carlyle confidently assured friends that it would be forthcoming in good time, while Carlyle himself said that the whole affair was a bore which must be endured patiently, since certain friends had been kind enough to take trouble and interest in it. He found himself unable to adhere to the usual practice of writing a speech in advance; and an additional uncertainty about whether the speech would actually be delivered was thus added to the normal hazards of travelling, which assumed always a monstrous aspect in Carlyle's eyes. To alleviate as much as possible the agonies he must endure Carlyle arranged to break his journey to Edinburgh for a short stay with Lord Houghton, formerly Monckton Milnes, at Fryston in Yorkshire; in Edinburgh he chose from several possible hosts his old friend Thomas Erskine, whose house might, he hoped, be out of the sound of railway whistles. As the time of departure from his Chelsea home approached, Carlyle became more and more apprehensive that he would break down; and he was not noticeably cheered by the further reflection that since he was old and weak, his breakdown would signify little. His wife's attempts to keep up his spirits were somewhat marred by her fear that he might fall into a fit or drop dead with excitement. She rejected because of her own poor state of health the idea of going with him. Supposing that she should drop dead too? "Then", as she mildly observed, "there would be a scene". She contented herself with making careful preparation of everything that her husband would need. When he had last delivered lectures, more than twentyfive years earlier, he had been much assisted by occasional nips of brandy; now she gave him her own small travelling flask with a single glass of brandy in it, to be mixed and drunk before delivering the address.

On the 29th March, 1866, the scientist John Tyndall called at the Carlyles' small house in Cheyne Row. Tyndall, T. H. Huxley, and Carlyle's Edinburgh host Thomas Erskine, were to receive the honorary degree of Doctor of Laws before the new Rector's installation; and Tyndall had agreed to take charge of Carlyle on the journey. The philosopher was punctually ready. He drank a tumbler of old brown brandy and soda poured by Mrs. Carlyle. Husband and wife kissed each other goodbye. Mrs. Carlyle said to Tyndall at the door, "For God's sake send me one line by telegraph when all is over"; and the two men drove away.

John Tyndall, who looked after Carlyle on this expedition "like an adoring son", was at this time fortyfive years of age, and already a famous man. The son of an Irish shoemaker who had become a member of the newly-formed Irish Constabulary Force, Tyndall worked as an ordnance and railway surveyor before finding fully congenial employment for his talents as a practical scientist. These had first been shown when he was appointed to teach mathematics and surveying at Queenwood, the "Harmony Hall" of early Socialism; the inscription "C of M, Commencement of the Millennium" was worked into the brickwork of this experimental school, which was the first in England to adopt practical field and laboratory work in teaching applied science. From Queenwood Tyndall graduated to the poorly-paid but influential post of Professor of Natural Philosophy at the Royal Institution. A collaborator of Faraday and the intimate friend of Huxley, Tyndall was one of those wonderfully practical and penetrating men of science, with an immense range of energies and interests, who flourished in the Victorian age. His researches included experiments into the nature of magnetism, light, heat and electricity, into the cleavage of rocks and into the character of the atmosphere as a vehicle of sound; he was an ardent mountaineer and a writer of remarkable fluency, whose essays on subjects as diverse as the sabbath, the rainbow, and common water, can still be read with pleasure.

The bent of Tyndall's mind, like that of most Victorian scientists and physicists of his generation, was towards rationalist explanations of natural phenomena; and Carlyle was known to abhor all kinds of rationalism, believing that life "is a mystery which will for ever baffle us". If not an atheist, Tyndall was an agnostic, who was very dubious about the idea that God had created the world; and if there was one thing that angered Carlyle more than another it was an expression of doubt about the existence of a creator. When he heard of Huxley's saying: "In the beginning was hydrogen", he observed that "Any man who spoke thus in my presence I would request to be silent— 'No more of that stuff, sir, to me. If you persevere, I will take means, such as are in my power, to get quit of you without delay.'" It is difficult to see at first what such a mind as Tyndall's could have in common with such a mind as Carlyle's: but in expressing surprise that Tyndall should have been numbered among Carlyle's adherents we forget the attraction that certainty holds for those who doubt. The Victorian scientists, physicists and rationalist philosophers were often appalled by the cold vistas of intellectual doubt and emotional insecurity opened up by their own discoveries and theories: there were many besides Tyndall who warmed themselves at the fiery certainty of Carlyle. Even in the field of science these men respected the certainty they did not possess. When Tyndall first listened to Faraday lecturing he was powerfully impressed by the fact that the great man "taught us as one having authority and not as the Scribes", so that "you could feel his powerful spirit, as it glowed underneath his utterance and made it deep and musical". He felt the same kind of reverence, for superior wisdom rather than superior knowledge, when first reading Carlyle. Tyndall was a young man of twentythree, living in Preston, when Carlyle's *Past and Present* came into his hands: and the author's passionate plea that philanthropists should look at the wretched condition of English workers before creating model farms for Africans found an echo in the heart of one who saw around him the "hunger-stricken, pallid, yellow-coloured" weavers that Carlyle described. Tyndall found in the book "strokes of descriptive power . . . thrills of electric splendour", and above all "A morality so righteous, a radicalism so high, reasonable and humane, as to make it clear to me that without truckling to the ape and tiger of the mob, a man might hold the views of a radical".

In person Tyndall, long-nosed and alert with a fringe of side-whisker, was said to present at this time the appearance of a clean-made, tall, athletic joiner. He was very conscious of the important trust with which he had charged himself—of the necessity for delivering the philosopher in good oratorical condition, as it were, to the Edinburgh authorities—and although he wore an appearance of imperturbability his spirits must surely have sunk a little at the unhappy effect of Carlyle's first night at Fryston. Lord and Lady Houghton received the travellers kindly: but dinner was served late, there was much talk during and after it, and Tyndall was disturbed to note that a menacing multiplication of railway lines clasped Fryston like a ring. Railway whistles were active all night. When the scientist visited Carlyle next morning his worst fears were realized. The philosopher had not slept, and was wild with suffering. "I can stay no longer at Fryston", he said. "Another such night would kill me". The dutiful Tyndall gave this message to Lord Houghton, who was naturally distressed, but agreed that the travellers had better move on as soon as possible.

After drinking a bowl of strong tea and milk with an egg beaten up in it, however, Carlyle expressed regret at his own ingratitude, and fell in with Tyndall's suggestion that they should take a pair of horses and ride through the neighbouring countryside. For five hours philosopher and scientist galloped through lanes, over fields, along high-roads and past turnpike-gates where Tyndall paid the toll. This strange remedy restored Carlyle to health. On returning he put on his slippers and grey dressing-gown, filled his long churchwarden pipe, and to the surprise of the servants sat on the carpet by the hall fire and began to blow smoke up the chimney as he did at home. He ate a simple dinner at his usual time, and when argument began Tyndall quickly stopped it, saying: "We must have no more of this". When retiring for the night, to a room in which a special attempt had been made to exclude both light and sound, Carlyle said that he had no hope of sleep and would come to Tyndall's room at seven.

At seven o'clock the next morning, however, it was not Carlyle who stood outside Tyndall's door, but the watchful scientist who stood outside Carlyle's, and noted approvingly the silence within. At eight he returned, and again at nine, when he found Carlyle dressing, his face glowing with happiness. "My dear friend", he said, "I am a totally new man; I have slept nine hours without once awaking".

*   *   *   *   *

So far, comparatively, so good. But the journey from Fryston to Edinburgh caused a relapse. After a first night in Edinburgh that he described as hideous, Carlyle felt again that speaking would be impossible, and that he would break down. His distress was shared by the Principal of the University, Sir David Brewster, who was horrified to learn that Carlyle, unlike all previous Rectors, had not written a word of his address. Other Rectors had not merely written their addresses but had seen them in print before the installation ceremony; and it is likely that in addition to Brewster's fear lest Carlyle might break down he felt also a certain nervousness that, speaking extemporaneously about the academic life and the state of society, this violent Radical might say things that were positively unfit for his young audience to hear.

The Music Hall, where the ceremony was to take place, was at that time the largest public hall in Edinburgh. Its doors were besieged long before the hour of opening, and by the time that Carlyle (who had not forgotten to drink the brandy given him by his wife) and the others were waiting in the ante-room, the audience numbered more than two thousand. The care of the patient Tyndall was extended up to the last possible moment. In the ante-room he went up to Carlyle, and looking at him earnestly, asked: "How do you feel?" Carlyle merely shook his head, and Tyndall improved the occasion. "Now you have to practise what you have been preaching all your life, and prove yourself a hero". Again Carlyle shook his head. A procession was formed into the hall, Carlyle took his seat in the Rector's chair, and the ceremony began. The honorary degrees were conferred with no untoward incident other than a little hissing of Huxley. Carlyle was proclaimed as Rector. He stood up to speak, throwing off the Rector's robe as he did so to reveal his carefully-brushed old-fashioned brown morning coat.

Among those who had made a special journey to Edinburgh to hear the address was an American clergyman and associate of literary men named Moncure Conway, who has left us a pen-portrait of Carlyle at this climactic moment of his life:

> The form, stately though slender and somewhat bent, conveyed the impression of a powerful organization; the head, well curved and long, moving but rarely from side to side, then slowly; the limbs, never fidgety, buttressing, like quaint architecture, the lofty head and front of the man: these characters at once made their impression. But presently other and more subtle characteristics came out on the face and form before us, those which time and fate, thought and experience, had added to the man which nature had given them. The rugged brow, softened by the silvered hair, had its inscriptions left by the long years of meditation and of spiritual sorrow; the delicate mouth, whose satire was sympathetic, never curling the lip nor sinking to sarcasm; the blond face with its floating colours of sensibility, and the large luminous eyes—these made the outer image of Carlyle.

Such was a somewhat idealised general impression. Other witnesses noticed particular things: the low plaintive voice drowned at first by thunderous applause, which developed into his typical rich utterance with its distinctive Annandale accent; the hesitation of the first few minutes, which cleared away to leave a style beautifully natural and free; his habit of raising his left hand at the end of each section in the speech, to stroke the back of his head as he debated what to say next; the nervous movement of his fingers. And most of all those who were present noticed the reverence of the audience, as applause and laughter died away to rapt silence. Tyndall felt the crowd below him "stirred as by subterranean fire". For an hour and a half Carlyle spoke without using a single note; and when he sat down Conway thought he heard "an audible sound, as of breath long held, by all present". Then a cry of exultation rose from the students. Many were waving their arms; some pressed forward and attempted to embrace the orator; others were weeping.

After the address Carlyle came out to the door, where a carriage was waiting for him; but he decided to walk. As soon as the students learned that the Rector was among them some hundreds of them organized a procession behind him, so that eventually he was forced to take a cab. As he did so he turned and waved his hand prohibitively, so that they gave only one more cheer. "Something in the tone of *it*", he noted, "which did the first time go into my heart". Before entering the cab he gave the ragged part of the crowd a steady, compassionate look, murmuring as he did so: "Poor fellows! poor fellows!"

The faithful Tyndall, in the meantime, had rushed to the nearest telegraph office, from which he sent a three word telegram to Mrs. Carlyle: "A perfect triumph".

*   *   *   *   *

The spoken word gains much of its effect from the emotions of those who hear it. When once the speaker has warmed an audience to belief in his own sincerity, it is only a short time before exercise of the critical faculty is suspended. The individual personalities that make up the audience merge imperceptibly into the speaker's personality: and the orator of genius will have judged so happily the desires and beliefs of those who are listening to him that while leading and instructing them he will seem to be merely their voice. The greatest practitioners of the art of oratory are, no doubt, those whose sincerity is both real and assumed: who are borne away by the verbal flood which, at the same time, they can perfectly control; who share the emotions of the audience and yet can pluck with precision the right string of indignation or humour; who, speaking in the name of the intellect, appeal invariably to the emotions. Such have been the distinguishing marks of the great orators of history, from Demosthenes to Hitler: and when the warmth of a passionate voice has faded from their words, when such notable oratorical feats as Sheridan's five hour speech impeaching Warren Hastings or Gladstone's apparently interminable flow of words on his Midlothian tour are revealed in print, it is no wonder that they seem to us as tasteless as cold bread pudding. Carlyle made on this occasion a remarkably successful speech: and, like the speeches of greater orators, it does not happily survive exposure to the hard logic of the eye.

He began with an allusion to the time, fiftysix years ago, when he had first come up to Edinburgh University; and, with a passing reference to his "dear old Alma Mater", expressed his appreciation of this acknowledgement that "he had not been an unworthy labourer in the vineyard". He lived, he observed, four hundred miles away, and his health was weak; he greatly feared that there was nothing worth the least consideration that he could do in a practical way for his listeners.

Meanwhile he had to address some words to them: and although he did not think much of advice, although advice that did not end in action could well be suppressed altogether, still there was one thing he must say to them, although it had been said a thousand times before, "That above all things the interest of your whole life depends on your being *diligent*". And, warming, to the point, he advised them also to read well and carefully, to avoid cramming, to be modest, humble, and assiduous in attention to their teachers. Above all, they should work, "For work is the grand cure of all the maladies and miseries that ever beset mankind,—honest work, which you intend getting done."

He advised them, further, to the study of history, in which he observed that no man or nation ever came to very much who refused to believe in the existence of an unknown, omnipotent, all-wise and all-just Being. And this led him, by way of anecdotal glances at British history and Oliver Cromwell, to remark that pure democracy was an impossibility; that no mass of men could ever govern themselves, and that the most beneficial form of government was that of a dictator. Looking back at the days when he had been writing about Cromwell, he recalled how he had been astonished, on looking into Collins's *Peerage*, to find that in the distant past the men created peers had generally deserved their appointment.

He spoke of his own past Radicalism and of the ardent reforming spirit which, he assumed, must animate his hearers. He too was still a Radical, but no longer of a popular kind: for he thought poorly of the spread of knowledge, as it was called, by which maidservants learned much of the ologies, but little of "brewing and boiling, and baking, of obedience, modesty, humility, and moral conduct". Then he referred to the time of anarchy and disintegration in which his listeners were

growing up to be men and women. They must observe this
time, make the best of it, try to change it: endeavouring to do
right, not caring for the good things of the world, but playing
their own parts firmly and truthfully without regard for the
consequences. He ended by reciting his favourite hymn of
Goethe's:

> The Future hides in it
> Gladness and sorrow;
> We press still thorow,
> Nought that abides in it
> Daunting us,—onward.

"Work, and despair not: *Wir heissen euch hoffen*, 'We bid you
be of hope!'—let that be my last word."

Such are the bare bones of the speech that caused some
to exult and others to weep: such is oratory, without the orator.
The speech was printed in full in many newspapers, and
comment on it was almost unvaryingly friendly. A rebel had
paid his tribute to respectability; instead of sounding a trumpet
call to destruction of the old order he had expressed himself in
terms almost acceptable to an orthodox Church of England
clergyman. His contemporaries were quick to discover that he
was not merely a great influence, but also a great man; many
voices that had been raised against him were stilled for the
rest of his life.

Tenniel produced a cartoon in *Punch* showing Carlyle and
John Bright depicted as "Wisdom and Windbag". Beneath
Carlyle's gravely respectable figure was an unexceptionable
extract from the Edinburgh address; below the figure of Bright
seen haranguing a crowd, was a quotation that began "The
House of Commons is little better than a Sham and a Farce".
It seems to have occurred to nobody at the time that Carlyle
had used harsher words than these about the House of
Commons. *The Times*, in a long leader, observed that a singular
mellowness had replaced Carlyle's old fire, although "There
were the old platitudes and the old truths, and, it must be
owned, here and there the old errors". His speech was contrasted with that of Gladstone who, "bidding farewell in
flowing and ornate diction" had "overwhelmed his hearers by
his exuberance" in talking for three hours about Homer.
Carlyle had shown himself "as simple and practical as his
predecessor was dazzling and rhetorical". *The Times* concluded

pacifically that no doubt the virtues of the two men complemented each other.

It is doubtful if Carlyle found any finer pleasure in his triumph than thought of the joy it would give to his wife. During nearly forty years of marriage she had never for a moment doubted his greatness, which she now saw acknowledged everywhere. When Tyndall's telegram arrived she was dressing to go out to dinner. She tore open the telegram, read it aloud to her maids and her cousin, who was staying in the house, and then fell into a brief fit of hysterics.

That evening she dined with John Forster, the minuscule Dr. Johnson of the Victorian age, who is remembered now by his long memoir of Dickens. Wilkie Collins and Dickens were at the party, and Carlyle's health was drunk with much enthusiasm. Mrs. Carlyle delighted Dickens by giving him the subject of a novel drawn from her own observation of a house in Cheyne Row. She invented the incidents of the story, with nicely blended seriousness and humour, from such things as the condition of the house's blinds and curtains, the visitors admitted and rejected, the pieces of furniture delivered and carried away. The story, she told the fascinated Dickens, had as yet reached no conclusion: but in a few days exciting incidents were expected, and she promised to give him the dénouement when they met again. She wrote almost daily letters to her husband, recording the overwhelming impression of personal goodwill in the tributes that poured in to Cheyne Row.

Carlyle, in the meantime, was engaging in some festivities at Edinburgh. A dinner attended by various academic figures was given in his honour; at another dinner, less formal, there was a song about the theories of Carlyle's one-time friend John Stuart Mill, with the chorus:

> Stuart Mill on Mind and Matter,
> Stuart Mill on Mind and Matter,
>   Stuart Mill exerts his skill
> To make an end of Mind and Matter.

Carlyle, to the general surprise, joined in the refrain. "Stuart Mill on Mind and Matter", he chanted, waving his knife to and fro like a conductor's baton.

All this, it seemed, must be pleasant; and it appeared to

Tyndall that Carlyle found it so. Nevertheless, he soon complained to his wife that he was "like a man killed with kindness,
all the world coming tumbling on him. Do me this, see me that!
above all, dine, dine!" After four days of seeing and dining he
left Edinburgh: he did not, however, return at once to Chelsea
as he had planned, but went with his brother John and his
sister Mary to the quiet farm at Scotsbrig in Annandale which
had been his family home. There his return was further
delayed by a sprained ankle. He was delighted by the cartoon
in *Punch*, unconcerned by a frosty note of congratulation on
the address sent by Mill. "Mill", he said, "Essentially is made
of sawdust". Slowly his ankle mended. He rode about, slept
well, enjoyed the clear air and the country scene. There seemed
no particular reason to hurry his return.

Tyndall had gone back to London, where he gave Mrs.
Carlyle an account of the journey in minute detail. "It is
the event of Tyndall's life!" she remarked. He found her in
high spirits, and glowing with pride in her husband. Everywhere she went people were talking of the address; a former
mathematics master at Eton, who had a private school of his
own, delighted her by saying that the address was read aloud
to the boys. She paid a two days' visit to her friend Mrs.
Oliphant at Windsor, and when she came back arranged what
was for her a large tea party, of eleven people, for Saturday
April 21st. She expected her husband to return on the Monday
following, and wanted to get the tea party over before his
return. On Saturday he had travelled as far as Dumfries. He
had been perturbed at Scotsbrig by a strange dream, prompted
by the fact that he had not received a letter from her that day.

> I had said, it is nothing, this silence of hers; but about 1
> a.m., soon after going to bed, my first operation was a kind
> of dream; an actual introduction to the sight of you in
> bitterly bad circumstances, and I started broad awake with
> the thought, "This was her silence, then, poor soul!"

But this letter did not arrive at Cheyne Row until two
o'clock on Saturday afternoon; and Mrs. Carlyle never
received it. She never finished, either, that story for Dickens,
who thought much of it afterwards. On Saturday she went to
lunch with the Forsters, who noted that she was in exceptionally
good spirits. "Carlyle coming home the day after tomorrow",

she told them; and she was also looking forward to her tea party that afternoon. She left them at about three o'clock in her brougham. In Hyde Park she put her little dog Tiny out for a run, and a passing vehicle knocked the dog over. Mrs. Carlyle pulled the check string of her brougham and hurried out almost before it had stopped. Tiny, however, was more frightened than hurt. Mrs. Carlyle lifted him into the carriage, and told the coachman to drive on.

He did so, but after going round the Park and repassing the scene of the accident he looked back to receive further instructions. Mrs. Carlyle was sitting motionless. Her hands lay in her lap, with one palm turned up and the other down. She was dead.

CHAPTER TWO

BACKGROUND OF A PROPHET

Though genuine and coherent, "living and life-giving",
he was nevertheless but half developed. We had all to
complain that we *durst not* freely love him. His heart
seemed as if walled in; he had not the free means to
unbosom himself. My Mother has owned to me that she
could never understand him; that her affection, and
(with all their little strifes) her admiration of him was
obstructed: it seemed as if an atmosphere of Fear repelled
us from him. To me it was especially so.

THOMAS CARLYLE: *Reminiscences.*

FIFTYSIX YEARS EARLIER, on a dark, frosty November
morning, Thomas Carlyle walked with his mother and father
through the street of his home village of Ecclefechan, on the
way to Edinburgh University. Carlyle was not quite fourteen
years old and his parents, as was customary, placed him in the
charge of an older boy named Tom Smail. The two boys were
to travel by themselves the journey of nearly a hundred miles
to Edinburgh—that also was customary; and when they
arrived Smail, who was already a student at the University,
was to find lodgings for both of them.

Such a journey, formidable as it may appear to us, was
common in the Scotland of that day. Many, perhaps most, of
the country students at Edinburgh and Glasgow Universities
came from poor families. Their parents' resources were strained
to the utmost by the payment of University fees; nothing was
left over for a seat in the coach, and there was no question of a
boy's parents travelling with him. The habit of self-reliance was
engendered by necessity. The means of life—oatmeal, potatoes,
salt, butter and eggs—would be sent to the students by carrier
from home; the returning cart took with it their dirty linen to
be washed and mended. With very little money in their
purses, and a background of Scottish Puritanism ordering
their minds, they were left to find their own diversions; these
generally took the forms of sightseeing, reading and the form-
ation of debating clubs. At the end of each term the University

scholars, as they were called, walked home in local groups.

Carlyle's first journey to Edinburgh was eased by the fact that the boys obtained a lift for part of the way in the cart of a man who was taking two loads of potatoes to the city. On the third day of the journey they arrived, found a clean and cheap lodging in a poor district, ate dinner and went out to see the sights. This was the first time that Carlyle had been more than a few miles from his home. Rediscovering, long afterwards, his impressions, he found that "The novice mind was not excessively astonished all at once; but kept its eyes well open, and said nothing". He was impressed, however, by Parliament House, with its red velvet Judges sitting on little thrones with enclosures while black-gowned advocates spoke to them eagerly, and the court criers stuck high up on the walls like swallows in their nests uttered "wildly plangent lamentable kinds of sounds". He settled down quickly into the routine of learning in the large classes; Scottish Universities offered at that time no individual tuition. His figure, tall, slender and awkward, a certain uncouthness in his manner, and the rawness of his Annandale accent, were not likely to attract favourable notice; and he responded to the indifference of his teachers with an unspoken contempt of his own. Professor Leslie, who taught him mathematics, noted that he showed uncommon ability, and after a few months recommended him as a teacher in algebra or geometry; apart from this recognition, such talents as he possessed remained officially unnoticed. His conversation was remembered by a fellow student as copious and bizarre, full of sarcasm, irony and extravagance. This flow of talk was shown, however, only to intimates; in the presence of those with whom he was unacquainted, or by whom he was disregarded, Carlyle was awkwardly silent, or given to even more awkward bursts of speech.

The roots of his character were firmly embedded in the village life of Ecclefechan, and the pattern of his thought was already strongly marked by the practical and verbal precepts received from his father and mother. Carlyle's father James and his mother Margaret Aitken were both, beyond doubt, people of remarkably strong character; and Thomas learned from them rules of action and an attitude of mind that profoundly influenced the philosophy of life which was to make him famous.

James Carlyle was a mason who had built his house with

his own hands: not, indeed, to live in but for sale in the ordinary course. The prospective purchaser tried to obtain a conveyance of the house without paying for it in full, and James Carlyle, ignoring promises, threats and lawyer's letters, settled in it himself. The house was divided by a central archway, and in the two upper rooms on one side of this archway James Carlyle lived. The ground floor was let to a baker, and James's brothers lived on the other side of the arch. To this house James brought his first wife, a distant cousin with the same surname as his own. She died of fever when they had been married little more than a year, and rather more than two years later, on the 5th March, 1795, James Carlyle married Margaret Aitken, the daughter of a bankrupt farmer, who was working as a domestic servant up to the time of their marriage.

To the mason, who had gained some knowledge of arithmetic and a fine antique handwriting during the three months at school that made up his formal education, and the domestic servant who could read with difficulty and at this time could not write at all, was born in the year of their marriage, on the 4th December, a son whom they called Thomas. He was, as his mother later remarked, a "lang, sprawling, ill-put-together thing". She was afraid to wash the child in case she should hurt him, and expressed her doubt that he would live to manhood. Thomas was succeeded by eight other children, born at intervals varying from twenty months to a little more than three years. One of these children died at the age of eighteen months: the others survived to maturity, composing in their childhood a narrow family enclave bound by common beliefs and jokes, and in later years by such curious habits as that of using a code to save the expense of letter-writing, when sending newspapers through the post. Thus two strokes underlining the address indicated that the sender was well, and had no news of particular importance.

Carlyle was thirtysix years old when his father died; and within a few days he sat down and wrote a memoir designed to discover "what I have lost, and what lesson my loss was to teach me." In the memoir he recreates his father's character and his own childhood with the strange power of giving actuality to the past that was one of his most distinctive marks as a writer. In one vivid phrase he uncovers the reality of their home life: "An inflexible element of Authority encircled us all".

Respect for authority, adherence to a strict, fanatical Protestantism and a furious hastiness of temper were the chief characteristics of the Carlyle family as far as their careers can certainly be traced, which is no further than the second generation from Thomas. Beyond that a line of descent goes dubiously back to Sir John Carlyle, created Lord Carlyle of Torthorwald in the time of the Bruces. The link between the noble Carlyles and Thomas is tenuous, and to James Carlyle was probably unknown.

James Carlyle's own fiery father was also a Thomas; he had been in his time an adventurous, vehement and passionate man who, after collecting money to pay his half-year's rent, troubled himself little with the welfare of his wife and six children, who were always poor and often hungry. In the childhood of young Thomas his grandfather, already almost a legend, lived on in Ecclefechan supported by his sons. Even more nearly legendary was Grand-uncle Francis, a great drinker and gamer, who had become a seaman, and helped to put down a mutiny on his first trip. Between Grandfather Thomas and Grand-uncle Francis there was some unrecorded cause of bitter dissension: but when Francis, a sea captain retired on half pay, learned that his brother was probably on his death bed he came in a cart to Ecclefechan, and little Thomas saw him for the first and only time. He remembered a man grim, broad and almost terrible, who had to be carried up the steep stairs because he was unable to walk. For twenty minutes the two brothers talked; then the chair descended again, and Francis was borne away.

From his father James Carlyle took a fierce and independent temper. In his youth he had been one of a band known as the fighting masons of Ecclefechan, who joined together to defend themselves against the gangs of Irish and other vagabonds who ravaged the surrounding countryside. James Carlyle and his brothers, known as the most diligent workmen in the neighbourhood, were known also as men with whom it was dangerous to meddle. But all this was long past in Thomas Carlyle's childhood, for by that time his father had become a member of a religious sect known as the Burghers, who had seceded from the Established Church of Scotland on the ground of its laxity. It is not likely that James Carlyle became more abstemious or frugal than he had been in the hard, hungry days of youth, or that his conversion much strengthened the passionate Puritanism which had prompted him while in his teens to throw a pack of playing cards upon the fire: but certainly the force of religious belief made him regret the physical violence of his early years. With his own children he was not loving or gentle, but he was strictly just; and his hand was never raised to strike them in anger.

As the eldest child in a large family Thomas Carlyle felt the full force of the rule exerted by his father. There is no evidence that he ever rebelled against this authority, or at the time thought it other than natural; but in the memoir that he wrote after his father's death he shows full realization that certain elements in his own nature had been suppressed in childhood. There were few games, and little spontaneous mirth, in the Carlyle home, and neither Margaret Carlyle nor the children were encouraged to chatter, for James Carlyle "absolutely would and could not hear" idle conversation, "but abruptly turned aside from it, or if that might not suit, with the besom of destruction swept it far away from him." The besom of destruction was contained in the particular intonation he gave to such a simple phrase as "I don't believe thee", or even his "tongue-paralysing, cold, indifferent 'Hah'". He was, however, a copious talker on ideas or matters of fact that interested him. Then his speech was brief, energetic, full of potent words accurately used, and of surprising rich peasant metaphors ("He was like a fly wading among tar", he said of a bad preacher). In anger, his son remembered, "his words were like sharp arrows that smote into the very heart".

Among Carlyle's recollections of his father one small incident stands out by its ocular vividness, its psychological implications, and by the fact that it is the only occasion on which the child felt that his father was spontaneously kind:

I can remember his carrying me across Main Water, over a pool some few yards below where the present Mainfoot Bridge stands. Perhaps I was in my fifth year. He was going to Luce I think to ask after some Joiner. It was the loveliest summer evening I recollect. My memory dawns (or grows light) at the first aspect of the stream, of the pool spanned by a wooden bow, without railing, and a single plank board. He lifted me against his thighs with his right hand, and walked careless along till we were over. My face was turned rather downwards, I looked into the clear deep water, and its reflected skies, with terror yet with confidence that he would save me. Directly after, I, light of heart, asked of him what these "little black things" were that I seemed sometimes to *create* by rubbing the palms of my hands together, and can at this moment (the mind having been doubtless excited by the past peril) remember that I described them in these words: "Like penny-rows" (rolls) "but far less". He explained it wholly to me: "my hands were not *clean*." He was very kind, and I loved him.

At about this time James Carlyle began to teach his son the principles of arithmetic, and soon afterwards sent him first to the village school, and then to a school at Hoddam, a mile away. This was the usual limit of village education; but after much heart-searching James Carlyle decided to extend it by sending his eldest son to a new Academy at Annan, six miles distant. This step, taken when the boy was ten years old, was a decisive one, for he stayed with an aunt from Monday to Friday each week, and so was cut off from the family life at home. His mother seems to have had no voice in reaching this decision: but she extracted from him a promise that under no circumstances would he fight with another boy.

The child who thus left home was not well equipped to fend for himself among schoolboys. From much listening to his father and his friends, as they sat discussing religion or the state of the world, he had learned to talk like a man; this, together with the habit of forceful expression taken from his father, made him appear both bitter and conceited. His case is far removed from that of the rejected aesthete of a later generation who has become familiar to us through many school stories, for Thomas Carlyle was not at all contemptuous of bodily sports, or averse from vigorous exercise. But he was possessed from an early age by the tiger of pride, and there can be little doubt that he asked not to be accepted as an equal but to be respected as a superior by his fellow schoolboys at Annan. The ruthlessness with which they destroyed this dream left a permanent mark in Carlyle's heart.

In an uncompleted story called *The Romance of Wotton Reinfred*, the first serious creative work Carlyle attempted, Wotton while at school imagines himself in the future as "by turns a hero and a sage, in both provinces the benefactor and wonder of the world". His progress at school was, we are told, "the boast of the teachers", and he would have been a universal favourite in any community less selfish and tyrannical than that of the schoolboys who jeered at and tortured him. The theme is elaborated in *Sartor Resartus*, which describes the persecution endured by the hero at the Hinterschlag (Smite-bottom) Gymnasium from those boys who "obeyed the impulse of rude Nature, which bids the deerherd fall upon any stricken hart, the duck-flock put to death any broken-winged brother or sister." And *Sartor*, Carlyle remarked in a note on his early life, did not tell half the truth of what he had suffered at the hands of the "coarse unguided tyrannous cubs" who were his schoolfellows. For a long time he obeyed his mother's injunction not to fight, but at last took off his clog and struck with it a big boy who was tormenting him. His determination to fight back changed the persecution of his schoolfellows to an attitude of, as it were, armed hostility. He was respected: but nothing could make his schoolfellows like a boy who, according to the testimony offered by one of them long afterwards, "was aye saying bitter, jibbing things".

He learned at Annan to read Latin and French with fluency, and became proficient also in geometry, algebra and arithmetic. But probably the most important element in his education in these five days of the week when he longed for Friday and his return home was the circulating library of a cooper named John Maconachie. From this library Carlyle borrowed the works of Smollett, and Robertson's history of Charles the Fifth, by both of which he was profoundly impressed; and he found other books from which he worked out mathematical conundrums. He was recognized as a good, and what was more remarkable as an eager, scholar; but the years at Annan did not change him in any essential respect. He went there a raw, clumsy, dogmatic young boy, in desperate earnest about everything he said and did; he left Annan no less raw and clumsy, with a thin, easily-broken crust of silence now covering his natural extravagance of speech and feeling.

* * * * *

The early years of Thomas Carlyle lend themselves obviously enough to interpretation in terms of psychoanalysis: and, in fact, such an interpretation has been attempted recently in the form of a "psychosomatic biography", in which Carlyle's later career is analysed in terms of the "anal sadism" developed in his childhood. Such an analysis has its own dogmatism, since it rests on the medical interpretation, asserted with all the certainty of holy writ, of certain events in Carlyle's childhood, and the unexplained neglect of others. The passage in which Carlyle describes his father's carriage of him over a stream, for instance, is certainly a strangely exact feat of memory (or memory plus unconscious invention), with a strong under-tone of physical feeling in it; and yet, to the layman, it seems hardly to justify the psychiatric interpretation that the "little black things" were "possibly the equivalent of the precious faeces", or even that the incident represented an "anal sadistic attack on the father". It may be true, also, that Carlyle's acts and writings were characterized by a compulsive anal sadism: but this interpretation must seem to us less valuable when we learn from the same authority that anal sadism is widespread in the world today, and is perfectly manifested in, for example, the liquidation of political opponents. To charac-terize a man by a compulsion apparently so common is hardly to characterize him at all. There are—if we can believe Carlyle's psychiatric interpreter—hundreds of thousands of anal sadists in the world today: but they do not write or think like Carlyle.

Bating these dubious rigidities of dogma, there is no doubt that in a sense psychiatrists would consider superficial, Carlyle's relation to his parents profoundly affected his character. The awe and respect in which Carlyle held his father did not proceed from any particular parental harshness: on the contrary, this frugal, puritanical man behaved with con-sideration and generosity towards his eldest son. It was un-common in those days for the son of a Scottish working man to carry on his education up to the age of nineteen without need for concern about earning money, and Carlyle was able to do so only because his father made sacrifices to keep him at the University. When, in his early twenties, the young man shifted uncomfortably from one occupation to another, the father never reproached his son for a vacillation utterly remote from his own temperament: this irascible and choleric man recognized and respected some remarkable merit in his son long before it was manifested in any outward form to the world. The few letters from father to son that have been preserved are written with an almost open acknowledgement of the son's superior attainments.

The factor in James Carlyle's character that at once alienated his son's emotional sympathy and earned his deepest respect, was the acceptance by James of many dogmas that Thomas, at an early age, began reluctantly to question. His father, Thomas Carlyle observed, was never visited with doubt. He believed without question in the literal truth of the Bible; he believed literally in a Hell where sinners should burn eternally. And, absorbed in the delights and terrors of worship ("His Reverence . . . was considerably mixed with Fear", wrote his son), he had no fear to spare for the troubles of everyday. The son noticed, approved, and tried to emulate his father's indifference to public opinion, his disinterest in money, his contempt for trivialities of speech and conduct, his silence about "what was disagreeable and past". But from his early teens he began to question the literal truth of many things recorded in the Bible.

It is not likely that Carlyle expressed what he thought to the father of whom he stood so much in awe: but no such barriers existed between the boy and his mother. Margaret Carlyle's belief was much gentler in expression than her husband's, but it was equally profound: and she was deeply shocked when one day her son asked ironically, "Did God Almighty come down and make wheelbarrows in a shop?" When later he questioned the symbolical significance of the Song of Solomon she was so much distressed that afterwards he kept silent about his doubts, and read the *Evidences of Christianity* in the hope of stilling them. The simple piety of Margaret Carlyle had been shocked by the glimpse given her of the thoughts moving in the mind of her much-loved eldest son: and he was for her ever afterwards a strayed sheep who might be recalled to the flock by constant admonitions, dutifully given in all her letters, to read every day a chapter from the Bible.

The influences at work on the mind of the youthful Carlyle were, then, a reverence for his father's person, habits and mode of life combined with a doubt, which in time became definite rejection, of the unquestioning faith upon which the revered way of life had been built. Can there be works without faith? Works, that is, of precisely the same kind as those achieved when faith is the mainspring of action? For the rest of Carlyle's life a war was to be waged, with varying intensity at different times, between the keen iconoclasm of his intellect and his emotional need for a faith which should comprehend the faith of his father. If the intellect destroyed accepted shibboleths, its verdict must be accepted: but destruction alone could never be good. Carlyle needed a prophetic gospel to still the doubts about the nature of God and society that his intellect had first revealed: and since he found all other prophets unacceptable, he enunciated the gospel himself. But the only completely successful prophets are those who are, as their followers say, inspired; or, as disbelievers put it, insane. In Carlyle the gift of prophecy wrestled always with a keen intellect, now winning and now losing a fall: for the passionate force with which this prophet was to speak sprang not from the strength of his belief but from his psychological need to emulate his father, and his intellectual difficulty in doing so. Such was the background of his lifelong struggle to expel with the magic of dogma the hydra-headed monster of doubt.

CHAPTER THREE

THE DOMINIE

> The hungry young (at the University) looked up to their
> spiritual nurses, and for food were bidden eat the east
> wind. What vain jargon of controversial metaphysics, ety-
> mology, and mechanical manipulation falsely named
> Science was current there, I indeed learnt better than
> most. Among eleven hundred Christian youths there will
> not be wanting some eleven eager to learn. By collision
> with such, a certain warmth, a certain polish was com-
> municated; by instinct and by happy accident I took
> less to rioting than to thinking and reading, which latter
> also I was free to do. Nay, from the Chaos of that library I
> succeeded in fishing up more books than had been known
> by the keeper thereof. The foundation of a literary life
> was hereby laid. I learned on my own strength to read
> fluently in almost all cultivated languages, on almost all
> subjects and sciences. A certain ground-plan of human
> nature and life began to fashion itself in me, by additional
> experiments to be corrected and indefinitely extended.
>
> THOMAS CARLYLE: *Sartor Resartus.*

AFTER WHAT HAS been said about the growth of doubt
in Carlyle's mind about the verities of Christianity, it may
seem odd that he should have accepted without apparent
reluctance the idea that he should enter the ministry. But when
the biographer analyses, with superior hindsight, the course of a
man's life he renders with deceptive clarity actions and motives
that were at the time of action deeply confused.

Among the forces that pressed Carlyle to acceptance of the
ministry as a vocation were the eagerness of his parents that he
should be a preacher; the hard fact that few occupations were
open in Scotland at this time to the son of a working man who
did not wish to follow his father's pursuits; and, strongest of all
perhaps, the young man's own uncertainty of any occupation
for which he might be perfectly suited. At the age of eighteen
he wrote at the end of a book of Greek prose his hope that "With
a heart of independence, unseduced by the world's smiles,
and unbending to its frowns, I may attain to literary fame. And
though starvation be my lot I will smile that I have not been

born a king!!!" These brave words were backed by no attempt
to write: they were rather a gesture of defiance designed to still
the fears, expressed by the young man in letters to his friends,
that he had no talent for literature. These friends, the eleven
out of eleven hundred as Carlyle called them later in *Sartor
Resartus*, were few but staunch. They were, like Carlyle himself,
the sons of working men. Like Carlyle again, they saw no
opening for themselves in life outside the ministry or school-
teaching; but unlike him they looked for nothing more and,
when the vague aspirations of youth had vanished, settled
down contentedly to their obvious lot in life. Carlyle's principal
friends and correspondents among these serious, virtuous and
priggish young men were Robert Mitchell, who was intended
for the ministry but became a schoolmaster, another future
schoolmaster named James Johnstone, and Thomas Murray
who in later years found relaxation from his occupation as a
minister in writing the history of his native county of Galloway.

Among these mild talents the light of Carlyle's conversation
shone brightly. One of his correspondents addressed him as
Jonathan or Doctor, in joking reference to Swift, while others
called him Parson; all recognized the force of his character and
intellect. But outside this small circle Carlyle was denied,
throughout his years at Edinburgh University, the success
which his talents deserved. His gangling awkwardness excited
some ridicule among fellow-students, and both students and
professors disliked his self-assertiveness. Carlyle showed openly
his contempt for the finicky delivery of Professor Brown who
taught Moral Philosophy; he sat grimly with notebook ready
when he was the sole student in the Natural Philosophy class
of Professor Playfair; only when learning mathematics from
odd, slovenly Professor Leslie, who in the hope of gaining a
young wife had dyed his hair a youthful black, among which
showed undesired streaks of pink and green, did the young
student feel himself welcomed and appreciated.

It was John Leslie who, about a year after Carlyle had left
the University, gave him a letter of recommendation for the
post of teacher of mathematics at Annan Academy. Carlyle was
interviewed, approved, and obtained the post which carried
with it a salary of £60 or £70 a year—a small enough sum,
but one which meant that he was no longer a financial burden
on his father, who was already considering the possibility of
sending his son John to Edinburgh. Carlyle disliked teaching at

B

Annan almost as much as he had disliked being a pupil there: and he soon decided that he disliked, not merely teaching at Annan, but teaching of any kind. He taught conscientiously, nevertheless, and was not disliked by his pupils; and he showed an eccentricity not much approved by his seniors in his neglect of the strap as a means of correction. There were other, and more considerable, reasons for disapproving of the young teacher. He refused almost all invitations from local society and visited instead a local minister named Henry Duncan, who was looked upon doubtfully because of the unorthodox evangelical- ism of his ideas and his acknowledgement of a debt to the Quakers. At Annan as at Edinburgh, Carlyle added to his un- popularity by the sarcastic violence with which he responded to attempts by his elders to show the young man his properly subordinate position in local academic society. In front of an awe-struck class he replied to a senior teacher who had con- temptuously asked him for a definition of virtue with the words: "Sir, if you have no notion of virtue within your own breast, I despair of ever communicating to you any adequate conception of it."

*   *   *   *   *

From the trials of life at Annan Carlyle found relief in the society of his family, in reading and in letters to his friends. James Carlyle had moved when his eldest son was two years old from the house in Ecclefechan to a small double cottage in the district, described in *Sartor Resartus* as "a roomy painted cottage, embowered in fruit-trees and forest-trees, evergreens and honeysuckles; rising many-coloured from amid shaven grass-plots, flowers struggling-in through the very windows". Then in 1815 James Carlyle, finding that his business as a mason was declining, took a lease of a farm on the main road two miles north-west of Ecclefechan. This farm, called Mainhill, now became the family home. Its situation was high, bleak, treeless, utterly exposed to the wind: remote enough from the pleasant double cottage with its flowers and fruit trees. There were stables, cow-byres, a washhouse and a dairy. The house was a long, low whitewashed cottage of one story, which contained as living quarters a kitchen and two bedrooms, one large and one small. In these three rooms James and Margaret Carlyle lived with the seven children who were at this time still at home. We have no details of how this large family lived and slept, here and in their earlier homes, in three rooms: but presumably the small bedroom was occupied by the parents and the small children, and the large room by the others.

On one weekend Thomas volunteered to sit by the bedside of his uncle, who had come to Mainhill to be nursed by Mrs. Carlyle. During the night the sick man died, and Carlyle remembered the bright blue eyes that "kept wide open until the life went out of them about three in the morning". Long afterwards he was asked if he had any kind of orthodox belief in his mind at that time, and answered that he had given up such belief long before, although he said nothing about it: but that was perhaps a deceit of memory, for at this time Carlyle was still formally a rural Divinity student, who had three years to pass in preparation before he finally decided whether or not to enter the ministry. In the letters he exchanged with Robert Mitchell, however, there is plainly no warmth in either young man for his future vocation. Christianity, Carlyle reminded his friend, was itself "only supported by probabilities; very strong ones certainly, but still only probabilities". He felt no reluctance to prepare the trial discourse required of apprentice preachers by Divinity Hall in Edinburgh, and the sermon he delivered on "The Uses of Affliction" won much approval from the Professors. At the same time the course of his reading was enlarging his scepticism. In a letter written to Mitchell on his first arrival at Annan he spoke, as one apprentice preacher to another, of the bigoted scepticism of David Hume and his blind prejudice in favour of infidelity: but within a few months he was confessing his admiration for the philosopher who maintained errors with so much ingenuity that one would be sorry to see him dislodged. And he went on to consider, with a heretical ingenuity of his own, the origin of character in physical circumstances rather than in moral causation.

The extent and nature of Carlyle's reading, during his student years and afterwards, was indeed almost incompatible with the simple life and beliefs of a minister. His sympathies ranged from Shakespeare (a writer unnamed by his teachers in Edinburgh, and regarded even by Hume as a barbarous genius lacking in taste and learning) to such a book as Franklin's *Treatise on Electricity*, which was one of the many little-read quarto volumes that he found in the college library. In the early parts of the correspondence with Mitchell Carlyle is reading Bossuet's *History of Mathematics*, and arguing with his friend over mathematical problems. Within the space of a few months we find him reading Wood's *Optics*, *Evaid* and Newton's *Principia*; Cicero, and Lucan, Voltaire and Fenelon; a good deal of idealist philosophy including the Scotch philosopher Dugald Stewart; and a large number of modern writers from Byron and Scott to the lady novelists of that day. Against such a background, "wrestling with lexicons, chemical experiments, Scotch philosophy and Berkeleian Metaphysics", he prepared his second discourse for Divinity Hall, an exegesis in Latin upon "Natural Religion". This too he delivered successfully: but he lacked the company of Mitchell, who had come with him when the first discourse was delivered. Mitchell had made up his mind not to enter the ministry, and Carlyle was unable to persuade him to visit Edinburgh.

Behind the religious doubt and the thirst for all kinds of knowledge that marked Carlyle at this time, there was also an eagerness to attempt creative work under the stimulus of a friendly eye which is both comic and pathetic. He took up with enthusiasm a plan proposed by Mitchell that they should exchange essays with each other. "We need be at no loss for subjects", he wrote. "Literary, metaphysical, mathematical, and physical are all before us". It would be an excellent way to spend the summer, "and you who are the *projector* will surely never draw back from what you yourself proposed, and therefore *will not fail* to send me your production the very next opportunity." But alas, this proposal for prolonged intellectual correspondence was entertained seriously on one side only: and although Carlyle tempted his friend with the news that he had on hand an explanation of the rainbow, and strove to stimulate his interest by exposing the errors of John Hamilton Moore, author of a book called *Practical Navigation*, who believed that "the attraction of a boat to a ship, or a ship to a rock, is caused by *gravitation*" instead of by capillary attraction, the sluggish Mitchell made only rare response.

Carlyle remained at Annan for nearly two years, stuck in a mire of intellectual discontent from which he was rescued by the friendly Professor Leslie, who remembered his former pupil when he was asked to recommend a classical and mathematical master for the Burgh School of Kirkcaldy. Carlyle was seen, and again approved: "There are few young men of his standing who have directed their studies to greater variety of objects, or have acquired a more extensive range of knowledge", the interviewer reported to the Council. He left Annan for Kirkcaldy, and so began the richest and most satisfying intellectual friendship of his life.

* * * * *

A long time before Carlyle went to Kirkcaldy, at a time near the end of his miserable schooldays at Annan, a young man entered the big, airy classroom. A native of Annan and formerly a scholar at the Academy, he was known at least by repute to most of the boys: for sixteen year old Edward Irving, who had for the past three years been a student at Edinburgh University, had a man's assurance and dignity, and spoke to the hard old English master Adam Hope as to an equal. The appearance of this tall, swarthy young man, his black coat and tight pantaloons worn in the fashion of the day, caught Carlyle's attention; and a slight preciosity in the pronouncia-tion of certain words (as it seemed to an ear which had then heard no dialect but that of Annan) was also noticed. This straight, handsome, singularly mature young man who stood chatting so easily to Adam Hope about the great world of Edinburgh seemed to the schoolboy altogether enviable. Or almost altogether: for the impressive effect of Irving's appear-ance was marred by a glaring squint, which gave a sinister look to a countenance otherwise frank and open. Such was Carlyle's first view of the man who, he said at the end of Irving's strange and tragic career, was "the freest, brotherliest, bravest human soul mine ever came in contact with . . . the best man I have ever, after trial enough, found in this world, or now hope to find."

The first meeting between the two was delayed for another seven years, and when it came was unpromising enough. In the interval Carlyle had heard much of Irving: of the distinc-tion he had shown in his studies, of his great success as a teacher, first at Haddington and then at Kirkcaldy. Irving had, more-over, joyously and easily passed through the trials of Divinity Hall, and had begun to preach. An incident that took place during his first sermon shows the young man's self-possession, and gives a hint also of the quality that made some stay away from his sermons because they felt that he showed too much grandeur. In the full flow of delivering his sermon, Irving tilted the Bible in front of him, and the manuscript from which he had been reading fluttered to the floor. The preacher bent his great height down over the pulpit, picked up the manuscript, stuffed it into a pocket, and went on talking as fluently as he had previously been reading. The gesture was immediately successful; and yet there was something in the ease with which it was done that was not altogether approved.

Such slight shades upon Irving's youthful fame were, however, hardly known to Carlyle; and when, after delivering the exegesis on "Natural Religion" which, he had written to Mitchell, "in the mind's eye seems vile, and in the nostrils smells horrible", he met Irving in Edinburgh at the house of a cousin, it was with a preconceived mistrust of the other's self-assurance. When Irving, who was at this time living in Kirk-caldy, subjected him to a battery of questions about social and domestic affairs in Annan, he felt both conspicuous and unhappy; for it was precisely in the social life of Annan that he had refused to mix. Carlyle was quick to notice, too, the air of "conscious unquestionable superiority, of careless natural *de haut en bas*", which had fretted some churchgoers in Kirk-caldy. His answers to questions about marriages and babies became shorter and shorter, and when at last he answered two or three questions in succession with a simple "I don't know", Irving said in a "gruffish yet not ill-natured tone", "You seem to know nothing". Carlyle's reply is typical of the bursts of sharp and ill-considered speech that punctuated his awkward silences: "Sir, by what right do you try my knowledge in this way? Are you grand inquisitor, or have you authority to question people, and cross-question, at discretion? I have had no interest to inform myself about the births in Annan, and care not if the process of birth and generation there should cease and determine altogether!" Carlyle, blaming himself years afterwards for his part in this passage of words, contrasted the joyous swagger in Irving's manner at this time with his own total lack of natural vivacity. "Not sanguine and diffusive, he; but biliary and intense."

Such was the past: now we return to the present and to Kirkcaldy, where Carlyle was going as, of all things, Irving's rival. Irving's teaching success in the village of Haddington had not been altogether repeated in this town, where he had been appointed master of a new school patronized by professional people and well-to-do shopkeepers, who wished to give their children a better education than that offered by the parish school. Perhaps some of the shopkeepers felt distrust of a dominie who appeared in a tartan morning coat wherein red was the predominating colour; certainly they disliked his unorthodox methods of teaching astronomy and surveying by field work, and very many resented the severity with which he beat his pupils. After Irving had been at Kirkcaldy for three years a number of his patrons decided to reorganize the parish school, appoint a new and livelier teacher, and send their children to him. This was the background of Carlyle's appointment.

The second meeting of the young men could hardly have taken place under less auspicious signs: and yet when Irving met his rival by chance one day in Annan, after Carlyle had been appointed but before he had taken up office, the "biliary and intense" schoolmaster was given an almost brotherly welcome. Two Annandale people, Irving said, must not be strangers in Fife. His house and everything in it was free to Carlyle's use. Carlyle still felt some doubts of his reception; they were finally dispelled when in Kirkcaldy Irving took him into the room containing the "rough, littery, but considerable collection" of books that made up his library, flung out his arms and said: "Upon all these you have will and waygate".

The friendship thus begun continued without a breath of dissension upon either side, until Irving's death. Carlyle found in him what he had searched for vainly in Mitchell and other friends; a man prepared to talk endlessly on philosophical, mathematical and ethical problems. He found in addition a spirit for reforming the world as keen as his own, a wholehearted religious faith that he admired, and a joyful exuberance in the physical aspects of life that delighted him. And what did Irving find in Carlyle? Beneath the surface brashness and awkwardness he must have discerned a churning energy still uncertain of its purpose, and a breadth of knowledge and understanding, vague in outline, but impressive in its latent power.

The two young men strolled on summer evenings along the mile-long Kirkcaldy sands and talked against the background of the sea, "one long wave coming on, gently, steadily, and breaking in gradual *explosion*, accurately gradual, with harmless melodious *white*, at your hand all the way (the *break* of it, rushing along like a mane of foam, beautifully sounding and advancing, ran from south to north, from West-burn to Kirkcaldy Harbour, through the whole mile's distance)".

They thought little of walking thirty miles a day at weekends to see a trigonometrical survey on the Lomond Hills; and here Carlyle saw with the most pleasant envy how the warm courtesy of his friend persuaded the man in charge, at first coldly mono-syllabic, to ask them into his tent where they looked through his theodolite at the signal column on top of Ben Lomond sixty miles away. They undertook, with Irving's assistant, a voyage to the remote small island of Inchkeith one afternoon, in a small rowboat; there they looked at the lighthouse, its keeper ("the most life-weary looking mortal I ever saw", thought Carlyle), and his wife and children. They returned to Kirkcaldy, five miles away, at night with the tide running against them, and found friends in much anxiety about their safety. At vacation time they went on a walking tour to the Trossachs with two other schoolmasters, and home to Annan by Loch Lomond, Greenock and Glasgow: in Carlyle's richly evocative remin-iscences of this and another tour, the long walks by daylight, the clean coarse beds, the simple people with their legends and half-mythical recollections, Irving plays always the principal part. He was acknowledged as the captain of any such ex-pedition; he knew the country and the people and was always at home, whether skilfully persuading shepherds with whom they lodged to reach into their stores of local anecdote and memory, or standing cudgel in hand, gigantic in breadth and height, ready to defend the party against threatened assault by gypsies.

On Sundays Carlyle listened often to the free and flowing eloquence of Irving's probationer sermons, and was impressed by the strength, clearness and melody of his voice, and by the "Old English Puritan style" of his diction, which influenced Carlyle's own use of words. The passion and rashness of Irving's preaching, the "trifle of unconscious playactorism" evident in such incidents as that of the dropped manuscript, continued to give offence; and once in Kirkcaldy Kirk the door of a pew in front of Carlyle suddenly opened and a middle-aged little man bolted out of it and strode from the church in fury.

The influence exerted by Irving on Carlyle was very great in all spheres except that of religion. Irving, emerging from a background very similar to Carlyle's (his father was a tanner who, like James Carlyle, dealt austerely with his children) had accepted from early adolescence his vocation for the

ministry; and Carlyle's hinted scepticism must have appeared
extraordinary to him. Both the young men were interested in
social questions; and both adhered to a vague but strongly-
held Radicalism, although their feelings were no more precise
than to give them a general sympathy for the oppressed workers
and peasants.

In the aftermath of the Napoleonic wars the Scottish
weavers and cotton-spinners suffered want and in many cases
starvation, and Irving as he went among them wrote to his
brother-in-law: "If I should report from my daily ministrations
among the poorest class and the worst reported-of class of our
population, I should deliver an opinion so favourable as it
would hardly be safe for myself to deliver, lest I should be
held a *radical* likewise." Carlyle, in Edinburgh at the same
time, saw the departure of the Lothian Yeomanry for Glasgow,
and the strange and menacing shout of the crowd that watched
them. He noted with bitter anger the old powdered gentlemen
in silver spectacles talking exultantly about "Cordon of troops,
sir", and when told by an acquaintance who was hurrying
along, musket in hand, for training as a gentleman volunteer,
that he also should have a musket, replied ironically that he
was not sure on which side to use it.

But Irving, Carlyle, and the many who felt with them
(Carlyle's father, even, held to a kind of Radicalism in his
later years, seeing that the lot of a poor man was growing worse
with every season, and believing that mighty changes must be
on the way since the world could not last as it was) had no
political feeling in any sense easily understood by the twentieth
century. Their sympathy was not logical, but emotional: put
in logical terms, it would amount simply to a complaint that
the weavers had been governed badly, whereas they deserved
to be governed well. The idea, to which almost all modern
adherents to Socialism and Communism are at least theoretic-
ally committed, that less government is a good thing in itself,
did not even occur to them. Irving's attitude to the great
changes that, the young men agreed, were impending in the
world, was less complicated than Carlyle's: for, accepting un-
hesitantly his lot as a preacher, he was concerned simply to
interpret the wishes of Almighty God in relation to such
changes. But what did Carlyle believe? The vast extent of his
reading, which he carried on at Kirkcaldy, had convinced
him only of his unfitness for the church, and he failed to attend

Divinity Hall to enrol for a third year. He seems to have made no specific statement abandoning the church, but the fact that he had done so soon became known to his family. His father and mother must have been sincerely grieved, but both of them accepted his decision without a word of question or remark.

Carlyle found teaching at Kirkcaldy little more agreeable than teaching at Annan. Here also he was notable for the fact that, unlike Irving, he was able to keep order without beating; on the other hand he lacked Irving's capacity for inspiring love in his pupils. His large glowing eyes were commonly scornful, his scowl hushed the whole school, and the grinding of his teeth as he uttered the words "dunce" and "blockhead" terrified his pupils more than a beating. Carlyle was aware that teaching, like preaching, was not his proper work: "I continue to teach", he wrote to Robert Mitchell, "with about as much satisfaction as I should beat hemp, if such were my vocation". He found refuge, as always, in voracious reading. He read Gibbon at the rate of a volume a day, "alternately delighted and offended by the gorgeous colouring with which his fancy invests the rude and scanty materials of his narrative; sometimes fatigued by the learning of his notes, occasionally amused by their liveliness, frequently disgusted by their obscenity, and admiring or deploring the bitterness of his skilful irony".

Now, in his early twenties, he had no idea of what he wanted to do in the world; the pawky innocence of his prolonged adolescence is visible in the letters written to his friends and his family. The letters often turn into stiff, awkward little lectures on literature or mathematics, through which Carlyle's longing for intellectual companionship and for the capacity to express himself with the clarity and ease of his friend Irving can easily be seen. His relations with Mainhill were maintained chiefly by correspondence, for he was able to visit his family only in vacations. He tried to convey in his letters a contentment that he did not feel, and he often sent a present of a scarf or a shawl to his mother. Her state of health gave him anxiety; for during the change of life Mrs. Carlyle had temporarily lost her senses. She was sent for a time to a farm near Dumfries where she surprised the farmer's wife by escaping from her room, mounting an unsaddled horse and riding it round a field. After she recovered Mrs. Carlyle continued to send her son letters, in her recently-achieved handwriting, expressing equally anxiety about the state of his clothing and the state of his soul. "Oh Tom mind the golden season of youth and remember the creator in the days of your youth. Seek God while He may be found. Call upon Him while He is near. We hear that the world by wisdom knew not God. Pray for His presence with you and His counsel to guide you. Have you got through the Bible yet? If you have, read it again."

To such exhortations Carlyle returned evasive answers, and behind the attempted ease of his letters home his parents caught glimpses of deep gloom and dissatisfaction. They must have been more distressed than surprised when, on returning to school after the summer vacation of 1818 he wrote to his father that his prospects as a schoolmaster in Kirkcaldy were not good (a third teacher had set up there, and had taken a number of pupils from both Irving and Carlyle). Moreover, he was "very much tired of the trade"; Irving was going away to Edinburgh, so that he would have no friend in Kirkcaldy; and "in short, I only wait for your advice, till I give in my resignation against December". He received a reply to the effect that his father was unable to give him any advice, and that he might do what seemed to him good. Carlyle recorded later on that his father inwardly disapproved of the step as imprudent, but had the forbearance to say nothing. His mother, to whom Carlyle had just sent a new bonnet which his father thought too gaudy, expressed herself characteristically: "I have been rather uneasy about your settlement but seek direction always from Him who can give it aright and may He be thy guide Tom." She ended this letter as she ended many others: "Tell me honestly if thou reads a chapter every day and may the Lord bless and keep thee."

So the die was cast, and Carlyle followed Irving to look for fortune in Edinburgh. Their prospects, however, were very different: Irving had friends, a certain reputation, and (if Carlyle's speculation is correct) some hundreds of pounds at the back of him; Carlyle, friendless and unknown, had a total capital of £85, out of which he sent a draft for £15 to his father towards support of the household at Mainhill. He thought that he would be able to live upon the remainder for two years, with the help perhaps of some private teaching. And after that? "I have thought of trying the law, and several other things", he wrote to his father, and added casually, "But I have not yet got correct information about any of them."

A long letter to Mitchell, portentously-phrased and choked

with fragments of learning (in the course of it he mentions familiarly Diogenes, Lucian, Voltaire, Plato, Sabatier, Cleanthes, Zeno, Epictetus, Kepler, Johnson and Gibbon), gives glimpses of his loneliness and frustration. Had he lived in Athens, he says, he might have been happy like Diogenes in his tub. But in these times, "when . . . the aberrations of philosophical enthusiasm are regarded not with admiration but contempt—when Plato would be dissected in the *Edinburgh Review*, and Diogenes laid hold of by 'a Society for the suppression of Beggars'—in these times—it may not be . . . *Therefore I must cease to be a pedagogue.*" What would he do? "I have meditated upon the profession of a lawyer, or of a civil engineer; though what person would afford me any assistance in executing either of these projects, I cannot say." In the meantime: "Mineralogy is to be my winter's work. I have thought of writing for booksellers. *Risum teneas*; for *at times* I am serious in this matter. In fine weather it does strike me that there are in this head some ideas, a few *disjecta membra*, which might find admittance into some one of the many publications of the day."

Above all, however, this harsh and awkward spirit felt the need to find among others the warm and generous sympathy accorded to him by Irving. "The desire, which, in common with all men, I feel for conversation and social intercourse, is, I find, enveloped in a dense repulsive atmosphere—not of vulgar *mauvaise honte*, though such it is generally esteemed—but of deeper feelings, which I partly inherit from nature, and which are mostly due to the undefined station I have hitherto occupied in society."

To find fame and congenial companions, to discover his proper station in society: with these objects Thomas Carlyle abandoned the safety of life as a schoolmaster, and launched himself upon the great world of Edinburgh from one small room in a poor part of the city. At the time he left Kirkcaldy he was within a month of being twentythree years old.

CHAPTER FOUR

EDINBURGH

Thou must act, thou must work, thou must do! Collect
thyself, compose thyself, find what is wanting that so
tortures thee.

THOMAS CARLYLE: *The Romance of Wotton Reinfred.*

AMONG CARLYLE'S OTHER causes for discontent almost
any modern reader will be inclined to emphasize his lack of
contact with the opposite sex. "In general", Carlyle noted
of Irving and himself in Kirkcaldy, "we were but onlookers
. . . not even with the bright 'young ladies' (what was a sad
feature) were we on speaking terms." This was hardly true of
Irving, whose charm and self-possession were much appreciated by women. During his time in Kirkcaldy Irving indulged
in two or three semi-serious flirtations with young women of the
district, and finally entered into an engagement, in circumstances to be considered later, with one of his pupils. But it
was certainly true of Carlyle, who had at this time as much
social grace as an argumentative bear; and it was probably in
consideration for the feelings of his friend that Irving, while in
his company, abstained from feminine society. In the autumn
before Carlyle went to Edinburgh, however, he was introduced
by Irving to one of his former pupils. Her name was Margaret
Gordon: and Carlyle was impressed by her wit, her intelligence,
and her air of being alien to Kirkcaldy provincialism. He
must also have been pleased by the fact that this fair-haired,
softly elegant and vaguely aristocratic girl showed a distinct
inclination to be impressed by his own sallies and monologues.

At the time she met Carlyle Margaret Gordon was just
twenty years old. The daughter of an army surgeon named
Alexander Gordon, she was born in Charlottetown, on Prince
Edward's Island, Nova Scotia, where Alexander Gordon had
married the daughter of the island's first Governor. Gordon,
after a series of financial misfortunes, left Nova Scotia for
Scotland, apparently to look after some small property; he
died on ship, leaving his wife and four children practically
penniless. Margaret Gordon, and her sister Mary, were

adopted by Doctor Gordon's widowed sister, Elizabeth Usher, who lived in Kirkcaldy. Elizabeth Usher had married a Scottish clergyman, who died a few years after the marriage leaving his wife nothing whatever beyond the furniture and other effects of her household. For the maintenance of herself and the two children Mrs. Usher had her own pension of some £30 a year, and a grant of £8 a year made by the Army Compassionate Fund to each of the children. Mrs. Gordon had, after three years of widowhood, married another army surgeon named Doctor Guthrie, who later became famous as founder of the Royal Westminster Ophthalmic Hospital and president of the Royal College of Surgeons. Rather curiously, it does not appear that at this time Mrs. Usher received any financial help from Doctor Guthrie or his wife.

The air of aristocratic aloofness that marked Margaret Gordon was, then, an acquired one. She felt considerable pride in her connection with the Gordons of Logie in Crimond, who could trace their descent back to the eleventh century: but from the time she was five years old she could have left Kirkcaldy only on short visits to Edinburgh and elsewhere. A water-colour miniature painted six years after she first met Carlyle indicates at least the nature of her charm. Beneath an enormous hat ornamented with ostrich feathers lies a pensive oval face framed with chestnut hair in ringlets; the mouth is small and the deep blue eyes are set wide apart. Margaret Gordon was tall, and had a beautiful figure; she moved gracefully and her expression, although haughty, was full of animation.

Such was the first girl seriously considered by Carlyle as a possible wife: or perhaps one would be touching a truth more nearly in saying, such was the first girl to discover the passionate intelligence blazing behind his awkward exterior. It is possible that a wish to establish himself in the eyes of Margaret Gordon may have been one of the motives that prompted Carlyle's departure from Kirkcaldy: possible, but not likely, for he had, now and hereafter, a sure conviction of his own talent and never felt the need to offer proof of it either to himself or to others. His feeling for her, however, exists as a background to his first two years in Edinburgh. He visited her frequently at Kirkcaldy: but it must soon have been apparent to him that his visits were not regarded with any friendliness by Margaret's aunt. Mrs. Usher had endured some privations in order to educate these two adopted children, and she can hardly be blamed for not wishing to see one of them married to a penni-less, grim schoolmaster who seemed to have no idea of the need for making his fortune, and whose bursts of loquacity were even more disturbing than his uncompromising silences. Carlyle and Irving spent their Christmas holidays in Kirk-caldy, and during that time Carlyle must have seen Margaret Gordon, for he wrote to a friend that these holidays "Were the happiest, for many reasons which I cannot at this time ex-plain, that for a long space have marked the tenor of my life".

In the meantime he did not prosper in Edinburgh. His winter's work, we know, was to be mineralogy, but after attending two of the lectures given by Professor Jameson, then a noted figure in the city, Carlyle's verdict was scathing:

> He is one of those persons whose understanding is over-burthened by their memory. Destitute of accurate science, without comprehension of mind,—he details a chaos of facts, which he accounts for in a manner as slovenly as he selects and arranges them. Yesterday he explained the colour of the atmosphere,—upon principles which argued a total ignorance of dioptrics. A knowledge of the external character of minerals is all I can hope to obtain from him.

Mineralogy was soon abandoned: and for some months he made no attempt to discover means of making himself proficient in civil engineering or the law. Instead he read books, following no systematic plan of study but devouring all kinds of reading-matter as a hungry man eats food. His spare time was spent in learning Italian and German; at Kirkcaldy Madame de Staël's *l'Allemagne* had made him curious about German culture: and an acquaintance had told him that he would find what he was looking for in Germany.

What was he looking for? It is not likely that he knew. His logical mind had rejected Christianity: what he sought for was a basis of belief outside Christianity as firm as that possessed by his father and Irving inside it. The search for some kind of spiritual truth appeared to him the only pursuit of any value or interest. The knowledge that one is in pursuit of such truth is apt to lend its possessor a cloak of self-conscious virtue that is rarely pleasing to others: so Carlyle, when he attended a meeting of the Royal Society, contemptuously noted the concern of its members to decide "that a certain little crumb of stone is neither to be called *mesotype* nor *stilbite*." So also, when he attended the breakfasts given by Irving in his lodgings to various Edinburgh intellectuals, the facility with which he demolished their most firmly-held beliefs made him generally disliked. "Your utterance", Irving wrote to his friend, "Is not the most favourable. It convinces, but does not persuade; and it is only a very few (I can claim place for myself) that it fascinates".

Carlyle went to see Professor Leslie who had recommended him for his positions both at Annan and Kirkcaldy; now, apparently weary of this intransigent figure, the Professor advised him to learn engineering and go to America. Carlyle also presented a letter of introduction to Doctor Brewster—that same Brewster who, as Sir David, was Principal of Edinburgh University at the time of Carlyle's installation as Rector. Brewster had for some years been editing the *Edinburgh Encyclopaedia*, which had by this time reached the letter "M", and Carlyle hoped to get some work from him. He was kindly received, and his address taken, but there was no mention of any work.

During this period he helped to maintain himself by private teaching, doing three hours' work a day at two guineas a month an hour. He taught astronomy to a young officer of the East India Company, and geometry to an old man from Jersey named Saumarez, with whom he argued also about Newton and natural philosophy; this work had come to him on Irving's recommendation. The hour with Saumarez, between 8 and 9 o'clock each morning, began Carlyle's day. He walked the mile to Saumarez's lodging and the mile back, and then ate his breakfast of porridge. Then he set out to visit the East India Company officer, who lived in the same district as Saumarez, and stayed with him until midday. After that he went home and read until two o'clock; attended a Natural History class for an hour; ate a frugal dinner; and read till midnight. "This is a picture of my life", he wrote to his mother, "and notwithstanding a fair proportion of anticipations and forebodings I am not at all uncomfortable."

His mother's chief concern, however, was for his spiritual welfare, since she was convinced that in practical matters "You will be provided for as He sees meet for you." But was he reading his Bible daily? He confessed that he had "not been quite regular" in doing so, but tried to assuage her fears with a tenderness which, where those he loved were concerned, was almost unfailing.

I entreat you to believe that I am sincerely desirous of being a good man; and though we may differ in some few unimportant particulars, yet I firmly trust that the same Power which created us with imperfect faculties will pardon the errors of every one (and none are without them) who seeks truth and righteousness with a simple heart.

In the same letter he expressed his intention of coming down to stay at Mainhill "accompanied with a cargo of books, Italian, German and others"; and he told her that he was reading D'Alembert, "one of the few persons who deserve the honourable epithet of honest man". Mrs. Carlyle, who can never have heard of D'Alembert, and knew nothing of the destructive rationalism of the French *Philosophes*, was nonetheless obscurely alarmed. "God made man after His own image therefore he behoved to be without any imperfect faculties", she wrote. "Beware my dear son of such thoughts let them not dwell on your mind".

"You are not to think I am fretful", Carlyle wrote to his mother; but when he came home to Mainhill for the summer, after six months spent in Edinburgh, fretful was an inadequate word to express the depth of his spirits. The only literary work he had obtained was some translations of articles on chemistry, magnetism and crystallography given him by Doctor Brewster; and Mrs. Usher must by now have made plain her disapproval of him, although since no letters between Carlyle and Margaret Gordon written at this time have survived we do not know its terms. In addition, he had begun to suffer the pains of what he called dyspepsia, a condition which lasted, with occasional alleviations, until almost the end of his life. He felt pains in the upper abdomen which often prevented him from sleeping, or woke him from sleep; and he was chronically constipated, a condition which he tried to rectify by the liberal use of castor oil.

Sick and ill-tempered, he wandered about Annan and the district, with gloomy ideas about his future. He thought vaguely of taking Leslie's advice about leaving Britain, and among the cargo of books he sent to Mainhill for summer

reading was one called *America and her Resources*. But this summer
he found even reading difficult and, abandoning his books,
went for lonely walks in which his mind swayed between
deceitful hopes and a kind of mulish patience. He wrote an
account of his sloth to Mitchell, and added ironically: "Do you
know of a more edifying life?" The good advice Irving gave his
friend, to "Fill up with the softness of rural beauty, and the
sincerity of rural manners, and the contentment of rural life,
those strong impressions of nature and of men which are already
in your mind", must have seemed almost perfectly inappro-
priate to its recipient.

A month or two after writing this letter Irving came to
Annan, with the news that he had been invited to become
assistant in Glasgow to Doctor Chalmers, the most noted
preacher of his day, who believed that "If the fear of Hell can
keep the crowd in order, they cannot have too much of it."
Carlyle accompanied his friend on foot for thirty miles of the
way, and at parting he can hardly have refrained from comparing Irving's bright prospects and assured part in life with
his own unhappy sense of wasted months and years. At Glasgow
the gigantic Irving with his *panache*, his overflowing eloquent
earnestness, his dark handsomeness and his terrible squint, was
an immediate success. He was mistaken by various members of
Doctor Chalmers's church for a brigand, a Highland chief and
a cavalry officer; stories of such exploits as his wrenching a
church door from its hinges when unjustly refused admittance
were vaguely circulated; his sympathy for the poor weavers
made him much liked, and the solemnity with which upon
entering their wretched homes he said invariably, "Peace be
to this house", left those who heard it awestruck by its prophetic
oddity.

Irving's success, however much Carlyle rejoiced at it, made
him more thoroughly aware of his own failure. He must have
known, also, the profound discomfort and distress he was
causing his family; when ten people are living together in three
rooms it is essential that they shall live harmoniously. After
six months spent at Mainhill in miserable indecision he
returned to Edinburgh and enrolled himself—it is hardly too
much to say in desperation—in the Scots Law class. Perhaps by
this action he seemed to himself to have signed a decree of
divorce from all literary aspirations, and to have entered on an
occupation which even Mrs. Usher must approve; certainly

before he finally (as he must have regarded it) dedicated himself to the law he went to Fife and saw both Margaret Gordon and the "lean, proud elderly dame" who "talked shrewd *Aberdeenish* in accent and otherwise", as Carlyle later described her.

He had now abandoned literature, and embarked without money on that profession for which, he had said some months earlier, several hundreds of pounds' backing would be needed. But one does not redirect so easily the course of ambition. From the first Carlyle's interest in the law was expressed chiefly in negatives. "I prophesy I shall not dislike the science", he wrote to Mitchell. "If health continue, I shall feel for it all the ardour which is naturally inspired by the prospect (however dubious) of its affording a permanent direction to my efforts. I shall require, moreover, to investigate the history, antiquities, manners, etc. of our native country—a subject for which I feel nothing like repugnance". Disinterest could hardly be expressed more clearly: and within a short time Carlyle was expressing contempt for the lecturer at the law class, and hinting darkly to his mother that his success in the profession "must depend on several circumstances". After less than four months he wrote to Mitchell: "Law, I fear, must be renounced; it is a shapeless mass of absurdity and chicane", and to his friend James Johnstone he recounted his disgusted refusal to learn "Long-winded, dry details about points not of the slightest importance to any one but an Attorney or Notary Public; observations upon the formalities of customs which ought to be instantly and for ever abolished; uncounted cases of blockhead A *versus* blockhead B, with what Stair thought upon them, what Bankton, what the poor *doubting* Dirleton."

This rejection of the law had also a personal and emotional basis. As Carlyle entered upon his studies in the hope of gaining Mrs. Usher's consent to his approaching Margaret Gordon as a suitor, so he abandoned them when it had at last been made plain to him that she would never become his wife. There is remarkably little material in Carlyle's generally well-documented life bearing on his love for Margaret Gordon: hints in the reminiscences Carlyle wrote nearly forty years after the affair was over, and two letters from Margaret Gordon to Carlyle are almost the sum of published and fully authenticated information. Carlyle said in his reminiscences that his friendship with her "Might easily have been more, had she, and her Aunt, and our economic and other circumstances liked!" Was

Margaret Gordon, then, in love with Carlyle? That is something we shall never know: but there is some evidence in
Carlyle's own writings which, for what it is worth, should be
put into the scale.

The first lengthy creative work Carlyle attempted was called
The Romance of Wotton Reinfred. The book was cast in the form
of a novel, with philosophical interludes; and after he had
written some 30,000 words Carlyle abandoned it. Much of the
book is plainly autobiographical; Carlyle is Wotton Reinfred,
and the heroine Jane Montagu has been adopted by a poor,
proud and strong-minded aunt who has "high hopes from her
niece" and does not approve of Wotton as a suitor.

At the beginning of March (he had begun his study of law
in the preceding November) Carlyle went to Kirkcaldy, and
learned from Margaret Gordon that she was going to live in
London with her mother and stepfather. Such a scene is
described in *Wotton Reinfred*, when Jane tells Wotton that he
must cease to visit her. "One whom she entirely depended on
had so ordered it, and for herself she had nothing to do but
obey." Wotton presses for an explanation which is refused, and
at last bids her an angry goodbye. Then:

> She put her hand in his; she looked in his face, tears started
> to her eyes; but she turned away her head, hastily pressed
> his hand, and, sobbing, whispered, scarcely audibly, 'Fare-
> well'. He approached in frenzy; his arms were half raised to
> encircle her; but starting back she turned on him a weeping
> face—a face of anger, love and agony. She slowly motioned
> him to withdraw.

So far, fiction; which bore, it is likely, some near relation to
fact. On June 4th Margaret Gordon wrote to Carlyle thanking
him for his visit to Kirkcaldy and saying that she should have
thanked him personally, but "*You* know the cause that
prevented me. If your call had been merely one of ceremony
such as I am accustomed to receive from the ordinary *herd*
of men, I should neither have seen nor declared any obligation."
His visit to her "appeared not only a proof of the noble triumph
you had obtained over your weakness (forgive the expression),
but seemed to be an intimation that I was still thought worthy
of that esteem with which you formerly honoured me." She
went on to say that her visit to London was to be for a twelvemonth, and expressed her hope that he would not desert his

true course in life. "It is true, it is full of rugged obstacles, interspersed with little to charm the sense; yet these present a struggle which is fitted only for minds such as *yours* to overcome. The difficulties of the ascent are great, but how glorious the summit! Keep your eyes fixed on the end of your journey, and you will begin to forget the weariness of the way." So, having "taken the liberty of a friend, I had almost said of a *Sister*, who is probably addressing you for the last time", Margaret Gordon ended her letter.

Perhaps it is not surprising that, on receipt of such a letter, Carlyle should have written again, and apparently with passion: at least her reply begins: "What a risk did you run in sending your letter". This reply finally convinced Carlyle that his cause was hopeless. Margaret refused to correspond with him because such a correspondence would be an encouragement of "that 'weakness' it has been my object to remove". She would be anxious to hear of his welfare, "but (think me not severe) from another source my information must come". And this letter, altogether remarkable in its maturity and coolness for a young woman of twentytwo, ended with some observations which must have been as unpalatable as they were acute:

And now, my dear friend, a long long adieu. One advice, and as a parting one consider, value it:—*cultivate the milder dispositions of your heart, subdue the more extravagant visions of the brain.* In time your abilities must be known; among your acquaintances they are already beheld with wonder and delight; by those whose opinion will be valuable, they hereafter will be appreciated. *Genius* will render you *great*. May *virtue* render you *beloved*! Remove the awful distance between you and ordinary men, by kind and gentle manners; deal mildly with their inferiority, and be convinced they will respect you as much, and like you more. Why conceal the real goodness that flows in your heart?—I have ventured this counsel from an anxiety for your future welfare; and I would enforce it with all the earnestness of the most sincere friendship. 'Let your light shine before men', and think them not unworthy this trouble. This exercise will prove its own reward. It must be a pleasing thing to live in the affections of others.—Again, Adieu. Pardon the freedom I have used, and when you think of me, be it as a kind Sister, to whom your happiness will always yield delight, and your griefs sorrow.—

Yours with esteem and regard

M. GORDON.

Written on the margin of the first page was a teasingly ambiguous postscript: "I give you not my address because I dare not promise to see you."

A few days after she wrote this farewell letter to Carlyle, Margaret Gordon went to London; she was seen on to the boat at Glasgow by, of all people, Irving. For Irving's highly susceptible heart, already engaged in Kirkcaldy, had also been touched by Margaret Gordon's charms: and after her departure for London Carlyle received a letter from his friend which must have turned a knife in the wound, caused by her departure. Irving told him in detail of the delightful time he had spent on a walking tour "with what Maiden do you think? One whose name will thrill you as it does me; one of whom I am very proud, and with whom I am well nigh in love, 'Sed Parcae adversae vetant'—Margaret Gordon." With a characteristic dash of rhetoric Irving added: "Such another scene of heart-content I shall never pass again: the brief time of it lies in my mind like a hallowed sanctuary in a desert, or like a piece of enchanted ground in a wilderness."

Once settled in London Margaret Gordon's attitude to her friends in Kirkcaldy developed a certain hauteur. When Irving visited her some eighteen months later he found himself received like a country visitor who must be made thoroughly aware of his own clownishness. She was, he said, good-natured enough, but still he felt indisposed to return. In spite of his affectations in dress and manner Irving's nature was essentially frank and simple, and he noted sadly upon this last visit: "I feel I am not master of the *haut ton* of intercourse."

In 1824 Margaret Gordon married an Aberdeen banker, wine merchant and manufacturer ten years older than herself, named Alexander Bannerman. Much later Bannerman was knighted and appointed Governor of Prince Edward Island, so that his wife had the pleasure of returning as the Governor's lady to the island her father had left at the nadir of his fortunes when she was a small child. She lost none of her haughtiness with the years. When any coarse observation was made in her presence she slowly raised her head and closed her eyes without speaking, in a way that was found awe-inspiring; and on first arrival in the Bahamas, when her husband had been appointed Governor there, she caused offence by looking through her eyeglass at the houses and saying: "Very colonial". In these days she spoke more of Irving than of Carlyle, and said nothing to her friends about any past romance between her and the most famous living Scotchman.

Carlyle never spoke to her after their farewell at Kirkcaldy; but he saw her twice some twenty years after. On the first occasion she was in Piccadilly with her maid, and apparently did not see him: but the second time they met face to face, both on horseback, at Hyde Park Gate, and "Her eyes (but that was all) said to me almost touchingly, 'Yes, yes; that is you!'"

* * * * *

In the meantime Carlyle had obtained some work from Doctor Brewster, in composing the biographies for the *Edinburgh Encyclopaedia* which had formerly been written by Thomas Campbell. It has been noted already that the *Encyclopaedia* had reached the letter "M" and he was delegated to write therefore on Montaigne and Montesquieu and Lady Mary Wortley Montagu, on Necker and the Netherlands and Pitt; and he did such work conscientiously, as anybody can discover who cares to read these pieces, written in a style obviously derived from Johnson's but altogether lacking Johnsonian weight and power.

Since his mode of life was absolutely frugal the small returns from such work, and from his teaching, were sufficient to maintain him in Edinburgh: but the period after his rejection by Margaret Gordon shows a marked decline in his spirits and his health. In a letter to his brother John, now a master at Annan and showing some inclination to the literary life, he strongly advised him not to "play the same miserable game that I have played, sacrificing both health and peace of mind to the vain shadows of ambition". He recommended to John, indeed, two of the occupations that he had himself rejected, teaching and the church, and added to them medicine; it was important, he said, to settle into a profession. He generously offered to John, and to his less scholastic brother Alick, financial help out of his own small savings. In other letters home he cries: "O for one day of such vigorous health and such elastic spirits as I have had of old", and talks of his long bloodless bony fingers, his lean and sallow visage, and his despair of ever doing any work for which he might be fitted. These periods of self-disgust conflicted with others when he was angrily conscious of his own frustrated talent. At such times he felt within himself some distinguishing marks of difference from and superiority to the mass of mankind: and then he resolved that if once he emerged from the bogs and quagmires in which he seemed so inextricably immersed, "I shall make some fellows stand to the right and left—or I mistake me greatly." A passionate desire for self-expression combined with inhibitions that peremptorily checked its use, a deep awareness of creative power held back by clearly-remembered but faintly understood influences and taboos from his childhood—these were the contradictions that he tried in vain to reconcile.

His thoughts moved always on the condition of Britain and the future of the world; and they were marked by a sharper Radicalism than ever appeared in his published writings. He saw around him poverty, misery, abortive risings; he heard the news of Peterloo; and his sympathies were emphatically on the side of the workers. "The substantial burghers and other idle loyalists of the place are training themselves to the use of arms for suppressing the imaginary revolts of the lower orders", he wrote sarcastically to his brother John; and writing of the failure of the Cato Street conspiracy to assassinate a number of ministers he observed that assassination was horrid, but that the germ of such attempts lay in the indifference or ridicule of the government. He was moved deeply by the sight of groups of men journeying about in search of food, and the fate of a shoe-maker from Ecclefechan who, coming to Glasgow to buy leather, met some fellow-Radicals and declared himself "delegate from Ecclefechan", an act which led to his speedy imprisonment. It seemed to him that unless the times altered "folks will all be Radicals together": and he and Irving felt equally, as Carlyle afterwards phrased it, that "revolt against such a load of unveracities, impostures, and quietly inane formalities would one day become indispensable", a feeling which had a "quasi-insolent joy in it; mutiny, revolt, being a light matter to the young."

In considering the nature of Carlyle's lifelong physical suffering we are confronted by the curious, although un-remarked, fact that he seems never to have suffered pain in company. In the minute survey of his life and habits, as they were observed by many would-be Boswells, there is practically no occasion on which he left any company because he felt unwell, or even complained of feeling pain at that especial moment of time. This was not stoicism, for he complained often enough of anguish in the past, and looked forebodingly into the unending agony of the future. It would seem, quite simply, that he did not suffer from pain, in the ordinary physical sense. Even on the dismal journey made to deliver the Edinburgh address he said to Tyndall only that he could not endure another night like the last, and not that he was suffering pain at the time of speaking.

This is not to say that his anguish was imaginary. It was very real: but its origins were psychic rather than physical. The trouble from which he suffered would probably be regarded today as a functional gastric disorder set up by various frustrations in his life, the desire to love, the desire to write, the desire for acknowledgement of his talent; the frustrations were deep-seated, and had become permanent long before their immediate causes disappeared. In a purely physical sense his condition would have been rendered more difficult to treat by the habit of tobacco-smoking, which he practised from the age of eleven, and by his lavish use of such an internal irritant as castor oil, to ensure daily evacuation.

This diagnosis finds much support in Carlyle's correspondence: at this time, for instance, he answered Irving, who had written to say that he did not wholly believe the bad report of his health, in terms equally passionate and unspecific:

> The state of my health you do not believe. My earnest prayer is that you may never believe. I was once as sceptical as yourself. Such disorders are the heaviest calamity life has in store for mortals. The bodily pain is nothing or next to nothing; but alas for the dignity of man! The evil does not stop here. No strength of soul can avail you; this malady will turn that very strength against yourself; it banishes all thought from your head, all love from your heart—and doubles your wretchedness by making you discern it. Oh! the long, solitary, sleepless nights that I have passed—with no employment but to count the pulses of my own sick heart —till the gloom of external things seemed to extend itself to the very centre of my mind, till I could remember nothing, observe nothing! All this magnificent nature appeared as if

blotted out, and a grey, dirty, dismal vapour filled the immensity of space; I stood alone in the universe—alone, and as it were a circle of burning iron enveloped the soul— excluding from it every feeling but a stony-hearted dead obduracy, more befitting a demon in its place of woe than a man in the land of the living!

From such sleepless nights, such minor bodily discomfort and such intense spiritual anguish, Carlyle sought relief, as always, in reading. He had indeed found much of what he looked for— or what, to put it more nicely, corresponded to his spiritual needs—in the work of Goethe and Schiller; and it was with the prospect in mind of long discussions about these literary idols, as well as of talk about the state of the world, that he paid occasional visits to Irving in Glasgow.

The sick and sour Carlyle found his friend now dressed more carefully and clerically than of old, with a long black frock and a wide-brimmed grave black hat; he was full of the work he was doing in St. John's, the poverty-stricken parish that Chalmers had chosen as a demonstration to show that with the aid of the church pauperism could be wiped out. By the standards of that time St. John's should have been full of paupers: but under the benevolent autocracy of Chalmers, assisted by Irving, all the needs of the poor in the district were supplied by the church. This was the work in which Irving was engaged; visiting the weavers, labourers and factory-workers, overcoming the barriers of distrust between many of them and the church, and persuading them to send their children to the schools that were being built for them. His sanguine temperament was not inclined to take Carlyle's pessimism seriously. It was impossible, he said, that such talent as Carlyle's should not cut its way clear one day, and with a pinch of self-mockery and an ounce of seriousness he declared that "One day we two will shake hands across the brook, you as first in Literature, I as first in Divinity; and people will say—'Both those fellows are from Annandale: where is Annandale?' "

In Glasgow Carlyle noted with irony the shining bald or white-haired heads of solid Scottish merchants and gentle-men, gossiping or reading their papers while—as the fierce inarticulate prophet thought,—the underpinnings of their security were rapidly rotting away. He met Glasgow philos-ophers in Irving's spacious ground floor room, amiable men "whom one did not find so extremely philosophical". He noted with interest the Glasgow young ladies upon whom, as well as upon elderly gentlemen, Irving paid his morning calls. He twice met the great Chalmers, the first time at breakfast when Chalmers was no more than absently kind; Carlyle noted the sorrowful glaze over his face and eyes and assumed that the preacher's thoughts were elsewhere. The second occasion was a solemn evening party; and here Chalmers, who had perhaps been told by Irving that this was a remarkable young man, and one who had doubts of the literal truth of Christianity, made an effort at conversion. Pulling his chair by the side of Carlyle's the Doctor talked earnestly about a scheme for proving the truth of Christianity by the fact that it so manifestly met the needs of human nature. Christianity was, as he put it, written in sympathetic ink; the Bible merely brought out what was, very obviously, there. Carlyle listened, as he thought respectfully: but perhaps after all he was not quite respectful enough, for Chalmers was unfavourably impressed by him. "That laddie", he said rather obscurely, "Is a lover of earnestness, more than a lover of truth".

It was on a visit at about this time that Carlyle revealed to Irving the depths and magnitude of his doubt. Irving had accompanied his friend, as was usual between them, part of the way home: the two went some fifteen miles, as far as Drumclog Moss in Renfrewshire before Irving turned back, leaving Carlyle to walk alone the ten further miles to Muirkirk. Carlyle has sketched the scene memorably in his *Reminiscences*: the silent world around them, a flat wilderness of pitted brown bog, remnants of heath and wide deep holes abruptly encountered, which became quagmires in winter. The talk, Carlyle remembered, had grown friendlier and more interesting with each passing hour: as the sun was setting, they leaned against a dry-stone wall, still talking. And here Irving "actually drew from me by degrees, in the softest manner, the confession that I did *not* think as he of Christian Religion, and that it was vain for me to expect I ever could or should". The confession seems not to have shocked Irving; he accepted it, Carlyle remembered, like an elder brother; and, as the sun set, turned for his long walk home.

The character of Carlyle, so far depicted, is likely to appear uncongenial to most contemporary readers. A conviction of superiority, combined with inability to manifest it; inner strivings that appear at best obscure, at worst ridiculous; a burning heart hidden behind a manner at once provocative and gauche: all these can appear tolerable only if their ultimate ends seem admirable and sympathetic. Few readers today feel much sympathy with Carlyle: yet he will be judged unjustly if the generosity, the need for love, and the desire to make a better and juster social order, that lay beneath the gauche façade are ignored; or if it is forgotten that the physical troubles besetting him, whatever their origin, were painfully real. "The heart longs for some kind of sympathy", he wrote to his brother John in a cry which is moving because of its very rarity.

He found in his twentyfifth year hardly such a sympathy, but at least the opportunity to use a little of his pent-up store of idealism. In the May of 1821 Irving came to Edinburgh to see his friend and found him, as usual, in low spirits. Irving proposed a walk to Haddington, which had been the scene of his early success as a teacher. The day was fine, and in the course of the sixteen mile walk Carlyle became more cheerful. "This is nearly all I recollect of the journey", he wrote much later. "The end of it, and what I saw *there*, will be memorable to me while life or thought endures."

CHAPTER FIVE

FROM JANE BAILLIE WELSH—

Mr. Carlyle was with us two days, during the greater part of which I read German with him. It is a noble language! I am getting on famously. He scratched the fender dreadfully. I must have a pair of carpet-shoes and handcuffs prepared for him the next time. His tongue only should be left at liberty: his other members are most fantastically awkward.

JANE BAILLIE WELSH to Bess Stodart, 1822.

IRVING BELIEVED THAT Carlyle's way of living was altogether too secluded: so, partly for his friend's benefit, he visited at Haddington as many friends and acquaintances as possible. In pursuit of congenial company they visited the local minister who had a daughter named Augusta, "tall, airy, shapely, giggly, but a consummate fool", Carlyle said: and the house of Mrs. Welsh, the widow of a local doctor. It was in the drawing room of this house that Carlyle saw Jane Baillie Welsh for the first time.

With his extraordinary capacity for recreating the past in visual scenes Carlyle shows us this drawing-room. It was, he tells us, the finest room he had ever entered; solid and correct and as clean as spring water; on the table "perhaps a superfluity of elegant whim-whams". But it is unlikely that he paid these things particular attention at the time, for he was too much delighted by the looks, speech and evident intelligence of Mrs. Welsh's daughter.

Jane Baillie Welsh was not quite twenty years old. She was four inches over five feet in height, slightly built, with a pale skin, a nose slightly tip-tilted, large and beautiful dark eyes which were more often mocking than tender, and a mass of curling black hair above her broad white forehead. She was called beautiful, although by ordinary standards her features were too irregular for beauty; but there was no doubt of the intellectual vivacity and intense spirit shown in her conversation. Plainly she was well read, intelligent, witty, full of sensibility; and yet, together with her arch and occasionally almost pert self-possession, went a marked humility in the presence of intellectual eminence.

She had dreams of becoming famous in her own right, and yet she was eager also to be the companion of a man of genius. Of genius and, one must add, sensibility; among Miss Welsh's idols were Byron and Rousseau, and she spoke half-seriously of marrying a Wolmar or a St. Preux. This tart-tongued and attractive provincial flirt had already a variety of would-be suitors whose absurdities she caricatured mercilessly for the amusement of her Edinburgh friend Bess Stodart. There was the gentleman who before dinner retired to the local George Inn and "vapoured back . . . in all the pride of two waistcoats (one of figured velvet, another of sky-blue satin), gossamer silk stockings and morocco leather slippers", and thus equipped told Mrs. Welsh and her daughter of the party he had attended on the previous evening *"with his arm under his hat;* and then he corrected himself, and said, *with his head under his arm!"* There was a local physician, Doctor Fyffe, there were James Aitken, James Baird, Robert MacTurk, Robby Angus and George Rennie, the handsome son of a rich engineer. There was Mr. Craig Buchanan, who "is about the age of Wolmar; but Wolmar had not a bald head, nor a lame leg, neither did Wolmar make puns or pay compliments". And now to this long list there was to be added Thomas Carlyle. One need feel no special indulgence towards Carlyle to find the fate in store for his gauche earnestness and ponderous playfulness a slightly pitiable one.

Carlyle and Irving stayed at Haddington, lodging at the George Inn, for three or four days. During this time they paid frequent visits to. Mrs. Welsh's house; and Carlyle, perhaps remembering his fate at the hand of Margaret Gordon's aunt Mrs. Usher, talked a great deal to Mrs. Welsh, leaving Jane to the company of Irving, who had in the distant past been her tutor. Grace Welsh was a tall and handsome woman, and Carlyle found no difficulty in talking to her, although later he discovered that she was fanciful and capricious. But while he talked to Mrs. Welsh he felt her daughter's bright eyes fixed enquiringly upon him; and he was in love with her from the time of this first visit. When the two friends returned to the George Inn that night Irving facetiously asked what Carlyle would take to marry Miss Augusta, and Carlyle made an equally facetious reply. "And what would you take to marry Miss Jeannie, think you?" "Hah!" Carlyle answered, "I should not be so hard to deal with there, I should imagine." With such thoughts in his mind he returned to Edinburgh and wrote to his brother Alick at Mainhill of his happy trip. "I came back so full of joy that I have done nothing since but dream of it."

Now the young man set out to turn his dreams into reality. During the course of conversation with Jane Welsh it had been agreed that he should assist her German studies, and generally advise the course of her reading; and this seemed to afford an excellent excuse for a letter. Perhaps it did: but not for such a letter as Carlyle sent to accompany a parcel containing Madame de Staël's book on Germany and the poetical works of Milton. His epistolary style had become noticeably easier and more colloquial during the past two or three years, but in writing to Jane Welsh he reverted to his most pedantic manner in asking whether she had "ever deigned to cast one glance of recollection on those few Elysian hours we spent together lately?" and in suggesting that he might come to Haddington and deliver "such a lesson on those Saxon Roots as you never heard". Such was perhaps the natural stiffness of a scholar: but what could be said of the clumsy attempt at intimacy which prompted him to begin with the words "My dear Friend" and to refer in the body of his letter to "Lady Jane" and even to simple "Jane"? "Positively, I must see you soon—or I shall get into a very absurd state. And then if I should come to visit Jane herself *professedly*; *what* would Jane say to it? What would Jane's friends say?" What Jane said was as short and sharp as possible. After a few days she returned the books, and Carlyle, searching the parcel for a letter, found merely a card on which she had written: "To Mr. Carslile, with Miss Welsh's compliments and very best thanks".

What might have seemed a knock-down blow to another man was no more than a temporary check to Carlyle. His mode of address had, he saw, been too familiar: with perhaps an excess of formality he changed it to "My dear Madam". He spoke of his dejection at discovering only "Miss Welsh's 'compliments' to Mr. Car*slile*, a gentleman, in whom it required no small sagacity to detect my own representative." But he was not deterred from sending further volumes of Madame de Staël's book, and he wrote of other books which they might undertake to read together. This letter drew half a dozen lines of formal reply addressed again, by what some will consider malice, others a Freudian error and others again simple weakness in orthography, to Mr. Carslile. Unable to write glowingly of the note's contents Carlyle rhapsodised about the seal which bore the motto *A l'Amista* ("Would you not pardon me, if the wish arose" that this "*were* in very deed the motto— once and evermore, between us!"). He suggested that she should give him permission to pay a visit to Haddington "*to inspect and accelerate your progress in the German tongue!*" There is no indication that such permission was given.

Few courtings, surely, have begun in a more curious guise than that of teaching German by correspondence. Yet Carlyle's instinct was not far out when it said that this was, at least for him, the way to Jane Welsh's heart. He was not a man physic- ally attractive to many women, although his ruddy face, rugged features, and flashing clear blue eyes made up an appearance which was in some ways almost handsome; and he was thoroughly conscious of his own lack of social and physical grace. When he pled humbly with Jane Welsh that she should "forget the roughness of my exterior, if you think me sound within", lamented his own absence of grace and said that "if Nature had meant me for a courtly person, she would have made me richer and more impudent", he was using effective arguments. He realized that he must please, if at all, by his intellect; and it was through the intellect that at last he won Jane Welsh. He had in his favour a gift of flattery effective because of its utter sincerity: he persuaded himself without difficulty that Jane Welsh of Haddington was another Madame de Staël, and wrote to her upon that intellectual basis. We can discover easily enough the defects and absurdities of Carlyle; it is not so easy to convey the intellectual power and con- versational brilliance that impressed even hostile observers. The lonely and miserable years that he had spent in acquiring knowledge were beginning to bear fruit, at least in his conversa- tion: his range and depth of knowledge were alike extraordin- ary, and the flashing and extravagant metaphors that constantly lighted up his speech were drawn from the most varied sources. And in his most bitingly ironical passages of conversation or argument he spoke not with cynicism but with a fervour and intensity in support of what he believed to be the truth that might have moved a heart less susceptible to high romanticism than that of Jane Baillie Welsh. Writing to her friend Bess Stodart, Jane compared Carlyle with her ideal St. Preux. Carlyle, she said, "Has *his* talents, *his* vast and cultivated mind, *his* vivid imagination, *his* independence of soul, and *his* high-souled principles of honour. But then Ah, these *buts*!— St. Preux never kicked the fire-irons, nor made puddings in his teacup. Want of Elegance! Want of Elegance, Rousseau says, is a defect which no woman can overlook."

Some three or four months after their first meeting Carlyle and Jane Welsh met in Edinburgh, and there he read Schiller, Lessing and Goethe with her. When, soon after her return, he spoke again of paying a visit to Haddington she attempted to dissuade him. In a letter to his mother Carlyle said that he had "a standing invitation, from a very excellent Mrs. Welsh, to go to Haddington, often, as if I were going *home*": but in fact Mrs. Welsh had changed her mind about Carlyle, and was no longer disposed to be friendly to him.

Mrs. Welsh was a capricious woman, and was also vain of her undoubted good looks; she was still in her forties, and it has been suggested that she was at first under the impression that Carlyle's attentions were directed to her, and that she became jealous when she found that he was in fact a suitor of her daughter. This may be true; but in the absence of any evidence it is more charitable, as well as more likely, to suppose that Mrs. Welsh simply disapproved of Carlyle as a possible husband for Jane Welsh. There were sound reasons, social, financial and psychological, why she should have done so.

The psychological reasons were those least likely to have disturbed Mrs. Welsh; they were nevertheless cogent. Jane Welsh was an only child; she had been indulged in childhood, and her natural tendency to self-assertiveness encouraged. She was eager to behave as much as possible like a boy, and to be treated as one. Her nature was fiery, passionate and romantic. At school she punched a boy on the nose, and made it bleed; at home, when told that a young lady reading Virgil should no longer possess a doll, she built a funeral pyre and burned her doll ceremoniously. Her wilfulness was increased by adoring grandparents and unchecked by her mother, with whom she frequently quarrelled; she respected only her handsome father and Irving, who was master of the local school, and gave her private instruction. Her eagerness to learn was remarkable. She got up at five o'clock each morning, and was very quickly proficient in mathematics and algebra. Her ambition, however, was directed towards literature, and at the age of fourteen she wrote a tragedy in verse.

The attachment between this spoiled tomboy and her

C

strikingly handsome and dignified father was strongly emotional. When he contracted typhus fever from a patient and she was refused admittance to his room, she lay all night on the landing outside his door. Within a few days he was dead: and Jane Welsh assumed the mourning black which she wore for the next six years.

Many things in Jane Welsh's character, as indicated in this brief history, made it unlikely that she would live a peaceful or happy life with Carlyle. As a suitor he found her wilfulness pleasant, and submitted to it, but plainly he would not tolerate such a quality in his wife. He respected and encouraged what he called her literary genius: yet she could not have known him long without realizing that he would expect a wife to undertake as a matter of course all the household tasks from which, in her home at Haddington, she was preserved. But most important of all, it is plain that this passionate young woman felt no physical love for Carlyle; her feeling for him had its origin in worship of her father's intellectual wisdom. "I had never heard the language of talent and genius but from my father's lips" she wrote when she had known him for eighteen months. "You spoke like him; your eloquence awoke in my soul the slumbering admirations and ambitions that *His* first kindled there." Such words express respect, even worship, but hardly passion.

It was the social and financial aspects of the possible match that are more likely to have concerned Mrs. Welsh. If the genealogies of the Carlyles and the Welshes are traced painstakingly back a lineage that begins with Lord Carlyle of Torthorwald is, as some of Carlyle's biographers have said, perhaps equal to the Welsh lineage traced back traditionally to Knox and Wallace. But this is looking after the event, and assuming a knowledge and a wisdom denied to Mrs. Welsh at the time. The facts known to her were that Carlyle was the son of a country mason, and that he bore very clear marks of peasant origin in his awkward manners, country clothes, and broad Annandale speech. The Welshes, on the other hand, had been for generations small gentry, lairds of their farm of Craigenputtock. John Welsh held the social position belonging to a country doctor who had married the daughter of a well-to-do stock farmer; the Welshes were the leading family in Haddington. In addition to his social defects Carlyle had no money, and for Mrs. Welsh this must have meant his positive disbarment as a suitor. Her husband, who was the eldest of a family of fourteen, had invested his savings in the purchase of Craigenputtock, which would eventually have come to him by inheritance. He had done this so that the money might be used to help his brothers and sisters: in consequence, when he died his widow and daughter were left with only the rent of the farm, about £200 a year, on which to live. Worse: the farm had, for some never-explained reason, been left to Jane. No doubt if she married well she would make over the money to her mother: but what if she married badly? Decidedly Mrs. Welsh had reasons for discouraging the courtship of Carlyle.

These thoughts, or some of them, were clearly perceived by Jane Welsh: but not by Carlyle, who in his simplicity saw no reason why the son of a mason should not wed the daughter of a doctor, and who was not for a moment inclined, either now or later, to let considerations of money play any important part in shaping his life. He did not very readily understand the mercurial changes of the young woman who had been his devoted pupil in Edinburgh, or appreciate her annoyance at being, ever so slightly, taken for granted. She reproved him with a mixture of waspishness and coquettishness for the familiarity with which he wrote. "One would almost believe the man fancies I have fallen in love with him, and entertain the splendid project of rewarding his literary labours with my self. Really Sir I do not design for you a recompense so worthless." About the suggestion that he should come out to Haddington she wrote that "As you neither study *my* inclinations nor consider *my* comfort, it is in vain to say how much I am averse to your intended visit, and to how many impertinent conjectures it will at present subject me in this tattling, ill-natured place. I leave it then to yourself to accomplish it, or not, as you please, —with the warning that if you come, you will repent it." If he consulted her wishes he would communicate with her "some weeks hence".

When she wrote this long and savage letter Jane Welsh was expecting a visit from George Rennie, who was perhaps her favourite among all the young men surrounding her; and she was anxious that Carlyle should not be present when this—as it seemed to her in prospect—crucial meeting took place. She was not pleased, therefore, when she received in reply a letter from Carlyle, a letter pathetically humble, indeed ("This conflict of sarcasms can hardly gratify or punish any very noble feeling in either you or me; and I am content to have my vanity humbled, since you wish it so"), but expressing an unshaken determination to come out to Haddington. "I have persuaded myself", he wrote, "that you will not be angry at this proceeding": but when he made his visit he found that he had persuaded nobody else. Mrs. Welsh snubbed him as severely as possible, and her daughter held him strictly to German lessons, and showed plainly that she disliked the awkwardness of his manners. The visit as nearly as possible severed their relations: in a desperate letter written after his return to Edinburgh Carlyle begged her to treat him less harshly, and renounced all idea of being ever considered as a lover. "I understand what is your rank and what your prospects . . . I understand too what are my own." It is plain that Jane Welsh and her mother had given him a lesson in social values and differences.

Carlyle and Jane Welsh did not meet again for another year, and perhaps even their correspondence might have ceased had handsome George Rennie made his expected proposal of marriage: but here Jane Welsh received as rude a disillusionment as was given to Carlyle upon his visit. Rennie was, she knew, going to Italy to learn to become a sculptor; and he had called on Jane Welsh some days before when she was out—a visit which her mother, typically, had omitted to mention. On the day before his departure he paid another visit. Jane described the scene to Bess Stodart:

> He half-advanced to shake hands with me; I made him a cold bow. He placed a chair for me, and went on conversing with my mother. He looked well—handsome—quite in high health and seemingly in high spirits. I scarcely heard a word he said, my own heart beat so loud.

There was some indifferent and impersonal conversation, and then:

> He rose. He took leave of my mother; then looked at me as if uncertain what to do. I held out my hand; he took it and said "Good-bye!" I answered him, "Farewell!" He left the house! Such was the concluding scene of our *Romance*! Great God! He left the house—the *very room* where—no matter—as if he had never been in it in his life before— unfeeling wretch! It was a dreadful trial to me to be obliged

to save appearance even for some minutes *after* he was gone; but I went through it bravely! I returned his letters that night, and now I am done with him *for ever*!

*   *   *   *   *

Carlyle's prospects, of which he had spoken to Jane Welsh with some disparagement, were brightened at this time through the agency of the ever-helpful Irving. When he had been for a year or more with Chalmers at Glasgow, Irving began to fret at his subordinate position; and he accepted eagerly the offer made to him of a small, decaying Scotch Church in Hatton Garden, with a congregation of some fifty persons. When his appointment was confirmed Irving astonished a minister with whom he was friendly by leaping over a gate. "Dear me, Irving", his friend said, "I did not think you had been so agile". Irving's reply shows his exultant certainty of success. "Once I read you an essay of mine, and you said, 'Dear me, Irving, I did not think you had been so critical'; another time you heard me preach, 'Dear me, Irving, I did not know you had so much imagination.' Now you shall see what great things I will do yet!"

Among those who listened to the sermon given by Irving on his preliminary visit to the Hatton Garden Church was Mrs. Charles Buller, the wife of a retired Anglo-Indian judge. The Bullers had three sons and were looking for a tutor to assist the two elder ones, Charles and Arthur, who were fifteen and thirteen years of age. Irving told them of his friend Carlyle, adding a warning note that he had seen little of life and was "disposed to be rather high in the humour, if not well used". Mrs. Buller promised that he should be well used, and well remunerated; the Bullers offered him £200 a year for teaching that would occupy him some four hours a day.

Carlyle met the prospective pupils and immediately liked them; he had been told by Irving that Charles, although clever and acute, was "all given to Boxiana, Bond Street, and pleasure." Carlyle, however, found him remarkably receptive and intelligent; Arthur also he thought a fine little fellow; and his good impressions were strengthened by familiarity. In fact Charles and Arthur Buller were both exceptional pupils. Arthur became, like his father, an Indian judge, and Charles a Radical politician who was prevented from reaching high political office only by his death at the age of fortytwo. There is no doubt that they genuinely liked Carlyle, and learned a great deal from him.

He was offered about this time, and refused out of hand, the editorship of a Dundee newspaper at £100 a year with a share of the profits; the refusal was made in the interest of that literary work which still remained a shade of his imagination. He projected a collection of essays on the Civil Wars and the Commonwealth, with sketches of Cromwell, Laud, Fox, Milton, Hyde and others; but it does not seem that this work was ever begun. From Brewster he obtained more work for the *Edinburgh Encyclopaedia*, and a commission to translate Legendre's *Elements of Geometry*. In the performance of such hackwork weeks extended to months. He was well and comparatively happy; he had obtained a new lodging on the outskirts of Edinburgh, and only a mile from the sea; every morning before breakfast he went down to bathe.

For one with Carlyle's few wants and sparing habits the money he received was much more than he needed for a livelihood, and almost every letter that he wrote to his parents at Mainhill was accompanied by a present. With one letter he sent two pairs of spectacles, one for his father and one for his mother; with the next he sent his mother a sovereign; later a piece of tartan for a cloak. Hard times were universal for farmers in Scotland, and the establishment at Mainhill felt the nibblings of anxiety over the future; Carlyle took upon himself the support of his brother John, six years his junior, who had now become a medical student. The later career of John Carlyle had about it, as may appear, something curious and entertaining, but at this time he was an earnest student both of medicine and literature. Carlyle did much to form his brother's literary taste, while firmly encouraging him to become a doctor; and not a mere general practitioner, but "a medical *savant* at length, bringing to bear upon his own science the mind of a man improved by literature and science in general, and looking forward to respectability in life, not merely because of a mechanical skill in his own particular trade, but also because of a general refinement of character; and a superiority both of intellectual and moral deportment". In pursuit of this formidable project John Carlyle came to Edinburgh and lodged with his brother.

Some six months after his unhappy visit to Haddington, at a time when he was sleeping badly, Carlyle had a curious experience of a kind that can only be called mystical. Like other mystical experiences, it can appear little more than merely bewildering or platitudinous when put down in plain print: but to Carlyle his passage from what he called "The Everlasting No" through the "Centre of Indifference" to "The Everlasting Yea" seemed afterwards both the prelude to manhood, and some kind of spiritual conversion. He later described his "Spiritual New-birth, or Baphometic Fire-baptism" in terms of the richest and most confusing rhetoric. Robbed of such rhetoric, painted with the dull colours of fact, this was what happened to Carlyle. He was walking down Leith Walk one day, on his way to the sea, when he asked himself suddenly what were the reasons for the obscure and pusillanimous apprehensions that he continually felt. What was he afraid of? What was the worse that could happen? Death. He must, then, meet death and the idea of hell, and defy them. "And as I so thought, there rushed like a stream of fire over my whole soul; and I shook base Fear away from me forever."

Such was the Spiritual New-birth. It is made intelligible in rationalist terms by the outline of the prophet's background that has already been given; and it may be observed here that the Spiritual New-birth by no means delivered Carlyle from obscure feelings of guilt, which in fact remained with him all his life. In mystical terms, of course, such revelations have an absolute value which admits of no argument or explanation; and the Spiritual New-birth, however we may interpret it, was valuable to Carlyle because it gave him some basis of belief which was essential to him before he could be committed to any kind of action. The word "belief" implied for him something opposed to the course of logical argument; some justification of the stern, hard way of life adopted by his parents, which remained with him as an ideal. It was at this time that he came to value very highly German idealist philosophy and German romantic poetry: he seemed to discern in them a fusion of the apparently contradictory ideas that moved in his mind, the instinct towards rebellion and the desire for order. The hero of *Sartor Resartus*, when he has passed from The Everlasting No to The Everlasting Yea says: "Close thy *Byron*; open thy *Goethe*." Byron, for Carlyle, has come to represent that purely rebellious and destructive spirit whose value is great indeed, but negative; Goethe contains all that is best in Byron, and much of a more positive good.

The philosopher fortunate enough to embrace The Everlasting Yea has made some other discoveries. He has learned that life only properly begins with the renunciation of worldly values; that man was not put on earth to be happy, but to work; that in every situation, even the despicable one of the present, there is an ideal action to be performed. And with all of these things realized, darkness and chaos are replaced by a blooming, fertile world wherein the convert exhorts himself, in the terms of *Sartor Resartus*, to

Be no longer a Chaos, but a World, or even Worldkin! Produce! Produce! Were it but the pitifullest infinitesimal fraction of a Product, produce it, in God's name! 'Tis the utmost thou hast in thee: out with it, then. Up, up! Whatsoever thy hand findeth to do, do it with thy whole might. Work while it is called Today; for the Night cometh, wherein no man can work.

It was, at least, something in this spirit that Carlyle began at last the attempt to produce some literary work that should express what he had to say to the world. Irving obtained a commission for him to write an article on Schiller for the *London Magazine*, an article which in the writing became a book; and he was commissioned by an Edinburgh bookseller and publisher to translate Goethe's *Wilhelm Meister*. By the tortuous and self-concealing paths of translation and biography he sought to attain self-expression.

CHAPTER SIX

—TO JANE WELSH CARLYLE

I am going to be really a very meek-tempered wife.
Indeed, I am begun to be meek-tempered already. . . .
And this is my last Letter! What a thought! How terrible,
and yet full of bliss! You will love me forever will you not
my own Husband?

JANE BAILLIE WELSH to Thomas Carlyle, October 1826.

"The Last Speech and *marrying* words of that unfortunate
young, woman Jane Baillie *Welsh*" I received on Friday
morning; and truly a most delightful and swan-like melody
was in them. . . . My last blessing as a Lover is with you;
this is my last letter to Jane Welsh: my first blessing as a
Husband, my first kiss to Jane Carlyle is at hand! O my
Darling! I will always love thee.

THOMAS CARLYLE to Jane Baillie Welsh, October 1826.

BETWEEN EDINBURGH AND Haddington the correspondence
flourished. For some time Carlyle refrained from expressing
again the hopes of a suitor, but wrote to Jane Welsh simply as to
a woman of intellect equal to his own. It was as such that he
regarded her; and she did not find this perfectly sincere flattery
displeasing. In a world where all are snobs, whether open or
inverted; where the nature of an accent or the cut of a coat
are still material for decisive judgements on spiritual and
social values: Jane Welsh was that harmless and almost virtuous
thing, an intellectual snob. She wished to be regarded as
talented, knowledgeable and witty, but she wished even more to
see great men and to hear their conversation: and her early
life was, in a way, a training which ensured that she would
not disgrace herself in such company. She had a sense that
there was something great about Carlyle; or she understood,
at least, that he was like no other man she had known. The
dozens of love letters that passed between these two make up a
correspondence which in its revelations of contrasted tempera-
ments, its intellectual quality, and its flashes of pathos and
comedy, is unexampled in its kind. Throughout the correspondence we can see the volatile, eager, independent talent of

Jane Welsh being slowly subdued and moulded by the massive and ponderous intellect of Carlyle.

After his visit Carlyle reverts to "My dear Madam" as a form of address; and the contents of both his letters and Jane's are, from the point of view of Mrs. Welsh, impeccable. She submits her German translations; he corrects them. He applauds her expressed intention to produce some work of literature, since her nature shows, he feels, the very essence of dramatic genius. Will she adopt the tragic or the comic mode? He sets out in some hundreds of words the possibilities of both, and offers her as a subject a tragedy to be constructed from the story of Boadicea, whose history he obligingly outlines. Miss Welsh feels none of his enthusiasm for Boadicea, and Carlyle, not at all cast down, suggests that they shall exchange a set of verses every fortnight. To this she agrees and sends at once a translation of some verses by Goethe, following it up by other original poems and translations and the suggestion that the Siege of Carcassone (described in Sismondi, whom she has been reading) might provide the material of a tragedy. Carlyle responds with poems of his own, regrets that the Siege of Carcassone will hardly do (although if she feels deeply in favour of it he will search out all possible information), and thinks that after all perhaps she should try a comedy.

Both participants in this exchange deprecated their own poetic talents: and the verses they wrote are chiefly interesting for the light they throw upon their authors. The best of the poems, Carlyle thought, were these lines by Jane Welsh— "The ideas are brilliant, the language emphatic and sonorous, the rhythm very musical and appropriate", he wrote:

I love the mountain torrent dashing
   Downward in thunder loud and hoarse;
With snow-white foam, in fury lashing
   The rugged rocks that break its course.

I love the thunder rumbling, crashing,
   Peal after peal along the skies;
While from the clouds the lightning flashing
   In deathful splendour strikes, destroys.

I love the soul no danger fearing,
   Still onward rushing to its goal,
All that impedes its course down-bearing,
   Proud, fiery, brooking no control.

Behind the stiffness and the Byronic diction we catch a genuine expression of the pent-up intellectual romanticism of Jane Welsh's nature. In emphasizing Carlyle's gaucheness and ill temper and Jane Welsh's flirtatiousness and love of gossip, we should not forget that they belonged to the small intellectual *avant garde* of their time. It is difficult for us to imagine the inspiration both of them drew from the novels and philosophical writings of Madame de Staël; to rediscover the reasons for the mixture of prudishness and admiration with which Carlyle regarded Rousseau, or the open-hearted worship of him felt by Jane Welsh; or to understand the delighted consciousness of outraging orthodoxy that informed their joint admiration of Byron. When Carlyle heard the news of Byron's death he felt as if he had "lost a Brother!" and thought: "O God! That so many sons of mud and clay should fill up their base existence to its utmost bound, and this, the noblest spirit in Europe, should sink before half his course was run." And Jane Welsh replied to him: "I was told it all at once in a room full of people. My God if they had said that the sun or the moon was gone out of the heavens it could not have struck me with the idea of a more awful and dreary blank in the creation than the words Byron is dead!"

The idea that Carlyle was leading Jane Welsh down these dark heretical paths had little basis in fact. She had, as she said, changed her religion and become "a sort of Pagan" after reading Virgil in her early teens; she had read *La Nouvelle Héloïse* and admired its unchaste heroine (although "*I do not wish to countenance such irregularities* among my female *acquaintances*") before Carlyle had any influence over her. When, however, Carlyle went on from Rousseau, Byron and Madame de Staël to Schiller and Goethe, Irving for one felt that somebody should protect Jane Welsh from such loose thinkers. There was, he said darkly, "too much of that furniture about the elegant drawing-room of Jane Welsh"; and he feared that unless she was given some more sober companions she would stray altogether from the sphere of his influence.

This influence was now being exerted publicly and with effect. Irving's success in the little Hatton Garden chapel was immediate. The oratorical style that had seemed affected in Kirkcaldy and Glasgow was immensely impressive to those who heard him in London. The little chapel was filled almost from his first sermon and the seal was placed upon his success when Canning, then at the height of his fame, made a reference in the House of Commons to one of Irving's addresses as "the most eloquent sermon he had ever heard". Canning's words brought the curious, the intelligent, the devout and the fashionable to hear the preacher: but those who came out of curiosity returned again and again, fascinated by his magnificent appearance and his earnestness, as well as by the strange beliefs to which he gave utterance. Within a very few weeks Irving was famous, the subject of violent lampoons and angry leading articles. His church was crowded every week with upper class men and women of all beliefs; Theodore Hook observed ironically, and not without truth, that the entry to the church was closed only to the pious poor. All roads to Hatton Garden were blocked for miles by carriages and pedestrians; early arrivals waited in long queues for admission; there was a ready sale of tickets for half a guinea apiece.

This triumph was due, in large part, to Irving's power as a speaker; De Quincey's praise of him as "by many, many degrees, the greatest orator of our times" had several echoes. But his audience was fascinated by the words he spoke, almost as much as by the passion with which they were uttered. With the fervour of a latterday Savonarola Irving reproached his fashionable audience for their indifference to the condition of the poor and the growth of unbelief, as well as for the casual spiritual conduct of their own lives. Those who heard him may not have been convinced by his words, but they were certainly disturbed by them; and few remained unaffected by the evident belief of the preacher that he was himself inspired. His first book, the *Orations* and the *Argument for Judgment to Come* sold three editions very quickly, in spite of the fact that it was greeted with scurrilous hostility from newspapers and reviews which attacked his grammar, his taste and his arrogance, and did, not fail to notice his squint.

So half of Irving's prophecy was fulfilled: he was "first in Divinity", in the sense that in the space of a few months he had become the most famous orator in Britain. Carlyle greeted his friend's success with sincere pleasure in which some jealousy was mingled. He felt himself forgotten because Irving, busy in London, did not write to him; moreover, the *Argument for Judgment to Come* had its inception in Irving's detestation of the *Vision of Judgment* written by Carlyle's much-loved Byron. It is not surprising, therefore, that writing to his brother Alick,

Carlyle should have reflected that although few men living deserved success more than Irving, such popularity would not suit his own taste; or that, writing to Jane Welsh, he should have thought it a pity that Irving's preaching had taken such a turn, and said that it would have been better for him to have become: "What he must ultimately pass for, a preacher of first rate abilities, of great eloquence and great absurdity, with a head fertile above all others in sense and nonsense, and a heart of the most honest and kindly sort". In the struggle between jealousy and generosity the latter, after all, won the day: "I could wager any money that he thinks of you and me very often, though he never writes to either; and that he longs above all to know what we do think of this monstrous flourishing of drums and trumpets in which he lives and moves". In the same letter Carlyle mentioned casually that Irving was soon returning to Scotland to marry that Isabella Martin of Kirkcaldy to whom he had contracted an engagement some years before.

Jane Welsh had her own reasons, unknown to Carlyle, for viewing Irving's success with mixed feelings. Between the gigantic teacher and his charming and talented pupil existed a relationship which remains obscure, in spite of many efforts made to disentangle it. Irving's susceptibility to feminine charms has been noted already, and there can be no doubt that among the young women upon whom he cast an appreciative eye Jane Welsh was included. He wrote her letters addressed to "My dear and Lovely Pupil"; and among the extravagant phrases characteristic of him are some which it is difficult to explain except on the assumption that he was in love with her, and wished to be free from his engagement to Isabella Martin. On the back of a sonnet he wrote to her are some cryptic and incomplete lines, part of the letter which she destroyed while preserving the sonnet: two of them read, "I have resolved neither to see Isabella nor her father before I" and "cannot brook the sight of either until this be explained and until". It seems probable, in the light of these words, that Irving went to Isabella's father and asked for his release: if so, he did not get it. Later he wrote to Jane Welsh that his regard for her "would long ago have taken the form of the most devoted attachment, but for one intervening circumstance" and that only with the help of heaven could he hope to find power "to satisfy duty to another and affection to you".

There is not much evidence that these warm feelings were

altogether reciprocated. Jane Welsh told Carlyle, on an occasion to be recorded, that she had once loved Irving passionately: but she had been passionately in love two or three times in her twenty-odd years, and Irving's name does not once appear among the long list of lovers that she sent to her friend Bess Stodart. Whether she would have married Irving had he been free; whether she would have been happier with Irving than with Carlyle; whether her brilliant sanity and commonsense could have saved him from the tragic fate that lay ahead: these questions will never be answered, any more than we shall know what song the sirens sang, or whether Marlowe would have been as great a dramatic poet as Shakespeare had he lived another twenty-odd years. Jane Welsh was, at any rate, sufficiently piqued by Irving's marriage to write about it with an edge of malice: "Tell me how he gets on with a wife; it must be very laughable"; sufficiently aware of the chance she had missed to refer with consistent irony to Irving's extravagances, absurdities, and neglect of his friends; and sufficiently annoyed by the comparison between successful Irving (who became daily more remote) and unsuccessful Carlyle (who was, in a postal way at least, only too ready at hand) to scold the latter for his foolishness in ignoring worldly success:

When shall a world know your worth as I do? You laugh at the stir I make about fame; but I suspect my sentiments on that subject, stript of the "garb" of my expressions, which is at times fantastic enough—are not very dissimilar to your own—You are *not satisfied* living thus—bowing a haughty genius to the paltry necessity of making provision for your daily wants—stifling the fire of an ambitious soul with hard-learned lessons of humility; or expending it in idle longings and vague, colourless schemes—"The wheel of your destiny *must* turn"—I have heard you say so—and you have power to turn it—great power. But when shall the effort be made? When will your genius burst through all obstruction and find its proper place? it *will*,—"as the bolt bursts on high from the black cloud that bound it"!—of *that* I have no fear; but when? Oh that I heard a nation repeat your name.

She encouraged him to work on the life of Schiller and the translation of *Wilhelm Meister*: but she made no attempt to

conceal her disappointment that he should be so deeply
involved in work that absorbed so much of his time and so
little of his talent. Carlyle agreed with her heartily. The
inadequacy of his biography of Schiller filled him with dismay,
and he was little better pleased with the translation of *Wilhelm
Meister*: he was infuriated by the disparity between the second-
hand nature of the task and the high view he held of his own
ability. He gloomily prophesied that nobody would buy a
copy of the translation, and added that Goethe was "the
greatest genius that has lived for a century, and the greatest
ass that has lived for three".

From these frustrations sprang other troubles. It was not to
be expected that Carlyle's first idyllic view of the Bullers, in
which he pronounced Mrs. Buller "one of the most fascinating
refined women I have ever seen" and her husband "an honest,
worthy, straightforward English Gentleman", should survive
long acquaintance with them in the humble position of tutor.
The Bullers were an intelligent and generous couple: Mrs.
Buller had in London been the centre of a group of Radical
intellectuals, and her husband was a hard-headed man who
enjoyed Carlyle's keen sarcasm. They realized that they had to
do with a strange and exceptionally talented man, and they
treated him with great tolerance. Carlyle was not unapprecia-
tive of such kindness: he told his brother John that the elder
Bullers treated him almost like a son, and the younger ones like
a brother; yet he was fretted by their expectation that he should
present himself in their drawing-room in the evenings to
drink tea and engage in polite conversation, and he was not
altogether pleased by a certain changeableness in Mrs. Buller's
disposition.

After staying a winter in Edinburgh the Bullers decided to
take furnished Kinnaird House in Perthshire, not far below the
mouth of Killiecrankie Pass. Carlyle, by his own wish, did not
lodge with them, but in an old mansion nearby also called
Kinnaird House, "a queer, old-fashioned, snug enough,
entirely secluded edifice, sunk among trees, about a gunshot
from the new big House". He went for long rides by horseback,
continued to write about Schiller and to translate Goethe: in
this loneliness his health seemed to become worse and worse,
and his spirits sunk lower and lower. It was a lifelong illusion
of Carlyle's that he disliked company, and was happy only in
solitude: in fact he was generally a cheerful and often a gay

companion, and became profoundly miserable when left alone for any length of time.

This loss of spirits was reflected in his view of his employers. It was in vain that, when he found his sleep disturbed and attributed it to the change in his hour of dining, they made arrangements immediately for him to take his meals alone at any time convenient to him; that he was left to join the family or to spend the evening alone as he wished; that he was treated in all respects as an equal. Carlyle reflected that he would be an unreasonable blockhead if he complained of their behaviour to him: yet his temper grew steadily worse in face of such incitements to irritation as the presence of some slightly fashionable guests who took great care to go out properly wrapped up and were immensely excited by their success in shooting two small fawns. There was, moreover, the difficulty of food. Sometimes Carlyle thought that Mrs. Buller was an exceptionally bad housewife, sometimes he regarded her as a beneficent figure whose good intentions were thwarted by the incompetence of the sluttish harlots (as he called them) who carried them out. Eating had worse effects, if that were possible, than abstinence. "If I take any of their swine-meat porridge, I sleep", he wrote to his brother Alick. "But a double portion of stupidity overwhelms me, and I awake very early in the morning with the consciousness that another day of my precious, precious time is gone irrevocably, that I have been very miserable yesterday, and shall be very miserable today. It is clear to me that I can never recover or retain my health under the economy of Mrs. Buller. Nothing, therefore, remains for me but to leave it."

Such despair, however, was always succeeded by good resolutions. Enormous efforts were needed to overcome the monstrous evils surrounding him; and enormous efforts should be made. "I say, Jack, thou and I must never falter", he wrote to his brother John, then placidly continuing his studies in Edinburgh, who must have been mildly surprised by such adjurations. "Work, my boy, work unweariedly. I swear that all the thousand miseries of this hard fight, and ill health, the most terrific of them all, shall never chain us down. By the river Styx it shall not. Two fellows from a nameless spot in Annandale shall yet show the world the pluck that is in Carlyles."

At times it seemed to Carlyle, as it must certainly appear

to the reader, that such lamentations and heroics were expressed in a manner altogether incommensurable with their cause: and in fact he did not at this time throw up his position, although he often threatened to do so. Perhaps gratitude to the Bullers restrained him, perhaps he realized that he would not, essentially, be better off in Edinburgh or anywhere else. He stayed with the Bullers at Kinnaird House for nine months and when at the end of that time they went to London, he was given three months' leave to arrange for the printing of *Wilhelm Meister* and to visit his family at Mainhill. Then, in June 1824, he followed the Bullers to London. Jane Welsh had hoped to pay a visit to London at the same time, so that they might both be guests of the now-famous Irving: but Irving wrote to Carlyle that his house was not in a condition to receive a lady, and to Jane Welsh that "My dear Isabella has succeeded in healing the wounds of my heart, but I am hardly yet in a position to expose them", and suggesting that she should delay her visit for a year when he would be "worthy in the eye of (his) own conscience" to receive her. Whether or not this letter from the man now called by Jane "that stupendous Ass the Orator" was inspired by his wife's jealousy, it put an end to her dream of visiting London with Carlyle. Equipped with letters to the poet Thomas Campbell and the engineer Telford, and in possession of the £180 paid him for the translation of *Wilhelm Meister*, Carlyle set out alone on a six day voyage by yacht to the great city.

Irving, with his usual optimism, was convinced that his friend need only be introduced to the London intellectuals for his capacity to be acknowledged: Carlyle thought differently, and knew better. His dogmatically-expressed opinions were likely to offend, and the broad burr of his speech might make them appear ridiculous; the enormous range of his reading not merely in literature, but in history, philosophy and science, would be appreciated only by the few people prepared in advance to give his views respectful attention; his earnestness and lack of light humour were not likely to be endearing. Carlyle expected little from London, and so was not disappointed.

The journey was, it is almost unnecessary to say, most melancholy: partly from the cross winds, storms and calms encountered, and partly from the stupidity of the society on board. The portraits of his companions that Carlyle cast off in letters foreshadow in their sharpness and concreteness his most brilliant writing of a later time. Sir David Innes, we learn

> Had a large long head like a sepulchral urn; his face pock-pitted, hirsute and bristly, was at once vast and hatchet-shaped. He stood for many hours together with his left hand laid upon the boat in the middle of the deck, and the thumb of his right hand stuck firmly with its point on the hip joint; his large blue rheumy eyes gazing on vacancy, the very image of thick-lipped musing.

At last the journey was over, and Irving met: and Irving, as always, exceeded in kindness what Carlyle had hoped or expected. Their last parting had been unfortunate. Carlyle had accompanied Irving and his wife upon part of their honeymoon through the Highlands: and on the last day that they were together a servant came up on behalf of a local peer with an invitation to dinner; a minute or two later the invitation was reinforced by the arrival of the peer himself. Perhaps it might have been stretched to include Carlyle; but in fact he saddled his horse and rode home alone.

In London all this was forgotten, if by Irving it had ever been remembered: he was, as always, eager to help his friend. On the very first afternoon Carlyle found himself in a whirl of religious Radicals and bluestockings, including a pretty and bashful cousin of Charles Buller's named Kitty Kirkpatrick, who attracted Carlyle's attention by twitching off in the lobby the label sticking to his trunk and taking it away with her; an action, it may be said, that has never been explained except on Carlyle's own dubious hypothesis that she took away the label to show to another cousin named Mrs. Strachey. Kitty Kirkpatrick and Mrs. Strachey had very handsomely furnished the Irvings' drawing-room in their absence: such were the blessings showered upon the fortunate Orator. Was Irving happy? Carlyle did not think so, finding that his friend was trying to conceal his inner confusion by persuading himself that he was conferring benefits from heaven upon the crowds that gathered continually around him.

At first impact, London literary society made no favourable impression upon Carlyle. He presented his letter of introduction to Campbell, whose "Hohenlinden" he had once thought a great poem. The conscientiously rustic Carlyle disliked the poet's dapper appearance; "the blue frock and trowsers, the eye glass, the wig, the very fashion of his bow, proclaim the literary dandy". To this appearance Campbell added the sins of an unwelcoming manner and a wife who spoke with a Celtic accent. Were these, Carlyle wondered after his visit, the rewards of literature—"a stupid Gaelic wife, with the pitiful gift of making verses, and affections cold as those of a tinker's cuddie, with nothing to love but my own paltry self and what belongs to it?"

More disappointing than Campbell was Coleridge, of whom Carlyle left a pen-portrait, in writing to his brother John, which is marvellous in its visual power, and in its indication of the way in which Carlyle identified mental characteristics through physical ones:

> Figure a fat, flabby, incurvated personage, at once short, rotund, and relaxed, with a watery mouth, a snuffy nose, a pair of strange brown, timid, yet earnest-looking eyes, a high tapering brow, and a great bush of grey hair; and you have some faint idea of Coleridge. . . . He has no resolution. He shrinks from pain or labour in any of its shapes. His very attitude bespeaks this. He never straightens his knee-joints. He stoops with his fat, ill-shapen shoulders, and in walking he does not tread, but shovel and slide. . . . He *would* do with all his heart, but he knows he dares not. The conversation of the man is much as I anticipated—a forest of thoughts, some true, many false, more part dubious, all of them ingenious in some degree, often in a high degree. But there is no method in his talk: he wanders like a man sailing among many currents, whithersoever his lazy mind directs him; and, what is more unpleasant, he preaches, or rather soliloquizes. . . . I reckon him a man of great and useless genuis: a strange, not at all a great man.

Such was his view of the two most important men of letters he met on this visit. His general view of the literary life was even lower than his particular view of individuals. A rabble destitute not merely of high feeling, but of common honesty; ill-natured weaklings; not men, but mere things for writing articles: such were some of the hard words he used about the professional critics of the day. It would be interesting to know what they thought of this strangely-dressed intruder: but the eyes of those upon whom he gazed so keenly passed him over without notice.

Was it not, indeed, part of the offence of Coleridge that when Carlyle managed to get the philosopher to himself and tried to engage him with questions about Kant and about " 'reason' versus 'understanding' ", he received evasive replies?

This visit to London marked the end of Carlyle's career as a tutor. The changeableness of Mrs. Buller was now manifested in the kind of uncertainty about her movements that he found it impossible to endure patiently. She thought of spending some months in Boulogne, and in the meantime lodged Charles and his tutor in a house at Kew Green which Charles detested and Carlyle found tedious; then she thought of going to Royston in Hertfordshire. Was Carlyle prepared to go to France, and willing in the meantime to come to Royston? Thus confronted with the need to make an immediate decision, Carlyle rejected the Bullers' offer. He had no very obvious reason for doing so: but he was tired of teaching even such amiable young men as the Bullers, and he discerned—or thought that he discerned—a wish on Mrs. Buller's part that Charles should go to Cambridge.

The Bullers and Carlyle parted in amity. Charles Buller was "in a passion of sadness and anger", Mr. Buller a little distressed, his wife upon the whole rather pleased. Buller offered Carlyle twenty pounds as a parting gift. "With an excess of generosity which I am not quite reconciled to since I thought of it maturely, I pronounced it to be too much, and accepted of ten", Carlyle wrote to his mother. "The old gentleman and I shook hands with dry eyes. Mrs. Buller gave me one of those 'Good mornings' with which fashionable people think it right to part with friends and foes alike . . . I am glad that we have parted in friendship; very glad that we are parted at all." It must be remembered that Carlyle's letters are not always a fair representation of his conduct: he gives the impression here, for instance, of a sharpness in the parting that must have been largely imaginary. Mrs. Buller extended her fashionable 'Good morning' by an invitation to a party that same evening, and the whole family remained upon terms of sincere friendship with the strange tutor. Carlyle's irritation was often purely epistolary: and the strain he endured cannot be assessed except by those who, like him, have laboured at uncongenial work in which only a fraction of their energy and nothing of their genius has been occupied. It was in the interest of his genius that Carlyle chiefly felt happy in parting from the Bullers.

But what was the nature of this very long-maturing genius? It had been manifested by now in the life of Schiller and the translation of *Wilhelm Meister*. Carlyle afterwards referred to the life of Schiller as a weak and feeble little book. It is certainly very unlike what we think of as his characteristic work, but it is not by any means a dull or contemptible performance. The style owes a great deal still to Johnson, but has a balance, firmness and humour of its own. Even at this time the effect of his humour depends upon exaggeration. "Look at the biography of authors! Except the Newgate Calendar, it is the most sickening chapter in the history of man", is a fair example; or "Harte's *History of Gustavus*, a wilderness which mere human patience seems unable to explore, is yet enlivened here and there with a cheerful spot, when he tells us of some scalade or camisado, or speculates on troopers rendered bullet-proof by art-magic". The *Life of Schiller* contains much excellent analytical criticism as well as many remarks even more applicable to Carlyle than to his subject ("Above all, he has no cant; in any of its thousand branches, ridiculous or hateful, none."). But upon the whole the most remarkable feature of this biography, written in ill-health and low spirits, is its coolness and serenity: the air of academic evenness and objectivity is quite remarkably maintained. Such a style was wholly at variance with Carlyle's temper and mode of life; it is interesting to see how nearly he had mastered it.

The reception of the two books was generally amiable. *The Times* gave a friendly reference to the *Life of Schiller*, and *Wilhelm Meister*, Carlyle told Jane Welsh, "is growing a kind of small very small lion in London: the newspapers puff him, the people read him, many venerate him very highly." There was one exception to this veneration: De Quincey, reviewing the book in the *London Magazine*, made a savage attack on Goethe, and a sharp criticism of his translator. This criticism was not, surprisingly enough, based upon the errors in Carlyle's translation (he had taught himself the language with grammar and dictionary, and had had little or no opportunity of hearing German spoken); De Quincey objected to the "provincialisms, barbarisms and vulgarisms" of the translation. Such Scotticisms as "backing a letter" for "addressing a letter" and "I cannot want it" for "I cannot do without it" were reproved severely: this coarse diction, De Quincey surmised, sprung from the translator's lack of intercourse with society.

De Quincey's attack gives the measure of the task that Carlyle had set himself in sponsoring Goethe and Schiller. To us the German Romantic movement exists in literary history as a triumphant revolt against Voltairean scepticism, an affirmation of belief in civilized values joined to a kind of aestheticism, and backed rather vaguely by the ideas of German idealist philosophers. Literary critics have fixed to their satisfaction the places of Goethe and Schiller in European society, and have assessed the beauties in the fragmentary notes of Novalis and the tumultuous epithets of Richter. But in the early nineteenth century De Quincey expressed, with unusual violence certainly, the view of most English men of letters when he said that "Not the baseness of Egyptian superstition, not Titania under enchantment, not Caliban in drunkenness, ever shaped to themselves an idol more weak and hollow than modern Germany has set up for its worship in the person of Goethe".

Carlyle was almost alone in his high assessment of the German romantics. He rated them so high, to be sure, because some features of their work expressed his own so far inarticulate outlook on man and the world. The books that influence us enlarge ideas that exist already in embryo within our minds: but they may contain also other ideas, which we distort or ignore. Thus Carlyle rejected ruthlessly many aspects of Schiller's and Goethe's ideas. He was frankly bored by their insistent aestheticism, and by their view that culture in its most comprehensive sense could be advanced through drama and poetry. He discovered in Goethe (however odd it may appear to us that he should have done so) a kind of justification for modern Puritanism, a distrust and contempt for the body and its desires. He took from Kant, whom he read at the same time, not his attempted proof of the relativity of all knowledge, nor his condemnation of metaphysics, but the idea that in the modern world it was necessary to construct a new and bolder metaphysic. He did not assess Kant like a professional philosopher; he did not evaluate Goethe as an artist: to attempt such assessments and evaluations would have seemed to him a waste of time. He was looking for ideas that would help him to combine fervent Radicalism with an equally fervent mysticism, distrust of orthodox Christianity with admiration for the effects of Christian Puritanism: and he found them in the German romantics.

We can understand today how necessary to Carlyle was the
guidance and impetus given him by the German romantic
writers, how they helped to emancipate him from the narrow
piety of family life and open up vistas (of which it is true the
end was not even vaguely visible) of an approach to social
problems which should adhere to Christian morality while
ignoring Christian doctrine: biographers have been granted an
enviable hindsight into such matters. But to Jane Welsh these
things were not obvious: it seemed to her merely that Carlyle
was wasting his time in drudgery. She did not at first care for
Goethe, who was certainly different enough in temper from her
favourites Rousseau and Byron: but even when she began
to appreciate him she still thought it a pity that Carlyle should
spend time in translation; and she' received with no great
pleasure the news that more German translations were to be
undertaken, including this time specimens of the work of
several writers. It was part of Jane Welsh's romanticism to look
for fame, or the prospect of fame, in a husband; and there
must have been times when she felt that Carlyle's genius would
always be hidden in conversational sarcasm and epistolary
profundity, and would never shine bravely before the whole
wide world.

Carlyle's activities after he had parted from the Bullers can
hardly have impressed her with his determination to work. He
went first to stay in Birmingham with a chemist and physician
named Badams, to whom he had been introduced by Irving's
friend Mrs. Montagu. Badams had cured several patients of
stomach troubles; and he promised to cure Carlyle. His treatment consisted of regular exercise and a diet in which half-raw
eggs, floods of tea, and wine drunk before dinner were important elements. He was strongly opposed to the use of drugs.
Carlyle had recently taken the advice of a doctor who told him
to give up tobacco, and dosed him plentifully with mercury and
with castor oil. The treatment of Badams, who allowed the use
of tobacco, and told Carlyle to use castor oil only once every
four days, must have appeared positively gentle in comparison.
Badams, who was making a large amount of money from the
manufacture of sulphuric acid, kept two or three horses: he was
a brisk, eager and a friendly man who would come in and wake
Carlyle at six o'clock in the morning for a two hour gallop
before breakfast. Carlyle stayed at Birmingham for several
weeks, during which his health seemed to improve; then,

instead of returning to Scotland, he went south. Jane Welsh first heard from him at Dover and then at the Hotel de Wâgram in Paris.

This journey to France came about through the indirect agency of Irving. The Orator, as Jane Welsh and Carlyle now both called him in their letters, had gone to Dover with his wife and small son, and that Kitty Kirkpatrick who had abstracted the label from Carlyle's trunk; there Irving meditated, wrote and bathed, and there Carlyle joined him to meditate and bathe, although not to write. He wrote to Jane Welsh, it is true, dwelling pleasantly on the attractions of Kitty Kirkpatrick and on the absurdities of the Orator. Kitty Kirkpatrick, he wrote, was "a little black-eyed, auburn-haired, brunette, full of kindliness and humour, and who never I believe was angry at any creature for a moment in her life." Kitty had other attractions: she was twentyone, had fifty thousand pounds in her own right, concerned herself demurely with the housekeeping, and withal was the child of an Indian Begum and an English Colonial official. Her happiness, Carlyle thought, "lies in the blood; and philosophy can do little to help us". Irving and Carlyle had many long and friendly discussions: but Carlyle could not forbear describing to Jane Welsh the way in which the Orator cared for his new-born son:

It would do you good to look at him in the character of day-nurse to his first-born Edward! It is a feeble shapeless thing, as all children of six weeks are; yet Isabella and her Spouse could not be more attentive to the infant Lama, were they high Priestess and Priest of Thibet. The waking and sleeping and all the operations of "him" (as they emphatically name it) form a most important item in the general weal. "Isabella", said he, "I think *I* would wash him with *warm* water tonight?" "Yes, *Dear*", said the compliant Isabella; Kitty smirked in secret; and I made bold to dissent totally from the suggestion; declaring that in my view this was the Wife's concern alone, and that were I in her place I would wash him with oil-of-vitriol, if I pleased, and take no one's counsel of it. Oh that you saw the giant with his broad-brimmed hat, his sallow visage, and sable matted fleece of hair, carrying the little pepper-box of a creature, folded in his monstrous palms, along the beach; tick-ticking to it, and dandling it, and every time it stirs an eye-lid, "grinning horrible a ghastly smile", heedless of the crowds of petrified spectators, that turn round in long trains gazing in silent terror at the fatherly Leviathan!

At Dover the party was joined by Edward Strachey, a man in his fifties who, like Buller, had at one time been a judge in India; and by his wife, who was some twenty years younger. Mrs. Strachey was a sister of Mrs. Buller but, as Carlyle said, "no more like her than the diamond of Golconda is to that of Bristol"; she liked and admired Carlyle at once, and it is probable that she thought of Kitty Kirkpatrick as a suitable wife for him. It was at her suggestion that, in the company of Edward Strachey and Kitty Kirkpatrick, Carlyle went to Paris; Irving, his wife and the much-dandled infant remained in Mrs. Strachey's company at Dover.

Carlyle read French easily, but spoke it badly and with a marked foreign accent; Strachey's French was even worse, and in Paris he abandoned it altogether and spoke English which, with the aid of gestures, he found to answer much better. Carlyle enjoyed the visit, although his wonder at the palaces and picture-galleries and continual entertainments was limited by a feeling that such fripperies could not be approved by an adherent to German idealism. He enjoyed France, as it were, against his will. The Palais Royal, he noted, was the chosen abode of vanity and vice; he rejoiced that it was never likely to be copied in the British Isles; meanwhile, he often ate dinner in it. The French people sat and chattered and drank and ate away existence in a way that no moralist could approve; their houses were like toy-boxes, tricked out with mirrors; quacks and dandies, gulls and sharpers, were seen everywhere by a watchful Scotchman; and in the midst of all the racket, among the filigree and gilding, he saw in the Morgue the naked body of an old artisan who had drowned himself in the Seine, his face fixed in a scowl of despair, his patched and soiled clothes together with his apron and sabots hanging at his head. The need to contrast such a sight with the gaiety outside may seem to us a commentary on Carlyle; for Carlyle it was a commentary on French civilization.

His journey appalled the family at Mainhill. France, to the elder Carlyles, was still the enemy of England, and they seriously questioned if their son would ever return. Mrs. Carlyle stopped singing at her work, and if Carlyle's sisters

laughed or sang they were reproached with showing an un-
becoming lightness of heart; enquiries were made daily at the
Post Office for a letter that would announce their son's safety.
At last it came and they gave thanks that he had, as his brother
Alick put it, "visited the once-powerful kingdom of the great
Napoleon, at whose frown Europe crouched in terror." Mrs.
Carlyle had studied *Wilhelm Meister* with a kind of fascinated
horror, exclaiming against the wantonness of the women in the
book, but nothing could have shown her so well as this journey
to Paris the great gulf that separated her ideas from those of her
eldest son. She accepted at last, although she was never
reconciled to, the fact that he had strayed a long way from her
own sectarian strictness, and it can have been with little hope
that he would follow her advice that after his return to London
she wrote to him: "Tell me if thou readest a chapter often. If
not begin oh do begin! How do you spend the Sabbath in
that tumultuous city? Oh remember to keep it holy this you
will never repent."

At Haddington also the news of his visit was greeted, for
rather different reasons, with little warmth. Jane Welsh was
somewhat tired of hearing about the dangers and tediums of
the great world without having a chance to sample them. At
least, she wrote maliciously (and mistakenly) Carlyle would not
speak Annandale after having travelled; and she wondered
plaintively in another letter when she would see this delightful
South where everybody found friends. She reacted sharply, and
with the pride of possession, to Carlyle's praise of Kitty
Kirkpatrick:

> I congratulate you on your present situation. With such a
> picture of domestic felicity before your eyes, and this
> "singular and very pleasing creature" to charm away the
> blue devils, you can hardly fail to be as happy as the day is
> long. Miss Kitty Kirkpatrick—Lord what an ugly name!
> "Good Kitty"! Oh, pretty, dear, delightful Kitty! I am not a
> bit jealous of her, not I indeed,—Hindoo Princess tho' she
> be! Only you may as well never let me hear you mention her
> name again.

What good reason had she for jealousy? This letter was
written in October 1824, and by that time Jane Welsh had
made up her mind, however reluctantly, that she was going to

marry Thomas Carlyle, although she did not regard herself as firmly engaged to him until three months later.

The transition from teacher to lover had not been made easily; in the process Carlyle had been given many more shrewd reminders of his poverty and his social unworthiness. For a long time he wisely made no attempt to change their purely intellectual relationship; she was, he repeated over and over, a genius who need only study, write and publish, to be acknowledged. Few aspirants to literary fame find such words either distasteful or incredible: Jane Welsh was helped by them to pull through much history and philosophy that she found frankly tedious. Yet she did not altogether share his illusion about her genius; she never began her side of the novel on which he suggested they should work in collaboration, and of which he wrote in fact two chapters that went into the fire; but who could be other than pleased by the praise of a tutor so learned, and so plainly in love with her? She teased him by telling him of various suitors: the young man of about six feet two, slender and graceful, who wore an amethyst ring on one finger and a steel chain with an ingenious portable perspective to denote his occupation of artist; the farmer's son whose proposal she decisively rejected; the youth with "fair silky locks, the sweetest eyes in nature, and a voice like music," who was so distressed by her refusal of him that he wept himself into a fever, fainted while out walking with her, and then "lay for three days and nights without sleep and almost without sustenance, tossing on his bed and crying his lovely eyes out". By the side of this romantic young man the little local Doctor Fyffe who merely threatened to commit suicide when she refused him seems almost commonplace.

Carlyle was expected to laugh at these suitors, and to sympathise with Jane Welsh in bearing with them, but for a long time he was not encouraged to enter the lists himself. She wrote to him now as her dear friend and subscribed herself "Yours affectionately": but when, mistaking a phrase in a letter of hers, he wrote ardently that "Jane loves me! she loves me! and I swear by the immortal powers that she shall yet be mine, as I am hers, thro' life and death and all the dark vicissitudes that await us here or hereafter", he was briskly undeceived. The love she felt for Carlyle, Jane Welsh explained, was that of a sister, calm and delightful; it would continue such even if she were married. "Your Friend I will be, your truest

most devoted Friend, while I breathe the breath of life; but
your Wife! Never, never! not though you were as rich as
Croesus, as honoured and as renowned as you yet shall be".
Carlyle replied with a pathetic pretence of satisfaction that
she had put their relations "*on the very footing where I wished them
to stand.*" His diet during this courtship included more humble
pie than he ate during the rest of his life.

The story of this strange lovemaking has been told chiefly
through letters: and the occasions on which Carlyle and Jane
Welsh met during these years were remarkably few. Irving
took Carlyle over to Haddington in May 1821, when they
stayed three or four days; Jane came to Edinburgh at the end
of that summer and stayed five or six weeks, during which she
saw Carlyle often. He paid his unhappy week-end visit in
February 1822, and did not see her again until a year later,
when he came out to Haddington on Mrs. Welsh's invitation.
This time he was well received. In May 1823 they met in
Edinburgh, but only hurriedly, because Mrs. Welsh had again
expressed her disapproval of Carlyle; in November he paid
another short visit to Haddington. In February 1824 Jane
Welsh came to stay with her friend Bess Stodart in Edinburgh
and saw Carlyle frequently, and she saw him again for a day or
two in May before he went to London. And that was all.
When in January 1825 she regarded herself as formally engaged
to Carlyle, Jane had not seen him for six months.

Carlyle's actual proposal of marriage (or rather the proposal
which Jane Welsh, with several qualifications, accepted) was
complicated by a misunderstanding that was not without
importance. When describing his visit to Paris he wrote,
perhaps with a guilty feeling that he might appear to be
wasting his celebrated freedom in the pleasures of travel, that
he was thinking of retiring into Annandale or any other dale,
there to write and read, read and garden, and live according
to the Birmingham code of diet. When she said casually that
she approved of this plan Carlyle elaborated. If he had land of
his own, he said, he would become a farmer. "I think how I
should mount on horseback in the grey of the morning; and go
forth like a destroying angel among my lazy hinds; quickening
every sluggish hand; cultivating and clearing, tilling and
planting, till the very place became a garden round me! In
the intermediate hours I could work at literature; thus *compelled* to live according to the wants of nature, in one

twelvemonth, I should be the healthiest man in three parishes."
London, he said, was no place to live; it was a monster of a city
that would amuse her for a week; more and worse, there was
no truly intellectual person among Irving's friends, and barely,
indeed, one in the whole of London. In her lengthy answer
Jane Welsh dwelt on this last remark and ironically listed all the
improving and intellectual society that she had been told
awaited her ("*Your* 'Rosy-fingered Morn', too, the Hindoo
Princess, where is she?"); at the end of several pages she
dismissed the farming project in two lines: " 'If you had land
of your own you would improve it'! Suppose you improve
mine? It is to let at present, and I know none that has more
need of improvement."

She had dismissed the subject with a joke: but she should
have known better than to joke in such a way, and on such a
subject, with Carlyle. He accepted the idea enthusiastically.
Would she go with him, would she share his life at Craigenputtock? She had only to say "Yes" and he would send his
brother Alick over to rent the farm at once. He entered upon a
rhapsody of a country household. What was it, he asked, that
made bluestockings of women and magazine hacks of men?
Nothing but their removal from reality, their departure from
nature. He envisioned the faculties of order and elegance which
Jane Welsh spent now upon pictures and portfolios devoted to
the proper conduct of a household; he saw his own mind
enlarged and invigorated by contact with the soil. "The rose
in its full-blown fragrance is the glory of the fields: but there
must be a soil and stem and leaves, or there will be no rose.
Your mind and my own *have* in them many capabilities; but
the first of all their duties is to provide for their own regulation
and contentment: if there *be* an overplus to consecrate to higher
ends, it will not fail to show itself". And after a cursory mention
of the question of money, a difficulty which he thought generally
overrated, he invited her to "Consent, if you dare trust me!
Consent, and come to my faithful breast, and let us live and die
together!"

It is easy, in an age which finds something ridiculous in all
heroics, to see what is absurd in Carlyle's suggestion: the
contempt for money and disregard of fame that went with it
are marks of a true and valuable idealism which we prefer to
ignore. Jane Welsh was more impartial. She understood the
passion and potential power of Carlyle: but she was unwilling

to live in an air quite so rarefied. Nothing more nicely indicates
the differences of temperament between Thomas Carlyle and
Jane Welsh than the story of their walk down Princes Street
in the early days of their relationship when she responded to his
words: "How many things are here which I do not want",
with the reply: "How many things are here which I cannot
get." Jane Welsh was in the best sense worldly, and she was also
practical. Probably she would have liked to live in London:
quite certainly she did not want to live in such a bleak, wild
and desolate place as Craigenputtock, more than a mile away
from the nearest cottage, a place where life would be hard and
company lacking. What could be further removed from the
ideal life she had recently sketched out to Carlyle of "A 'sweet
house' calmly embosomed in some romantic vale; with wealth
enough to realize my ideal of elegant comfort; with books,
statues, paintings and all things suitable to a tasteful, intellectual manner of life; with the friendship and society of a few,
whose conversation would improve the faculties of my head and
heart." With such an ideal before her, who can blame Jane
Welsh for looking coldly on the prospect of life at Craigenputtock? "You and I keeping house at Craigenputtock!" she
wrote. "I would just as soon think of building myself a nest on
the Bass Rock."

Her reply to the rest of Carlyle's letter was frank enough.
She said that she loved him, honestly, serenely, simply, "but
I am not *in love* with you—that is to say—my love for you is not
a passion which overclouds my judgment, and absorbs all my
regard for myself and others." She did not wish for grandeur or
fortune: but she was not prepared to abandon the "station in
society" into which she had been born. Had he any fixed
place in her own rank of society? she asked. Or any immediate
prospect of attaining it? Had he any settled income, even a
modest one? Let him forget Craigenputtock, think how to use
his talents "to gild over the inequality of our births and then
—we will talk of marrying."

An engagement to marry was perhaps never discussed in
terms more logical or less warm. It seems at first surprising
that this should have been the first in a series of letters in which
these two contestants for superiority in married life (for so one
is almost bound to regard them) each stated and restated the
case from their own point of view, with a courtesy and a care
for the logical development of argument that would do credit

to many a professor. Few lovers could have endured the chilling reception Jane Welsh gave to Carlyle's most cherished ideas; few women would have examined with Jane's calmness and candour their feelings for the man they meant to marry. For that she did mean to marry him became ever plainer, even to herself, through the pattern of mutual compliment and finespun argument. When she declared to Carlyle that marriage with him was "her most probable destiny" she was acknowledging her fate.

To this contest of wills there could be but one end: for in the years of their correspondence Carlyle had established over her mind an almost complete ascendancy. Now and in the future she might mock him, be angry with him, use him as a strop on which to develop the razor-edge of her wit: but beneath all such surface rebellions she was submissive to a mind that had depths she could never plumb, to a genius that awed her by its very difference in nature from her own brilliant talent. Now, when Carlyle spoke of parting from her for ever she revealed her utter dependence on him: "I will not believe that you ever seriously thought of parting from me, of throwing off a heart which you have taught to lean upon you till it is no longer sufficient for itself! You could never be so ungenerous! . . . How could I *part* from the only living soul that understands me? I would marry you tomorrow rather!" Her destiny was not merely probable, it was settled: since she could not part from Carlyle she must marry him, and her objections took on more and more the character of rearguard actions to save her will from complete domination.

For as the months passed Carlyle found no fixed rank in society, and was no nearer to achieving that modest but fixed income which she had called a pre-requisite of matrimony: but their forthcoming marriage was spoken of openly as a soon-to-be-accomplished fact. He took some pains, indeed, to see that nobody should have the smallest justification in saying that he had married for money. At his wish Jane Welsh made over the life rent of Craigenputtock to her mother and put the house in which they lived at Haddington wholly at her mother's disposal. In spite of this action Mrs. Welsh could not bring herself to do more than tolerate Carlyle as a prospective son-in-law; at times she would go so far as to say that her daughter's mind had been bewitched and poisoned by contact with such a man.

However reluctantly, she gave her consent: now Jane had to be seen and approved by the Carlyles, who regarded their son as a sufficient prize for any woman. A farm named Hoddam had been taken for Carlyle two miles from the family home of Mainhill, although not he but his brother Alick was actually to farm it; his mother and one or other of his young sisters were generally there to cook and do the household work. At Hoddam Carlyle worked on a selection and translation of Specimens of German Romance; and to Hoddam came Jane Welsh for inspection. She was approved; she went riding with Carlyle, and they paid some local calls together; the visit was a success. There was now no objection to the marriage.

Or rather, there was one objection, soon overcome. Through the agency of Carlyle Jane Welsh had entered into a correspondence with Irving's friend, Mrs. Montagu, and this lady was aware that there had been some tenderness between Jane and Irving. With the exultant eagerness for another's self-sacrifice that marked a certain kind of nineteenth century bluestocking, she told Jane that skeletons must be taken from closets, and the secrets of the past revealed. Whether, without such prompting, Jane would have told Carlyle of her love for Irving (whether, indeed, there was much to tell) may be doubted: but now that she received Mrs. Montagu's communication, which bore with it the implication that Carlyle might hear this news from another source, she sat down and wrote at once a letter to her prospective husband in which she told him that she had "*once* passionately loved" Irving. This he would forgive, no doubt: but could he forgive her for concealing and disguising the fact? "I beseech you, instantly . . . let me know my fate". She must have received his reply with a relief that may have been tinged with vexation at the calmness with which he accepted her confession. The annoyance it caused him came, he said, from selfish sources, unworthy of notice. There could be no question of his offering forgiveness: for (and here he plunged into the abyss of self-analysis in which he so often, and so unprofitably, disappeared) his own faults were fifty times greater, and he could never make her happy. It would be well for her to leave him before she was destroyed. "It is but one bold step and it is done. We shall suffer, suffer to the heart but we shall have obeyed the voice of reason, and time will teach us to endure it." This offer of release for his own sins, generous as in a sense it was, must have been slightly disconcerting to Jane Welsh; but at least the confession had been made.

Now all was settled, except that the lovers had no house of their own; for Hoddam Hill had to be given up after a short tenure because of an argument about the lease. Jane Welsh had rejected Craigenputtock. Now she made a proposal of her own. Carlyle was to take on lease a "nice little house" that he had seen in Edinburgh, and Mrs. Welsh was to take one within a few yards of it, "so that we may all live together like one Family until such time as we are married, and after."

Such a suggestion showed a large misunderstanding of Carlyle's determination to have his own way in such matters. Just as he had had no thought of attempting seriously to improve his social and financial position, so now he gave a tolerant but absolute rejection of her plan. What a bright project it was! he exclaimed; and how impracticable! As a first objection Mrs. Welsh did not like him, and he thought would never like him; as a second, he did not wish to share Jane with other company, but wanted her wholly as his own; as a third, Mrs. Welsh's love of parties and visitors was altogether uncongenial to him. He added—and one feels that even Jane Welsh's hardy spirit must have blenched a little at the words: "The moment I am master of a house, the first use I turn it to will be to slam the door of it on the face of nauseous intrusions of all sorts which it can exclude; my prospective cottage would be calculated for different objects than your Mother's". With an amusement mingled with exasperation Jane Welsh complained that he was a singularly changeable person. First he wished to live in the country, and she tried to adjust her mind to that idea; then he thought of Edinburgh, and she was prepared to say goodbye to her flowers without a moment's hesitation: and now "Houses, walled gardens, conversaziones and all the rest of it, pass away like the baseless fabric of a vision; and lo! we are once more a solitary homeless pair." Perhaps, she wrote jokingly, they should take different roads after all. There was Catherine Aurora Kirkpatrick, was there not, "who has fifty thousand pounds, and a princely lineage, and 'never was out of humour in her life.' " Jane, no doubt, would be able to settle comfortably with her second cousin who was a Doctor at Leeds, or with an interesting widower who was prepared to make her mother to his three small children.

D

She was very witty: but this was wit of a kind Carlyle could not appreciate. He responded to her mockery with a letter of many pages, in which he tried to justify the whole course of his life and to defend himself from the charge of being changeable. He is no longer, as he has been lately, a suppliant; sure of her eventual submission, he writes now as a master and says that she must either accept or reject him wholly as he is:

> If . . . my heart and my hand with the barren and per-plexed destiny which promises to attend them, shall after all appear the *best* that this poor world can offer you, then take me and be content with me, and do not vex yourself with struggling to alter what is unalterable; to make a man who is poor and sick suddenly become rich and healthy. . . . Alas! Jane, you do not know me; it is not the poor, un-known, rejected Thomas Carlyle that you know, but the prospective rich, known and admired. I am reconciled to my fate as it stands or promises to stand ere long; I have pro-nounced the word *unpraised* in all its cases and numbers; and find nothing terrific in it, even when it means *unhonoured*, and by the mass of His Majesty's subjects *neglected* or even partially *contemned*.

This letter was answered by one so moderate in tone, so warmly loving and so sadly reproachful that it made him penitent: "You are an Angel of Light", he wrote, "and I am a mean man of earthly clay, who ought not to mete you by a standard fit only for vulgar natures".

Penitence, however, did not move him so far as to accept the suggestion that he should live with, or near, Mrs. Welsh. On the contrary: the lease of Mainhill had run out, and the Carlyle family had engaged to take Scotsbrig farm, two or three miles north-east of Ecclefechan. The domicile of Scots-brig was, Carlyle wrote cheerfully, one of the most monstrously ugly and uncultivated houses he had ever set eyes on: neverthe-less, he suggested that Jane should come and live there. Instead of Carlyle living with Mrs. Welsh, Jane was to be cast among the Carlyles. Later it occurred to him, when he discovered that Mrs. Welsh was, after all, giving up the house at Haddington and going to live as housekeeper to her father at Templand, that he and Jane might very well set up house at Haddington.

There was a certain coolness in the suggestion that Mrs.

Welsh's house would, as it were, become habitable once she had left it; and Jane placed an immediate veto upon it, chiefly for this reason and partly also perhaps because her former suitor Doctor Fyffe used part of the house for a surgery, and meetings with him would have been unavoidable. Scotsbrig, too, was seen to be unsuitable by Carlyle's parents, and even by Carlyle himself when Jane mentioned casually that her mother might come and stay there. It was clear, he wrote, that she totally misconceived the nature of life at Scotsbrig. "You talked of your Mother visiting us! By Day and Night! It would astonish her to see this same household. O no, my Darling! Your Mother must not visit mine."

Where were they to live, then? Although Jane said that she would cheerfully live anywhere except at Haddington, and Carlyle said that apart from stipulating quietness at night his toleration was "absolutely boundless", it seemed somehow impossible to find a suitable house or cottage. A certain sense of strain, though never of acerbity, begins to enter the letters; and their relationship was wholly epistolary, for at the time of these arguments they had not seen each other for nearly a year. Then suddenly the insoluble was resolved; Mrs. Welsh went to Edinburgh, and rented Number 21 Comley Bank, what we should now call a tenement house in the northwest suburbs, near Princes Street but free from smoke and noise. In front there was a small flower garden; the windows looked on green fields; within there was a drawing-room, a dining-room, a kitchen and three bedrooms; the rent was £32 a year.

So they were married: not without a sudden attack of biliousness suffered by Carlyle which made him very depressed, and led to an interchange of condolences upon the terrors of the ceremony. At last, however, the arguments, the complications and the distractions were over: on Tuesday the 17th of October, 1826, in the Welsh house at Templand, Jane Baillie Welsh became Jane Welsh Carlyle.

CHAPTER SEVEN

COMLEY BANK

Virtue *is* its own reward, but in a very different sense than
you suppose, Dr. Gowkthrapple. The *pleasure* it brings! Had
you ever a diseased liver? I will maintain, and appeal to
all competent judges, that no evil conscience with a good
nervous system ever caused a tenth part of the misery that
a bad nervous system, conjoined with the best conscience
in nature, will produce. What follows, then? Pay off
your moralist, and hire two apothecaries and two cooks.
. . . Heed not the immortality of the soul so long as you
have beefsteaks, porter, and—blue pills.

THOMAS CARLYLE: Journal, December 1826.

THE IDEAL BIOGRAPHY, no doubt, is that in which
no partial shadow of his own opinion is thrown by the biographer upon the clear grey reality of the past, so that its
creatures think and move exactly as they were. Such perfection,
however, is unattainable. The biographer who denies himself
the expression of opinion is still selective in his choice of
incident; the biographer who pretends to reach impartiality
through the words of his subjects can never be impartial enough.
Biography turns and shapes the past in the fire of the biographer's mind, and its end is not the attainment of abstract
truth, but the concrete recreation of a character or a society
as they appear to one set of more or less erroneous senses.
Yet impartiality, that philosopher's stone, is always sought for:
the conscientious biographer adopts unconsciously a partial
point of view while assuring himself of his own exquisitely
objective approach.

Such illusions are the essence of art in our age and society:
and they could hardly be shown more clearly than in biographical writings about the married life of Thomas and Jane
Welsh Carlyle. Partisanship is both unconscious and intense: it
has been expressed by the friends of Jane in an attempt to
depict her as the long-suffering wife of a crabbed, impatient,
neglectful and at times almost cruel man of genius; on the other
side Carlyle's more reverential admirers, not content with

pointing out Jane's occasional shrewishness and tendency to hysterical exaggeration, have gone so far as to suggest that she was a rather exceptionally plain girl who made a very successful match in Carlyle. In explanation of the undoubted friction that marked the married life of this strange man and woman Jane's supporters have asserted plainly that Carlyle was impotent, and Carlyle's have retorted briskly that Jane may have been frigid. Where so many strongly-held views have been so passionately expressed, is it not almost ludicrous for another biographer to advance his own ideas with the proud claim of —impartiality? But it is every biographer's illusion that, at last, he has discovered the philosopher's stone . . .

In looking back we may well wonder that any degree of harmony should have been possible between two such touchy and ill-assorted characters. Carlyle's idea of the proper function of woman was derived largely from the part that women played in his own family: he expected a woman to be a good housewife and an unquestioning executor of her husband's ideas. Brought up in a peasant home, he thought it no hardship to expect of a woman that she should scrub floors and bake bread. Yet, with these views, he had deliberately chosen as his wife a woman who had been preserved by her upbringing from any household duties whatever; who also, as we have seen in her letters, looked upon her union with a man as a relationship certainly intellectual, possibly passionate, but in all aspects well above the ground of everyday reality. It might be expected that these very different views of a wife's functions held by Carlyle and Jane would cause trouble: but, in the early days of marriage at least, they did not. Jane adopted without question the cares of a household and found time to read with her husband in the evening; and when she was ill one day Carlyle nursed her, she wrote, "as well as my own Mother could have done."

Almost as notable as this quiet adaptation to the workaday exigencies of married life is the way in which differences of temperament were, at this time, almost completely submerged by mutual goodwill. These differences were to become more and more important in later years: their nature can be grasped only by a full understanding of these two personalities. Beneath Carlyle's harshness of speech and confusion of mind there lay a deep humility and selflessness, reflected equally in his unquestioning acceptance of Jane Welsh's sarcasm and in his disregard of money and fame. The comments that, as a man unhonoured and little-known, he made upon his more or less famous contemporaries, are those of one speaking from a height which he had no apparent prospect of attaining; they are of the kind that we are accustomed to dismiss as the mere sourness of uncreation: yet such a dismissal is, in this particular case, thoroughly superficial. We may not share Carlyle's literary judgements, we may regard with distaste the view of the world which he was slowly developing, we may trace the nature of his lifelong internal struggle back to its psychological and physiological origins: but for the effort itself, distinct from its fruits or its origins, there must still be profound respect. If we believe at all in the idea of spiritual greatness achieved through the exercise of freewill, if we do not adhere utterly to the view that "greatness" is a simple product of historical circumstance, then it is difficult to deny that Carlyle was a great man. And even for those who acknowledge determinism as the only absolute in a world of otherwise relative values some human sentiments are more important than others: the force that drove Carlyle to imprint upon his letters the seal of a wasting candle with the motto *Terar dum prosim*—"May I be wasted so that I am of use"—had its potential value in any society.

Such impersonal nobility was outside the reach, although not beyond the understanding, of Jane. The humour that shows in her letters is earthly, the continual sparkle of her wit is founded upon a generally enjoyable and occasionally petty malice. She saw herself and others in the light of a capacity for observing and enjoying the ridiculous that never touched Carlyle: she found, or created, drama in the rejection of a suitor or the vagaries of a maidservant, in the baking of bread or the burning of coffee. The tribute paid by Dickens at the end of her life, that "None of the writing women come near her at all" will seem no more than justice to those who have read the letters in which the ironical glance of her irreverent imagination mocks the turns of speech and habits of thought of her husband and her friends. Living another life, married to another man, her great gifts of wit and irony might have found the public expression that she often spoke of but never attempted: as it was she lived in the light of a spirit much more intense than her own, and at times such a life seemed to her profoundly unsatisfactory. Many years later she was to say, with a characteristic touch of the dramatic, that she had married for ambition, and that "Carlyle has exceeded all that my wildest hopes ever imagined of him—and I am miserable". But those times were not yet: in the early days at Comley Bank she was content simply to sit and listen to him talking, or even "just sit and look at him, which I really find as profitable an employment as any other."

In spite of all this mutual tolerance and goodwill there was from the first something not quite right about the marriage. Carlyle was not the most cheerful of bridegrooms. In a letter written to his mother two days after the ceremony he admits to being "dreadfully confused, far from being at home in my new situation, inviting and hopeful as in all points it appears." Jane loves him devotedly and he has been, he says in a curious phrase, "mercifully dealt with": but still he is sick with sleeplessness, nervous, bilious and splenetic. A few days later, writing to his brother John, he says that he dare not let himself out about his matrimonial views, but hopes that he will "get hefted" to his new situation, and then be "one of the happiest men alive." Meanwhile he is still swallowing salts and castor oil, and his wife is the best of all wives. In the fourth week of his marriage he goes so far as to say that he has "positively nothing in the world to complain of", and that "Sometimes . . . we *are* very happy." The tone is hardly that common to newly-married husbands.

What was the cause of this disquiet? Why did Carlyle find it so difficult to accustom himself to the idea of being married; why after only two days of marriage did he feel "dreadfully confused" and say that he had been "mercifully dealt with"? It will hardly do to say that he was disappointed, as he may have been later on, that marriage did not effect a magical change in his way of thinking and feeling: his letters indicate a more immediate distress. These phrases must be put in the scale (although, to be sure, they are of no portentous weight) on the side of the view which maintains that Carlyle was unable to perform the sexual act.

We are gradually becoming accustomed to the idea that great literary fame could be achieved in the nineteenth century only at considerable risk of mental or physical unbalance. Dickens suppressed certain criminal tendencies, which emerged in his extraordinary public readings; Swinburne was a masochist to a pathological degree; Ruskin we believe to have been impotent, in spite of his gallant and interesting offer to give public proof to the contrary; Lewis Carroll liked to take photographs of little girls, but not of little boys, naked; Samuel Butler was a repressed homosexual, Oscar Wilde an open one. Perhaps other revelations await us. Victorian literary men, no doubt, were no odder than those of other periods: but the stiff cloak of bourgeois respectability made it difficult for them to indulge, and impossible for them to acknowledge, oddities of sexual behaviour.

There is nothing inherently unlikely in the idea of Carlyle's impotence: what is the evidence? It rests on a statement received by Carlyle's friend and biographer Froude from Mrs. Carlyle's friend Geraldine Jewsbury, to the effect that "Carlyle was one of those persons who ought never to have married". Froude added that "the nature of Carlyle's constitution . . . was an open secret." It is certainly true that there had been rumours to that effect about Carlyle, as there were about Ruskin. Geraldine Jewsbury's information, Froude said, was "coupled with too many singular details, to allow doubt to be possible." Some of the details were told, or invented, by Frank Harris in his frequently pornographic but rarely uninteresting auto-biography, *My Life and Loves*. By this account Sir Richard Quain, physician to the Carlyles, examined Mrs. Carlyle when she was in her late forties, and found that she was a virgin. Later Mrs. Carlyle obligingly gave Sir Richard an account of how, on the wedding night, Carlyle "lay there, jiggling like", until she suddenly burst out laughing. He then "got out of bed with one scornful word, 'Woman!' and went into the next room; he never came back to my bed again."

The attempted rebuttal of the charge is as vague as the evidence. Two maiden ladies living at Dumfries solemnly testified that Jane had consulted their mother about her prospects of having a child; in a letter written nearly five years after their marriage, Carlyle told her to "Take every care of thyself, Wifekin: there is more than thy own that thou carriest with thee"; after Jane's death a bundle of baby clothes was found in a drawer of her bedroom. Of such straws are bricks made: and it is beside the point to say that the evidence in favour of Carlyle's impotence is so conjectural that it would hardly require rebuttal in a court of law. In a case of this kind a biographer does not weigh evidence, but balances possibilities: and they suggest strongly that, if Carlyle was not impotent, he was a highly unsatisfactory lover, and that this lack of physical affection caused Jane much unhappiness. From an early stage of their life together husband and wife occupied separate rooms: and in all the hundreds of letters they exchanged there is much evidence of deep affection, but hardly a word of physical passion. We know, moreover, from Carlyle's work that he had a morbid distaste for, and pre-occupation with, bodily functions ... .

* * * * *

This was the unspoken and almost unobserved background of life at Comley Bank. In the foreground, and vitally import-ant to the newly-married couple, was the fact that Carlyle had no regular employment and very little money. "We are really very happy", Jane wrote to her mother-in-law. "When he falls upon some work we shall be still happier." Carlyle tinkered with the idea of a new literary paper, and drew up a draft of a "Literary Annual Register"; but these projects came to nothing.

He had recently completed the translations from the German romantic writers, Musaeus, Fouque, Tieck, Hoffman and Richter, together with prefaces to them. The task became more and more like hackwork, less and less like the introduction of new and surprising luminaries to the English scene, the longer it continued; and Carlyle's increasing distaste for the work is reflected in a preface which encourages intending readers by telling them that in Germany: "Interspersed with a few Poets, we behold whole legions and hosts of Poetasters, in all stages of worthlessness; here languishing in the transports of Sentiment-ality, there dancing the St.-Vitus dance of hard-studied Wit and Humour . . ."

Few readers are likely to dip into his translations nowadays: and this attempt to popularise the minor figures in the German romantic movement (with the addition of the major figure of Richter) did not meet with much approval even from those who had welcomed his Goethe translation and his life of Schiller. The book's sales were very poor: Tait, the Edinburgh bookseller who had published it, positively refused a year or two later to consider the History of German Literature on which Carlyle had been working. The small flurry of excitement about Germany that Carlyle and some others had created was now over, and magazine editors joined with Tait in thinking that anything German was best avoided.

The fear of a failing market was not at all in Carlyle's mind when, soon after his marriage, he began work on a didactic novel called tentatively *The Romance of Wotton Reinfred*. It is more likely that he hoped for a release in marriage from the conflicting emotional pressures that had so signally prevented him from producing an original work of art. The Calvinistic sense of guilt which made him think of all novels, even Goethe's, as trivialities unworthy of a grown man's attention, was not so easily dissipated: and *Wotton Reinfred*, begun with no very high hopes, was soon referred to in tones of desperation, and within three months abandoned altogether. Many years later the manuscript was stolen from Carlyle, and it was published after his death.

The Romance of Wotton Reinfred was sired by Rasselas out of the French *Philosophes*: the hero is recognisably intended as Carlyle, the heroine is Jane with an admixture of Margaret Gordon, the features of Irving and other friends appear in the minor characters who sit and talk philosophically about the fate and purpose of man. The style throughout is stiff and unhappy: and the experiment convinced Carlyle finally that he had no talent for fiction.

Lack of occupation always made Carlyle miserable; and after the abandonment of *Wotton Reinfred* he became very bilious indeed. The door of their house in Comley Bank was not always closed upon those nauseous intrusions he had mentioned so gleefully: they gave and accepted no dinner invitations, but on Wednesday evenings received visitors ranging from Doctor Brewster, who was still wrestling with the *Edinburgh Encyclopaedia*, to a Pomeranian lady who taught German and was accustomed to denounce bad translations by reading the original "in a high, shrieky tone". Such a life was unsatisfactory: and now that marriage had failed either to settle his confusion of spirit or to cure his biliousness, he began to cast wistful glances again upon the distant view of Craigenputtock. Within five months of marriage he had the project vaguely planned. His brother Alick would come down and farm the land; his brother John would become a doctor not very far away in Dumfries; and the rest of us (he wrote to his father) "would farm, and write, and labour each in his sphere". Away from the city, too, Carlyle was convinced that his health would improve. And what did Jane think of the idea? "Both Jane and I are very fond of the project", he assured his father.

The plan remained in abeyance while Alick Carlyle made up
his mind whether he wanted to become the tenant of a farm
upon these stern Scottish moors and to live there with his
stern and bilious brother. Meanwhile Carlyle meditated the
prospect of becoming Professor of Moral Philosophy in the
recently-created London University. This possibility opened
itself to him through an introduction given him by the poet
B. W. Proctor to Lord Jeffrey.

The personality of Francis, Lord Jeffrey, was not, one might
suppose, likely to predispose him in favour of Carlyle; Jeffrey's
philosophy of life was that of an amiable Epicurean, friendly
and helpful whenever possible towards his fellow-creatures,
but as far as possible from feeling, or even understanding,
Carlyle's passionate general concern for the fate of the world.
In manner he was gentle where Carlyle was rough; in politics he
was a cautious orthodox Whig where Carlyle was a violent
unorthodox Radical. These, one might think, were differences
enough to make Jeffrey think Carlyle a barbarian: and on the
other side Carlyle might have been excused for seeing in
Jeffrey a man who had succeeded fairly easily in everything
he had undertaken, where he had found any kind of achievement dismally hard.

Jeffrey was probably the most famous advocate in Scotland
at the time he met Carlyle: but his fame was also social and
literary. From the time when, a quarter of a century earlier,
he had founded the *Edinburgh Review* with Henry Brougham,
Francis Horner and Sydney Smith, his career had never known
a setback. The *Edinburgh Review* had an immediate appeal to the
speculative, hard-thinking right-minded middle-class on both
sides of the border: its moderate Whiggism and guarded
Utilitarianism were much appreciated, the literary judgements
and prejudices of its editors soon became vitally important
to writers and the small reading public. Of those early editors
only Jeffrey remained, and his enthusiasm for the review that
had done more than anything else to make him famous was by
now much dimmed. His failure of enthusiasm was reflected
in the contents of the *Edinburgh*, a fact of which Jeffrey was
aware; and he was certainly disturbed by the existence of
another literary magazine in Edinburgh. This was *Blackwood's*,
a magazine enlivened by the ebullient personality of John
Wilson, who under the pseudonym of Christopher North
contributed to *Blackwood's* those *Ambrosianae Noctes* which are

still perhaps the most readable and amusing criticism of the age.

It may be that the desire recently expressed by Jeffrey to a London friend to find "some clever young man who would write for us" had something to do with his first friendly reception of Carlyle: perhaps also he recognized at once the talent of the raw, oddly-spoken unfashionably-dressed man who presented Proctor's letter of introduction at his house one evening. The warmth of Jeffrey's welcome was, in any case, sufficient to dispel the sense of hardship lingering in Carlyle from the fact that seven years before he had submitted a contribution to *The Edinburgh Review* which had been altogether ignored, "no answer and no return of MS., absolutely no notice taken; which was a form of catastrophe more complete than even I had anticipated!" A pair of candles burned in Jeffrey's study; a baize-covered table was covered with books, and more new books were on the shelves; and there Jeffrey, "an homunculus of five foot one", as Southey called him, talked amiably about German literature, Goethe, Carlyle's recent book on German Romance. Carlyle had seen Jeffrey before, at the Law Courts and elsewhere; and he seems to have regarded him as a kind of charming doll, "a delicate, attractive dainty little figure", with bright black eyes, an oval face of which the expression rapidly changed from grave to gay, a clear, harmonious voice, and a laugh that was, regrettably, a kind of snigger. Soon afterwards Jeffrey paid, with his wife, a call on the Carlyles. He was delighted by Jane; and Carlyle wrote to his brother John that Jeffrey was "by much the most lovable of all the literary men I have seen".

The immediate result of this acquaintance with Jeffrey, which ripened quickly into friendship, was that Carlyle wrote two articles for the *Edinburgh*, the first on Richter and the second on "The State of German Literature"; but as acquaintance became friendship Carlyle received from Jeffrey a literary backing of which he was much in need, however ready he may have been to do without it. In the course of the calls made by Jeffrey, sometimes accompanied by his wife, to Comley Bank, and the visits paid by Carlyle and Jane to the Jeffreys' home at Craigcrook, the advocate became aware (if he had not realized it on the first meeting) that he had to do with a remarkable man. The attraction exerted by a passionate personality over a moderate one, the respect and irritation felt by a successful

man of talent in the presence of an unreasonable man of genius,
—these things, together with simple good nature and liking
for Jane, combined to induce Jeffrey to attempt to find
some sinecure for Carlyle which would make unnecessary
his immurement at Craigenputtock. Now he tried to use his
influence to get for Carlyle the professorship at London
University already mentioned; again he recommended Carlyle as
successor to Chalmers at St. Andrews University. It is apparent
from Carlyle's letters that he had hope of rescue from the
helotage of reviewing through one or other official appointment:
but the testimonials of Jeffrey and John Wilson, of Brewster
and Irving, of his former mathematics tutor John Leslie and
old Buller, were not sufficient. Like many other official positions
before and since, these had been decided in advance.

With these hopes gone, the Carlyles settled finally on going
to live at Craigenputtock. Carlyle went down to look at it with
his brother Alick and reported to Jane that he saw "Green
fields far greener than I had anticipated; Nature doing her part
to maintain her children; and such a scene of human sloth
and squalor, as I scarcely think could be paralleled within the
county." The wretched state of the property he ascribed to the
neglect of the tenant; his account of it might have chilled many
hearts, but it did not touch Jane's. Her reply shows that she
had either become reconciled to Craigenputtock, or that she
hid remarkably well any reluctance to go there; it suggests also
the spirited optimism she felt in these days, and contains
perhaps the nearest suggestion of physical intimacy in their
whole matrimonial correspondence:

Dear, dear, Cheap, Cheap,—I met the postman . . .
yesterday morning, and something bade me ask if there
were any letters. Imagine my agitation when he gave me
yours, four-and-twenty hours before the appointed time!
I was so glad and so frightened! so eager to know the *whole*
contents, that I could hardly make out any *part*. In the little
Tobacconist's, where I was fain to seek a quiet place, I did
at length however, with much heart-beating, get through
the precious paper, and find that my Darling still loved me
pretty well, and that the Craig o' Putta was still a hope; as
also that if you come not back to poor Goody on Saturday,
it will not be for want of will. Ah! Nor yet will it be for
want of the most fervent prayers to Heaven that a longing

Goody can put up; for I am sick, sick to the heart of this
absence, which, indeed, I can only *bear* in the faith of its
being brief. Oh, Dearest, I *do* love you in my very innermost
being, far better than words can tell or even kisses; though
these (when not the *experimental* sort) *are* rather eloquent in
their way; and, to me at least, have often told such things!
and they shall tell the same story over again, shall they not,
yet a thousand and a thousand times? "I expect but I doubt
not."

Alas the poor Craig o' Putta! what a way it is in, with
these good-for-nothing sluggards! I need not recommend
you to do all that is possible, nay, to "do the impossible"
to get them out. Even suppose we did not wish the place for
ourselves, it would be miserable to consign it to such hands.

Carlyle's reply shows a love equal to his wife's; it shows also
his belief that some magic spell in the country air would at
once improve his health and give him a clear understanding of
the way in which the world's troubles might be cured:

O Jeannie! How happy shall we be in this Craig o' Putta!
Not that I look for an Arcadia or a Lubberland there: but
we shall sit under our bramble and our saugh-tree and none
to make us afraid; and my little wife will be there forever
beside me, and I shall be well and blessed, and the latter
end of that man will be better than the beginning. Surely
I shall learn at length to prize the pearl of great price which
God has given to me unworthy; surely I already know that to
me the richest treasure of this sublunary life has been
awarded, the heart of my own noble Jane! Shame on me for
complaining, sick and wretched though I be! Bourbon and
Braganza, when I think of it, are but poor men to me.

The idea of living at Craigenputtock was clear enough; the
unsatisfactory tenant was replaced by Alick Carlyle, who began
to put things to rights; but the actual accomplishment of
taking up residence there was delayed for weeks, and the
weeks turned into months. There were in Edinburgh, after all,
chances of literary success that might not come at Craigenputtock. There were the friendship of Jeffrey, the aggressive
amiability of John Wilson and the dazzling conversation of
De Quincey ("What wouldn't one give", Jane said, "to have

him in a box, and take him out to talk"). There were such
pleasures as a visit from Irving, who had come up to Edinburgh
to deliver twelve lectures on the Apocalypse. The famous
preacher was now showing eccentricities of conduct which
brought some to question his sanity. The lectures were given at
six o'clock in the morning, and the crowds attending them at
this unusual hour filled to overflowing the largest church in
Edinburgh. The wildness, as it seemed to most of his audience,
of Irving's admonition to prepare for some soon forthcoming
Day of Judgement, provoked strong disapproval: and with
the wildness went an increasing oddity of speech, dress and
behaviour. He wore old-fashioned clothes with a waistcoat that
showed its tails half-way down the thigh; he began a theological
argument with the words, "Who art thou, O man, that smiteth
me with thy tongue?"; his long, magnificent black hair trailed
down his back. Carlyle's eighteen year old sister Jane was
staying at Comley Bank when Irving called there. She hid
behind some furniture, and was astonished to see him rise when
cakes and wine came in and say with unction: "Lord bless your
basket and your store, and the little maiden who abideth with
you". Irving stayed for only half an hour, but it was long
enough for Carlyle to note with uneasiness the strange exalta-
tion that possessed him. Old James Carlyle, who heard news of
Irving's doings, was more forthright. "What think'st a he
means, gawn up and down the country tevvelling and screech-
ing like a wild bear?" he asked his son.

These were reasons for staying in Edinburgh: they waited
also because Alick was longer than he expected in setting
Craigenputtock to rights. Little money could be spared to
make such essential alterations as the addition of a storey to the
original house, and the erection of a separate cottage for
Alick to live in; and such small troubles as a smoking kitchen
chimney loomed large in Carlyle's eyes. "Free air is the birth-
right of every free man", he wrote to his brother. "This kitchen-
chimney *must be cured*, my dear Alick; I say, *must* be, come of it
what will . . . and if we cannot cure it, we will blow up the
whole concern with gunpowder rather than leave it stewing
there." But at last everything was ready: and in the spring of
1828 Carlyle and Jane left Comley Bank. They stayed two
nights with Jeffrey and his family at Craigcrook, and then
followed the six carts that had already transported all their
belongings to the lonely house on the moors.

CHAPTER EIGHT

CRAIGENPUTTOCK

Here, in a mountainous district, through which the River Nith flows to the neighbouring sea, not far from the Town of Dumfries, at a place called Craigenputtock, he, with a beautiful and highly-accomplished Consort, established his simple country home.

GOETHE: Introduction to German edition of Carlyle's *Life of Schiller*.

THE LIFE AND surroundings of Carlyle are better-documented, perhaps, than those of any other English man of letters. Both Carlyle and Jane were voluminous correspondents who, when they sat down to pen, as they said, a few hasty lines, were as likely as not to write enough to fill three or four pages of print; and many of those who received their letters preserved them. Husband and wife, also, were assiduous keepers of letters: the usual biographical resources of more or less intelligent conjecture, and adroit evasion of obscure periods in the subject's life, is replaced by a wealth of first-hand material that is sometimes almost embarrassing. If interest is to be maintained chronology, in these exceptional circumstances, must at times be ignored: and it is only now that we can easily consider Carlyle's correspondence with Goethe, and his letters to his brother John, which had been conducted over a number of years and throw an interesting light on his character and hopes.

The correspondence between Carlyle and Goethe began when Carlyle was twentynine years old, and Goethe was seventyfive. The German moralist had settled serenely into his national fame; for half a century he had been attached to the Court of Weimar as Minister of State, moralist and poet. Nevertheless his fame was merely national, and he was pleased to receive from an unknown, but obviously youthful, admirer his translation of *Wilhelm Meister*, with a letter which breathed reverence and ended with the hope "That your life may be long, long spared, for the solace and instruction of this and future generations." Goethe's reply had the pleasant but formal

condescension of a great man receiving a deserved tribute; he
sent Carlyle a present of some poems. The letter, Carlyle
wrote to Jane Welsh, was "almost like a message from Fairy
Land; I could scarcely think that *this was* the real hand and
signature of that mysterious personage, whose name has
floated through my fancy, like a sort of spell, since boyhood";
and the spell is visible in the self-abnegatory Chinese courtesies
with which Carlyle sent, two years later, his *Life of Schiller*
and *Specimens of German Romance* to one whom he regarded, he
said, "with the feeling of a Disciple to his Master, nay of a Son
to his spiritual Father".

Goethe was not immune to the opinion implied in such words:
and the correspondence thereafter has features both instructive
and comic. With the letter enclosing the *Life of Schiller* Carlyle
sent a purse made by Jane, "the work . . . of dainty fingers and
true love." Goethe responded with a letter addressed to Sir
Thomas Carlyle, which was speedily followed by "the daintiest
boxie you ever saw." The box contained five volumes of Goethe's
poems, inscribed "for the valued marriage-pair Carlyle"; a
pocketbook for Carlyle and a black wrought-iron necklace with
a head of Goethe cut in coloured glass and set in gold for Jane;
a medal of Goethe, and one of his father and mother; and some
cards, each with a verse written on it. These gifts ornamented
the drawing-room at Comley Bank, which contained already a
large portrait of Goethe on the wall and others in portfolios:
the medals were placed on the mantelpiece, the books had a
place of honour, "and from more secret recesses your handwriting can be exhibited to favoured friends". With his next
letter Goethe despatched five more volumes of his works, a
little box and an almanac for Jane, and six bronze medals.
He asked Carlyle to present two of the medals to Sir Walter
Scott; the other four were to be distributed to admirers of
Goethe selected by Carlyle himself. Such a task could not be
undertaken lightly: Carlyle promised to dispose of these four
medals "not rashly, but worthily", and he brooded for a long
time over the appropriate recipients, weighing carefully the
merits of various candidates before making his final choice.
Now these gifts had to be reciprocated. A portfolio made by
Jane was sent to Weimar; it contained a copy of Cowper's
Poems, a Scotch bonnet and a lock of Jane's black hair. "She
begs . . . and hopes", Carlyle wrote, "that you will send her,
in return, a lock of *your* hair; which she will keep among her

most precious possessions, and only leave, as a rich legacy, to the worthiest that comes after her."

The request, made to a man in his late seventies, had a certain tactlessness: Goethe was much distressed by his inability to make the desired return:

I will mention first the incomparable lock of hair, which one would indeed have liked to see along with the dear head, but which, when it came to light by itself here, almost alarmed me. The contrast was too striking; for I did not need to touch my skull to become aware that only stubble was left there, nor was it necessary for me to go to the looking-glass to learn that a long flight of time had given it a discoloured look.

There Goethe left the question of hair, moving on to the more genial subject of the Scotch bonnet which he regarded, "including the thistle, as a most pleasing ornament"; but the whole incident plainly troubled him, and in the postscript of a letter written two months later he reverted to it.

A peerless lock of black hair impels me to add still a little sheet, and with true regret to remark that the desired return is, alas, impossible. Short and discoloured and devoid of all charm, old age must be content if any flowers at all will still blossom in the inner man when the outward has vanished. I am already seeking for some substitute, but have not yet been lucky enough to find one.

There the matter of the hair ended; but still more gifts and letters were exchanged. They terminated in the tribute sent to Goethe on his eightieth birthday from "fifteen English friends" including Wilson, Scott, Lockhart, Southey, Wordsworth, Proctor and Carlyle: this was a seal, where "amid tasteful carving and emblematic embossing enough" the words "To the German Master: From Friends in England", with the date, were printed on a golden belt circled by a serpent-of-eternity. The suggestion was Carlyle's, and Goethe was pleased by the gift although he did not omit to note that the words were in Old German Capitals "which do not bring out the sense quite clearly". The acknowledgement of this gift was the last message Carlyle received from Goethe; in his eithtieth year, full of honour, without any apparent suffering, Goethe died.

In his obituary article, written for Lytton's *New Monthly Magazine*, Carlyle celebrated the man whom he had called his spiritual father by saying that, like the old poets, he was a seer; he was the inspired thinker, the true sovereign, the wise man, moving the world towards "Insight, Spiritual Vision and Determination". The crowning achievement of Goethe, Carlyle wrote, was to have suggested in his work that "New Era" which must succeed the present age of necessary disorder and unbelief.

This, the highest that can be said of written Books, is to be said of these: there is in them a New Time, the prophecy and beginning of a New Time. The corner-stone of a new social edifice for mankind is laid there; firmly, as before, on the natural rock; far-extending traces of a ground-plan we can also see; which future centuries may go on to enlarge, to amend and work into reality.

This was what Carlyle praised: but it was not all that was to be found in Goethe, and there were other aspects of the master's ideas which seemed to the disciple obscure or ridiculous. Their correspondence shows Carlyle's devotion to an ideal Goethe partly of his own creation, and Goethe's appreciation of his disciple's originality and stern moral sense: but it reveals also divergences of viewpoint which make it unlikely that the meeting with his spiritual father which Carlyle promised himself would have been altogether harmonious.

At an early stage in the correspondence Goethe propounded the idea which had become a preoccupation of his old age: a comity of human relations, which should be achieved by the universal power of art. Whatever, in the art of any nation, contributed to a peaceful mind and a gentle spirit, should be borrowed by other nations. National characteristics should not, of course, be abandoned, for they were the very salt of such artistic intercourse as Goethe had in mind: but still, "what is truly excellent is distinguished by its belonging to all mankind".

For such vague internationalism, which did not then seem as commonplace as it does today, Carlyle had no use at all: his thoughts were moving in a much more Radical, and more arbitrary, groove. He replied cautiously that "so far as I have seized (the) full import" of the idea, it commanded his assent. This was merely a polite form of rejection. Such ideas were exactly what Carlyle thought ridiculous in Goethe, such idealism about the transforming power of art was exactly what made him say that "I could sometimes fall down and worship him; at other times I could kick him out of the room." And as the correspondence continues it is plain that Carlyle has had his fill of translating the work of other men, however notable. The suggestion of Eckermann, Goethe's friend and biographer, that Carlyle should translate *Faust* met with no reply; when Eckermann repeated it, saying that "If I were in your place, I should certainly undertake something for which my country would be grateful, by employing, for some years, my best leisure hours on a faithful translation of *Faust*", Carlyle returned a vague assent, and did nothing.

Goethe, on the other hand, had little interest in, and no sympathy with, Carlyle's gradually hardening view that the world could only be saved by some new religion embodying a new idea of social justice; the honoured dependent of the Double-Court of the Grand Duke of Saxe-Weimar would have been horrified by the conception that the French Revolution was a great and necessary overthrow of corrupt and decadent institutions. In vain did Carlyle try to obtain a pronouncement from Goethe about the evils of Utilitarianism and Benthamism in England, in vain did he ask what advance these pernicious doctrines had made in Germany: to such questions the sage returned no answer. When Carlyle received a letter from the revolutionary St. Simonian Society and asked Goethe's opinion of them, he received simply a warning: "From the St. Simonian Society pray hold yourself aloof". His further remarks about the St. Simonians remained unanswered.

Carlyle's official view of Goethe was embodied in his obituary article; his private one was put down in a letter to his brother John:

In my own heterodox heart there is yearly growing up the strangest crabbed one-sided persuasion, that all Art is but a reminiscence now, that for us in these days *Prophecy* (well understood) not Poetry is the thing wanted; how can we *sing* and *paint* when we do not yet *believe* and *see*? . . . Now what under such point of view is all existing Art and study of Art? What was the great Goethe himself? The greatest of contemporary men; who however is not to have any follower, and should not have any.

*   *   *   *   *

The relationship between father and son was repeated with several variations during Carlyle's life; his character was ordered, no doubt, by the attempt to compensate for his unsatisfactory childhood relationship with his own father. Irving, Jeffrey and Goethe all, in greater or less degree, represented surrogates for his father in the paternal nature of their influence on him; and on the other hand, Carlyle was never more benevolent and considerate than when exerting a paternal influence himself. Jane Welsh, we remember, was reminded by his wisdom and influence on her of her own much-loved father; and Carlyle's relations with his brother John, who was a little more than five years his junior, were more like those between father and son than the usual relationship of brothers.

We have, unfortunately, no memoir and little contemporary description of the rest of the Carlyle family: the fragments that remain with us show that they were almost all remarkably literate, considering their background. *Wilhelm Meister* and the *Life of Schiller* were read by most of the family: although when Carlyle inscribed the *Specimens of German Romance* to his father, he said that he knew James Carlyle would not read a word of it.

If, as we are told by one of Carlyle's biographers, Alick was the most talented of his brothers, John was certainly the most literary. A photograph shows him as a small version of Carlyle himself, with the same questioning look and the same underlip dogmatically outthrust, but without that fiery gaze, as of a man inspired even to his own destruction, that marked Carlyle from youth; and John Carlyle was in fact a tame version of his brother with an interest in literature and politics, a taste for chop-logic that many of his acquaintances found infuriating, and an incurable and lifelong distaste for work of any kind. Upon this amiable and slightly irresponsible young man, who was called in the family "Lord Moon" in reference to the roundness of his shining red face, Carlyle lavished his considerable resources of hidden tenderness and a good part of his slender store of money. He paid for much of John's education, and for his training in medicine when they shared rooms in Edinburgh; and when, at the end of John's medical training, he was invited by Baron d'Eichthal, uncle of two young St. Simonians, to come to Munich, Carlyle paid again a large part of his expenses.

To understand clearly Carlyle's generosity towards his family—for he also sent money to his father and mother— it must be remembered that he was living on his earnings from review articles, which amounted to some £250 a year; that lack of money prevented him from paying a visit to Goethe at Weimar; and that one of the principal advantages mentioned in relation to Craigenputtock was that living there would cost only about £100 a year, some half of what it cost in Edinburgh. Throughout his life Carlyle had no interest either in money or in the comforts it can provide: and he expected that his wife's attitude to money should be identical with his own. It was not: but neither now nor at any later time does Jane appear ever to have complained to or about her husband in this respect; nor did she ever suggest that he should compromise himself by trying to obtain through some comparatively distasteful work that small settled income which had seemed essential in the days before their marriage. More: although Carlyle had objected strongly to the idea of sharing a house with Mrs. Welsh, he expected her to live at Craigenputtock with Alick and to welcome his mother and sisters (and of course brother John) at Comley Bank. In all this his wife found nothing objectionable, so much was Jane Welsh Carlyle changed from Jane Baillie Welsh: she did not complain even when John Carlyle went upstairs to study the stars all the evening and came down to eat porridge at about ten o'clock "with a nose dropping at the extremity, and red as a blood-pudding."

The ostensible reason for John Carlyle's departure to Munich was that he might obtain there the surgical knowledge without which he felt unable to set up in practice: but once abroad he showed no inclination to return. He received placidly his brother's various moral exhortations, and perhaps kept a Journal of his activities as he was advised to do; but it is not likely that he carried out Carlyle's instructions to look into the political condition of Bavaria, and discover the nature of the social order and the degree of individual freedom permitted in that country. For a period of four months his family had no word from Lord Moon; and when they did hear, it was in a letter saying that he would like to spend another year in Germany if he had the means. He did not stay in Germany; but neither did he come home. For six months he lingered in

Vienna, supplied with money by Carlyle, who urged his brother
now quite frantically to come home and begin at least to
practise medicine. "It seems clear to me . . . that a man of
sound character and medical talent could not fail to have
eminent success at this time, in many places of Scotland,
perhaps in few others more remarkable than in our own
County, or Town, of Dumfries."

At last John Carlyle came home, but not to practise medicine
in Dumfries. He showed no sign of any desire to practise
medicine anywhere: after some weeks of cogitation spent at
Scotsbrig and Craigenputtock, he announced that he had
come to a fixed resolution—of living by writing articles. He
proposed an article on Animal Magnetism and another on
German Medicine: and Carlyle encouraged him with words
that have an undertone of despair. "For the thousandth time,
I repeat that I think there is *no* fear of you, so (you) will but set
your shoulder stoutly to the wheel. Write your Papers then,
the best you are able; think with yourself, take counsel with your
kind Friends; and dread no evil issue." With the best of intentions, the most fixed of resolutions, John Carlyle went off to
live in London.

*   *   *   *   *

What, meanwhile, of life at Craigenputtock, that lonely
spot where the mail was delivered once a week and the nearest
neighbours other than peasant families lived six miles distant?
Where once, in the winter, three months passed without any
stranger, even a beggar, calling at the door? The days and
weeks and months passed there in an unvarying seasonal round.
Carlyle rode about the moors, meditated on the fate and future
of man, tried to understand the French Revolution which more
and more occupied his thoughts, wrote essays praising the
German romantics once more and attacking German popular
playwrights, and critical-biographical studies of Burns and
Voltaire. The piece on Burns was written for the *Edinburgh*
but Jeffrey, in spite of the award to him of one of Goethe's
medals, had made up his mind that Carlyle had too much
"Teutonic fire" and that his high opinion of Goethe and others
was "erroneous". When he invited Carlyle to write on Burns
he said that he could not permit him to deprecate too freely
the poets of the age.

"Felicia Hemans is my delight, and for Moore I have the
most profound admiration . . . I will show you infinite passages

in Moore, to which I defy you to find a match in Goethe and his followers." From this time onwards Jeffrey, to whom this self-imposed exile in Craigenputtock seemed a deplorable eccentricity, tried to persuade Carlyle to modify what he thought affectations of peculiarity relating to life and literature, and to return from the desert of Craigenputtock to that Scottish Athens, Edinburgh. He disliked the note of urgency and the sense of mission that he found in Carlyle; and he suspected that Jane was neglected in the pursuit of what seemed to him mere chimerical dreams. "Be gay and playful and foolish with her, at least as often as you require her to be wise and heroic with you", he wrote. "You have no mission upon earth, whatever you may fancy, half as important as to be innocently happy."

These fears for the Carlyles' happiness were unjustified: in general they lived a contented enough life. There were two horses in the stables, and in the morning they rode on horseback together for an hour before breakfast. Then Carlyle wrote in his snug, green-curtained library while Jane inspected her house, garden and livestock, cut flowers and gathered eggs; after dinner Carlyle read while she lay on the sofa, sleeping, reading or daydreaming. Sometimes in the evening they read *Don Quixote* together, by way of learning Spanish. "On the whole I was never more contented in my life", Jane wrote to Bess Stodart. "One enjoys such freedom and quietude here." She congratulated herself that she had a knack of adapting herself equally to the busy life of Edinburgh or the "pretty extensive peat-moss" of Craigenputtock.

Those were the good days. There were also bad ones. Carlyle's health improved with the solitude, regular work and exercise, but Jane's did not. She had been delicate from youth, subject to mysterious headaches and nervous prostration; now her health grew worse, and she suffered from frequent colds, sore throats and constipation; like Carlyle she had a mistaken faith in the sovereign propensities of castor oil. Her natural gaiety was at this time not easily repressed; but on days when the front door would not open because of the drifts of snow outside she thought wistfully of the life of Edinburgh and cried for "a sight of the green fields again, or even the black peat-moss—anything rather than this wide waste of blinding snow!"

Life on the moors had some inconveniences but few

hardships. A maid came with the Carlyles from Edinburgh, and there was also a dairywoman and what Carlyle· called "a thoroughgoing, out-of-doors, good-humoured slut of a byre-woman." Jane can have had little more rough work to do than at Comley Bank: but when, many years later, she remembered these days on the moors, her strong dramatic sense came into play and, from the gloom of her middle fifties, she invested the past with largely imaginary trials and sorrows. Writing some thirty years later, as the wife of a famous man, Jane recalled Craigenputtock itself, and a particular incident there, through the darkest of spectacles:

I had gone with my husband to live on a little estate of *peat bog* that had descended to me all the way from John Welsh the Covenanter, who married a daughter of John Knox. *That* didn't, I am ashamed to say, make me feel Craigen-puttock a whit less of a peat bog, and a most dreary, un-toward place to live at . . . Further, we were *very* poor, and further and worst, being an only child and brought up to "great prospects", I was sublimely ignorant of every branch of useful knowledge, though a capital Latin scholar, and very fair mathematician!! It behoved me in these astonishing circumstances to learn to sew! Husbands, I was shocked to find, wore their stockings into holes, and were always losing buttons, and *I* was expected to "look to all that"; also it behoved me to learn to cook! no capable servant choosing to live at such an out-of-the-way place, and my husband having bad digestion, which complicated things dreadfully. The *bread*, above all, brought from Dumfries, "soured on his stomach" (oh Heaven!), and it was plainly my duty as a Christian wife to bake at home. So I sent for Cobbett's *Cottage Economy*, and fell to work on a loaf of bread. But knowing nothing about the process of fermentation or the heat of ovens, it came to pass that my loaf got put into the oven at the time that myself ought to have been put into bed; and I remained the only person not asleep in a house in the middle of a desert. One o'clock struck, and then two, and then three; and still I was sitting there in an immense solitude, my whole body aching with weariness, my heart aching with a sense of forlornness and *degradation*. . . . It was then that somehow the idea of Benvenuto Cellini sitting up all night watching his Perseus in the furnace came into my head, and suddenly I asked myself: "After all, in the sight of the Upper Powers, what is the mighty difference between a statue of Perseus and a loaf of bread, so that each be the thing one's hand has found to do?" The man's determined will, his energy, his patience, his resource, were the really admirable things, of which his statue of Perseus was the mere chance expression.

The story is well told: but it is less likely than Carlyle's account of the same incident in his *Reminiscences*, written at a time when he had had no opportunity of seeing that letter:

> I can remember very well her coming in to me, late at night (eleven or so) with her *first loaf*, looking mere triumph and quizzical gaiety: "See!" The loaf was excellent, only the crust a little burnt; and she compared herself to Cellini and his *Perseus*, of whom we had been reading.

      *   *   *   *   *

Visitors to Craigenputtock were few. Jeffrey paid a three day visit with his wife, his child, and the lap-dog that he carried everywhere. The visit was a great success. Carlyle remembered afterwards with pride that in spite of their comparative poverty Jane managed to invest everything with a coat of elegant, and even abundant, hospitality; and they were all delighted by the felicity with which Jeffrey mimicked various kinds of public speakers, strutting about, "full of electric fire" and varying his manner so that "his little figure (seemed) to grow gigantic if the personage required it", until at last the mimicry "ended in total downbreak, amid peals of the heartiest laughter from us all . . . the aerial little sprite, standing there in fatal collapse, with the brightest of eyes sternly gazing into utter nothingness and dumbness."

The next visitor was Irving, who eight months later came and stayed two nights, on another triumphal tour of Scotland. He was three hours in the pulpit at Dumfries, where he spoke to ten thousand people, and on the same day he preached another sermon four hours in length at adjacent Holywood. There were whispers that he held strange and heretical beliefs about the inspiration of the Bible; but as yet they were only whispers, and Irving talked seriously to Carlyle of the great Prophetic Conferences he had attended in London, and of the vague but momentous decisions that had been reached.

In the following year Carlyle's mother (for several weeks) and his father (for a fortnight) were their visitors; occasionally the Carlyles rode fourteen miles to see Mrs Welsh at Templand, and more rarely made the journey of nearly forty miles to Scotsbrig. The life they lived was certainly exceedingly lonely; if Jane endured it with, upon the whole, remarkable cheerfulness, that was because she not only loved her husband but also admired him. Carlyle's writings at Craigenputtock had confirmed her view that he would one day be acknowledged as a great man.

Isolated upon these grim moors Carlyle at last began to produce work of a rich and formidable originality. His articles on German literature were by now merely profitable by-products of what he truly wished to say: in defending German taste he was defending his own viewpoint, in applauding the wisdom of Goethe and the mysticism of Novalis he was concerned largely with the effect of their writings as an antidote to French rationalism. But his pieces on Burns and Voltaire and the article called "Signs of the Times" expressed some positive aspects of his attitude.

It is difficult now to understand the reason for Jeffrey's objections to the article on Burns. There are in it very few hints of Carlyle's fully mature style, although Johnsonian diction has been much modified and replaced by a tighter, slightly stylised prose. This tighter prose permits the use of epigrammatic phrasing: "No man, it has been said, is a hero to his valet; and this is probably true; but the fault is at least as likely to be the valet's as the hero's." Tom Moore and Felicia Hemans remain, after all, unmentioned: and the criticism of a certain unconscious affectation in Byron compared with the simplicity of Burns is both moderate and effective. There is a warmth and generosity of feeling in the whole study which does not always mark Carlyle's more famous work.

So it seems to us: but the article looked very different to Jeffrey. He objected to the tone and diction of the essay: such ideas as the one that poets "were sent forth as missionaries to their generation" were altogether uncongenial to him; he insisted on making cuts. Jeffrey hoped that these cuts would not be much missed, even by their author: although since the cuts amounted to a fifth of the essay this was an optimistic view. Carlyle restored most of the cuts when reading the proofs, and

Jeffrey was annoyed. His remarks were a foretaste of objections that Carlyle was to encounter again and again:

> I do not think I shall let you have any more proof sheets. It only vexes you, and does no good, for you correct them very badly. . . . I am afraid you are a greater admirer of yourself than becomes a philosopher, if you really think it material to stick to all these odd bits of diction—and to reject my little innocent variations on your inspired text. How can you dream of restoring such a word as *fragmentary*, or that very simple and well used joke of the clothes making the man and the tailor being a creator?

There were to be more and odder bits of diction before long, and that joke about the tailor and the clothes was to be used again, and very notably.

Part of Burns's attraction for Carlyle was his peculiarly Scottish character: part of his antipathy to Voltaire came from the fact that he represented (as it appeared to Carlyle) an "inborn levity of nature, (an) entire want of Earnestness" characteristic of the French. This may seem the most obvious and uninteresting Puritanism; but in Carlyle's hands such a point of view becomes dramatically enlarged to point an opposition between the rational mind that views history "not with the eye of a devout seer, or even of a critic; but through a pair of mere anti-catholic spectacles"; and the more valuable kind of mind—the mind, in fact, of Carlyle—that, appreciating the force and wit of such rationalism, is able to look beyond it and to apply its genius in the service of that New Era to which Carlyle confidently looked forward.

There are some further contrasts to be pointed: the vivid life of Voltaire and the Marquise du Châtelet, with its immense intellectual influence upon their age, was very much the life that Carlyle would have wished for himself and Jane—and at Craigenputtock such a life seemed very far away. One cannot read the account of Voltaire's last triumphal journey to Paris without feeling that at the back of the writer's mind there is the thought that he too might make such a journey, and more worthily. For although Carlyle thought that Voltaire maintained "a certain indestructible humanity of nature; a soul never deaf to the cry of wretchedness; never utterly blind to the light of truth, beauty, goodness", he nevertheless appeared to the serious moralist as nothing more than a master of persiflage, although "if we call him the greatest of all *Persifleurs*, let us add that, morally speaking also, he is the best." If the tribute seems ungenerous, it should be remembered that the article was not offered to Jeffrey, because so favourable a view of Voltaire's religious heterodoxy would have raised a storm of protest. Such words are rather those of a man struggling through antipathy to appreciation: those may call them ungenerous who have made the same effort in relation to Carlyle.

The ideas of Voltaire had prompted the French Revolution: what revolutionary change in English society would be heralded by the new seer? "The time may come", Carlyle wrote prophetically, "when Napoleon himself will be better known for his laws than for his battles; and the victory of Waterloo prove less momentous than the opening of the first Mechanics' Institute". In the article called "Signs of the Times" he considered for the first time directly the "Age of Machinery" in which the artisan was driven from his workshop, the shuttle dropped from the fingers of the weaver, and the sailor abandoned his oar. He suggested, as men are still suggesting today, that the machinery of the spirit was even more important than the remarkable addition of power to the social system achieved through mechanical production, which must inevitably change, and quickly, the old relations between rich and poor. To the Utilitarians, the orthodox advanced thinkers of the time, it seemed obvious that the advance of machine power must ensure human happiness; opposition to such a view was expressed practically by the Luddites, who smashed all the machines they could find. Carlyle welcomed the machine age, but insisted that it must be adjusted to a new structure of society:

There is a deep-lying struggle in the whole fabric of society; a boundless grinding collision of the New with the Old. The French Revolution, as is now visible enough, was not the parent of this mighty movement, but its offspring. . . . Political freedom is hitherto the object of these efforts; but they will not and cannot stop there. It is towards a higher freedom than mere freedom from oppression by his fellow-mortal, that man dimly aims. Of this higher, heavenly freedom, which is "man's reasonable service", all his noble institutions, his faithful endeavours and loftiest attainments, are but the body, and more and more approximated emblem.

The originality of such writing did not escape Carlyle's contemporaries, although the "Signs of the Times" excited alarm rather than favour, except among the St. Simonians, who opened a regular correspondence in the hope of converting him to their views on such points as the need for absolute equality of income. He was not far away from their ideas when he suggested in his journal that political economists should collect facts about the human condition, the number of manual workers and the average human wage; and when he noted the strange fact that there were certain individuals whose wages were equal to those of some seven or eight thousand others. "What do those highly beneficial individuals *do* to society for their wages?—*Kill partridges. Can* this last? No, by the soul that is in man it cannot, and will not, and shall not!"

It was with a view to playing his part in the reorganization of society that he was now writing what he described to his brother as: "A very singular piece, I assure you! It glances from Heaven to Earth and back again in a strange satirical frenzy, whether *fine* or not remains to be seen."

CHAPTER NINE

THE WRITING OF *SARTOR*

What is a man if you look at him with the mere logical sense, with the understanding? A pitiful hungry biped that wears breeches. Often when I read of pompous ceremonials, drawing-room levées, and coronations, on a sudden the *clothes* fly off the whole party in my fancy, and they stand there straddling in a half-ludicrous, half-horrid condition.

THOMAS CARLYLE: Journal, August 1830.

I N R E P L Y T O Jeffrey's frequent reproaches that he had buried himself and, worse, his wife, in a desert, Carlyle replied that he did not live in a desert from choice but because he had to earn at least £100 a year to meet current expenses. Jeffrey, in a most charming and graceful letter, immediately offered to give him this sum which, he said, "would not be felt out of my income; and I cannot but feel *ashamed* that I should either hoard it up, or squander it in useless vanities, when such a man as you might be spared some irksome and anxious hours." Carlyle refused the loan, not without some reflections in his journal on the folly of spiritual pride; two months later he wrote and asked Jeffrey for help. Jeffrey sent him sixty pounds where Carlyle had asked for fifty, "knowing that a man who supposes he wants the latter sum, is sure really to want at least £10 more."

If Carlyle was poor it was chiefly because of the contributions he made to the support of his brother John, whose situation in London became more and more unpromising. In letter after letter Carlyle encouraged his brother to do work that would provide some certain income. He offered some formidable suggestions about an article on diet, which Doctor John had mentioned casually. Were there any dietic habits peculiar to the continent? Did any governments there take charge of the people's health, as all governments should? How were boxers dieted in the present? What foods had athletes eaten in the past? "Say thus much at least: Man can live on all things, from whale-blubber (as in Greenland) to clay-earth (as at the mouth of the Orinoco, see *Humboldt*). Then you have all the

Passions, etc. influenced by eating . . ." The research necessary
for such an article must have been far from the thoughts of
Doctor John. He wrote little and sold less, and at last Carlyle
was driven to the conclusion that his brother had "no heartiness
in the business of medicine" and that he could not live by
literature. In the education and support of his brother Carlyle
had advanced nearly £250. Now what was to be done with
him? Again the recluse of Craigenputtock appealed to Jeffrey
for help; and the little Duke of Craigcrook, as the Carlyles called
him, first lent Doctor John money and then found him a post as
medical attendant to the Countess of Clare, who spent much of
her time in travelling about Europe. In this position Doctor
John received 300 guineas a year and expenses, and before
long began to pay back both to Jeffrey and to Carlyle the
money he had borrowed from them.

Doctor John was not the only cause of trouble. The farming
project at Craigenputtock, backed by Carlyle's money, had
been wholly unsuccessful, and after losing £80 a year for
three years his brother Alick decided to abandon an enterprise
"for which he is evidently not adapted", as Carlyle dryly put
it. Carlyle was further depressed by the death from tuberculosis
of his favourite sister Margaret, at the age of twentysix; by
the increasing difficulty he found in selling articles on German
literature, and by the rejection of his part-written *History of
German Literature*, which remained forever unpublished.

In these generally gloomy circumstances he comforted
himself with the doctrine of renunciation expressed in the
German word *Entsagen*, and expressed more and more emphatically his hatred of what he called gig-men and gigmanity.
These epithets were taken from the questions and answers in
a contemporary trial: Q. What sort of person was Mr. Weare?
A. He was always a respectable person. Q. What do you mean
by respectable? A. He kept a gig. In his journal he wrote down
the most widely-ranging and arbitrary thoughts and speculations, and struggled to dispart his true beliefs from mere
prejudices. How could he know England, how understand
English history? Was not the Church the half of it? "Am I not
conscious of a prejudice on that side? Does not the very sight of
a shovel hat in some degree indispose me to the wearer thereof?"
Did he not also "partly despise, partly hate, the aristocracy of
Scotland . . . This too should be remedied . . . All are not mere
rent-gatherers and game-preservers". The death of Schlegel,

the character of Luther, his papers on Voltaire and Novalis, all churned together in his mind and led on to thoughts of decaying institutions, and the uses of economics and philosophy. "Political philosophy should be a scientific revelation of the whole secret mechanism whereby men cohere in society . . . by what causes men are happy, moral, religious, or the contrary. Instead of all which it tells us how 'flannel jackets' are exchanged for 'pork hams'." Such thoughts mingled with exhortations to himself to stand alone: "Stand to it tightly, man, and do thy utmost. Thou hast little or no hold on the world; promotion will never reach thee, nor true fellowship with any active body of men; but hast thou not still a hold on thyself?" Within a week, however, these observations were contradicted: "I have strange glimpses of the power of spiritual union, of association among men of like object." Passionate pity for the poor, passionate hatred of the "grand dilettanti", Whigs and Tories, excitement about the quickly-crushed French Revolution of 1830—"Away with Dilettantism and Machiavellianism though we should get atheism and Sansculotism in their room!"—all these things succeed each other rapidly in the journal. In England the Whigs had come to power and Jeffrey was Lord-Advocate. "The Whigs in office, and Baron Brougham Lord Chancellor! Haystacks and cornstacks burning all over the south and middle of England! Where will it end? Revolution on the back of revolution for a century yet?"

*   *   *   *   *

There must be chaos in the mind, Nietzsche tells us, if we wish to breed a dancing star. Out of the chaos in Carlyle's mind came *Sartor Resartus*, literally "The Tailor Repatched". Into this extraordinary book he tried to pack all the mystical, Radical, anti-gigmanic thoughts that were passing through his mind, choosing as the vehicle an imaginary biography of Herr Teufelsdröckh (or Devil's Dung), Professor of Things in General at the University of Weissnichtwo (or Know-not-Where), author of a book on the Philosophy of Clothes, published by Stillschweigen (Silence) and Company.

In the year 1900 nine separate editions of *Sartor Resartus* were published: half a century later the book is so little read that a short account of it may be useful. *Sartor* is divided into three parts: the first describes, with many elaborate jokes and hesitancies, the career of Teufelsdröckh, and the way in

E

which the manuscript relating to him came into the supposed editor's hands; the second casts back into Teufelsdröckh's childhood and youth; the third gives details of the Clothes philosophy. The book is at once an intellectual and spiritual autobiography and a criticism of various aspects of British life written from the point of view outlined in "Signs of the Times".

Such baldness of description, however, cannot at all convey the manner or the effect of *Sartor Resartus*. The manner is, speaking very generally, that of Sterne; the Professor darts from aspect to aspect of his subject, moves from serious political argument to outrageous comedy, from the pedantic to the ludicrous, as the history of Teufelsdröckh is discovered in six paper bags marked with signs of the zodiac—paper bags which contain also such things as wash-bills and "a Meta-physico-theological Disquisition, 'Detached Thoughts on the Steam-engine' ". Then this comedy turns suddenly to the most savage satire in the Professor's comments on a scheme proposed by his disciple Hofrath Heuschrecke for an "Institute for the Repression of Population". Heuschrecke, an ardent Malthusian, is afraid that the people of the over-populated world will end by eating one another. The Professor comments:

> The old Spartans had a wiser method; and went out and hunted-down their Helots, and speared and spitted them, when they grew too numerous. With our improved fashions of hunting, Herr Hofrath, now after the invention of fire-arms, and standing-armies, how much easier were such a hunt! Perhaps in the most thickly-peopled country, some three days annually might suffice to shoot all the able-bodied Paupers that had accumulated within the year. Let Govern-ments think of this. The expense were trifling: nay, the very carcasses would pay it. Have them salted and barrelled; could not you victual therewith, if not Army and Navy, yet richly such infirm Paupers, in workhouses and elsewhere, as enlightened Charity, dreading no evil of them, might see good to keep alive?

The central character of *Sartor Resartus* is, of course, Carlyle himself, drawn self-mockingly as a man of "genial capability, marred too often by . . . rudeness, inequality, and apparent want of intercourse with the higher classes"; his book has "the gravity of some silent, high-encircled mountain-pool, perhaps the crater of an extinct volcano"; he is "a speculative Radical, and of the very darkest tinge; acknowledging, for the most part, in the solemnities and paraphernalia of civilised Life, which we make so much of, nothing but so many Cloth-rags, turkey-poles, and 'bladders with dried peas'." This character is created for us chiefly in the account of his opinions: but the second part of *Sartor* recounts fairly exactly Carlyle's schooldays (although Teufelsdröckh is brought in a basket to his foster-parents by a mysterious stranger), his affair with Margaret Gordon and his "conversion". Such a blend of autobiography and social fable would, in any case, have been sufficiently bewildering: Carlyle added to these confusions the obstacle of his remarkable prose style which is seen here, for the first time, in full flower.

The style of Carlyle remains unique in English. It is at once breathlessly colloquial and full of elaborate metaphors; connectives are eliminated to gain force; words become displaced in the sentences, as it seems by accident, but always with the effect of increasing power and urgency of expression; the parts of speech abandon their usual functions, and move into new and fantastic patterns. It is a style utterly removed from what was thought, in Carlyle's day, proper English prose: it is violent with the unordered fluency of life, where classicism was modish; it brings together in a single paragraph, sometimes in a single sentence, neologisms and compound words, strange nicknames like Teufelsdröckh, and fantastic metaphors: the whole informed with a humour at once extravagant and clownish, obscure yet overflowing with vigour. This style was profoundly influential in changing the shape of literature in the nineteenth century. As Wordsworth and Coleridge killed classical diction in poetry, Carlyle extinguished it in prose. He gave to historians a new freedom and flexibility, and suggested to novelists that they could deal with the most complex and serious material by the heightening and illuminating power of metaphor. Upon Dickens, Meredith, Browning and Ruskin his shadow was particularly cast, but there is hardly a single serious prose writer in the second half of the nineteenth century who remained uninfluenced by the style of Carlyle.

What, it is natural to ask, were its origins? Carlyle himself said that the form, at once abrupt and extravagant, was his father's common mode of speech and that the humour came from his mother. The statement is acceptable so far as it goes, but it does not tell the whole story. The florid manner of Irving was responsible for much of the transcendental rhetoric which is almost the least acceptable feature of Carlyle's writing today; and added to Annandale colloquialism and Irvingesque rhetoric was the influence of the German models so faithfully studied. There is no clearer exposition of Carlyle's style than his own account of the style of Jean Paul Richter which is "to critics of the grammarian species, an unpardonable, often an insuperable rock of offence":

> Not that he is ignorant of grammar, or disdains the sciences of spelling and parsing; but he exercises both in a certain latitudinarian spirit; deals with astonishing liberality in parentheses, dashes, and subsidiary clauses; invents hundreds of new words, alters old ones, or by hyphen chains and pairs and packs them together into most jarring combination; in short, produces sentences of the most heterogeneous, lumbering, interminable kind. Figures without limit; indeed the whole is one tissue of metaphors, and similes, and allusions to all the provinces of Earth, Sea and Air; interlaced with epigrammatic breaks, vehement bursts, or sardonic turns, interjections, quips, puns, and even oaths! A perfect Indian jungle it seems; a boundless, unparalleled imbroglio; nothing on all sides but darkness, dissonance, confusion worse confounded!

How can such a style be justified? Partly by reference to the question Carlyle asks of Richter, and answers in the affirmative: does the style represent his real manner of thinking and existing? But more, much more, by the fact that the kind of attack made by Carlyle upon the institutions and the formal thinking of his age could not be made in eighteenth century prose, that with "the whole structure of Johnsonian English breaking up, revolution *there* is visible as everywhere else."

"It is a work of genius, dear", Jane said on reading the book for the first time. She was right: but *Sartor Resartus* is not, judged by Carlyle's own standards and intentions, a satisfactory work of genius. There is something pathological in the preoccupation shown here and in his later work with normal bodily functions. "I think the world will nowise be enraptured with this (medicinal) Devil's Dung", Carlyle wrote to his brother John; and as the years pass his metaphors and similes become more frequently concerned with excretion. It could be maintained, indeed, that the style itself, with its air of continually bursting through invisible but perpetual restraints, has some relation to his chronic constipation. Such conjectures, however, can be left to the American professor who, even now, is doubtless completing his thesis on "The Effect of Constipation on Nineteenth Century English Writers, with special reference to George Eliot and Thomas Carlyle". That will be an instructive volume.

It is of more immediate concern that the book describes social chaos, but is itself chaotic: that the very liberating and revolutionary qualities that make the famous style an ideal vehicle for Carlyle's individual attack on society render it peculiarly unsuitable for charting the New Era. Revolution, and the New Era after it, were much in his mind. It could not be doubted, he wrote to the St. Simonian Gustave d'Eichthal, that the maxim *"to each according to its capacity, to each capacity according to its works"* was "the aim of all true social doctrine". There are no constructive ideas for the reordering of society in *Sartor Resartus*. Instead, there is—an account of Carlyle's journey from "The Everlasting No" through "The Centre of Indifference" to "The Everlasting Yea"! If only all men could experience such a conversion! If the whole world could be stripped of its clothes of affectation and its gigmanism, if all kinds of cant and unreality could be dismissed, and the executioner and his victim, the landlord and his tenant, the prince and his retainer, appear equally in the form of forked, ungainly radishes . . .

The book was finished in August 1831, and within a few days Carlyle was in London trying to sell it. Poverty must have approached very nearly at this time: he could find no publisher for the *History of German Literature* or for his translation of St. Simon's *Nouveau Christianisme*; and Macvey Napier, who had replaced Jeffrey as editor of the *Edinburgh*, was cautious of commissioning an article from this odd kind of Radical. In London he hoped to be able to sell one or all of his books; he still thought that Jeffrey, now living in London, might be able to obtain for him some sinecure; and he felt a certain hankering to see closely the progress of the recent social reforms which he viewed with such contempt. With the manuscript of *Teufelsdröckh*, as it was then called, in his pocket, and "a deep,

irrevocable, all-comprehending Ernulphus Curse . . . Upon—
GIGMANITY" on his lips, Carlyle came to London. In October
Jane followed him, and they stayed in the city together until
March of the following year.

This stay in London had certain decisive results. It fixed
quite clearly in Jane's mind that she wanted to live there; and
it fixed just as firmly the fact that publishers had no use at all
for *Sartor Resartus*, and not very much use for Carlyle. First of
all, a "staid, cautious, business-like man" at Longmans
listened with a smile to the description of the German Literary
History, and then politely refused it. *Sartor* was retrieved from
John Murray, after he had kept it for ten days without reading
it; Longmans refused it as politely as they had refused the
German History. Carlyle turned to Jeffrey: but Jeffrey was
extremely busy, with no time to talk to Carlyle privately. He
kept the manuscript for some days, and then said that he had
read only twentyeight pages of it, pages for which it was plain
that he felt no great enthusiasm. He wrote, nevertheless, an
encouraging letter to Murray, who made an offer of publication
upon not very magnificent terms (Carlyle was to receive
nothing at all from the first 750 copies, and after that was to
become sole owner of the copyright): even this offer was withdrawn upon the curious ground that Carlyle had already
submitted the book to another publisher. "The truth of the
matter", Carlyle wrote to Jane, was that "Dreck cannot be
disposed of in London at this time." The book was put away in
his trunk, tied up again with the tape that Jane had put round
it. Carlyle's patience and dignity in face of this rather casual
treatment were admirable: equally admirable was Jane's
sympathy. When he told her that Jeffrey had recommended
the book to Murray she doubted it. "I must smile at the idea
of Jeffrey recommending your manuscript to Murray. He will
not, Dearest, dare not." When Murray finally refused it she
wrote: "If they will not publish him, bring him back and *I*
will take care of him and read him and admire him, till we are
enabled to publish on our own account."

The letters written by Carlyle to his wife during their period
of separation give a wonderful picture of his pursuits and
preoccupations. He revived old friendships, and in some cases
enmities. At Enfield he found Badams, who five years before
had attempted to cure his dyspepsia, dying from drinking
brandy—"his *gig* has broken down with him all to shivers, at

full speed." Not very far from Badams lived Charles Lamb, whose blend of whimsicality and light humour could never have appealed to Carlyle: now he was appalled by Lamb's utter drunkenness, and bored by his frivolity to the point of thinking the famous essayist almost insane, and putting down in his journal: "Poor Lamb! Poor England, when such a despicable abortion is named genius!" He looked with the same hard ironic eye, with its power of deriving character from external appearance, at Jeffrey in the House of Lords, "the poor little Darling with a grey wig on it, and queer coatie with bugles or buttons on the cuffs—snapping away and speaking there, in a foreign country, among entire strangers", and at John Bowring, the Radical editor of the *Westminster Review*. "Figure to yourself a thin man about my height and bent at the *middle* into an angle of 150°, the *back* quite straight, with large grey eyes, a huge turn-up nose with straight nostrils to the very point, and large projecting close-shut mouth." Carlyle said that they talked copiously, "he utterly utilitarian and Radical, I utterly mystical and Radical".

In this spirit of mystical Radicalism he saw the philosopher of Anarchism William Godwin, who had long ago retreated from the intrepid thinking of his early manhood into the salutary caution of old age. One can envisage clearly enough, even without the humour Carlyle gives to the scene, the impatient mental stampings with which the lean frowning blue-eyed Scotchman waited at a tea party for the arrival of England's leading political philosopher, and the contempt with which he observed the presence of several figures from the theatrical world. At last came Godwin, "a bald, bushy-browed, thick, hoary, hale little figure . . . wears spectacles, has full grey eyes, a very large blunt characterless nose and ditto chin." He spoke with some spirit but, Carlyle was disappointed to note, said nothing but commonplaces. Godwin had been eyeing Carlyle, whether with interest or fearfully we shall never know, and "by degrees I hitched myself near him, and was beginning to open on him", when—Godwin was hustled off to play whist. Noisy children and chattering women clustered round him; two women crashed at a piano in tones "louder than an iron forge"; there was to be no philosophical argument. Carlyle stayed for an hour, looking "sometimes not without sorrow at the long-nosed whist player", and then went home.

The idea that Carlyle was an unsociable man, as distinct from being upon occasion a ruthlessly impolite one, is erroneous. In London, at this time and later, he was noted as a great hunter of acquaintances: and if he found little profit among his elders, he was much cheered by the emergence of what he called "the rudiments of a mystic school". Among these young men, most of whom were quite unmystical and who formed a school only in Carlyle's imagination, were Charles Buller, now a furious Radical, and a friend of John Carlyle's named William Glen who, Carlyle said, "looks up to me almost as his Prophet". Chief of them was John Stuart Mill, whose papers in the Radical *Examiner* Carlyle had read with appreciation. Mill had some links with Carlyle in the fact that his father was a Scotchman, but the differences in the characters, backgrounds and modes of thought of the two men were so great that it is surprising they should ever have been friends.

James Mill, John Stuart's father, was one of those Utilitarian political philosophers who, more than the most extreme Tories, infuriated Carlyle by their complacent belief in the beneficial nature of mechanical progress. Cold, inquisitive, critical and unimaginative, James Mill at once reflected and distorted the teachings of such intellectual liberators as Diderot, Rousseau and Voltaire. He had made a destructive attack on ethical ideas in an *Analysis of the Human Mind*, and had written a scholarly *History of India* which earned him a comfortable position at India House. James Mill applied his logical, analytical, precise and narrow mind to the education of his son. He began to teach John Stuart Greek at the age of three; and between the ages of three and eight the child read a number of works in Greek, including Aesop's *Fables*, the *Anabasis* of Xenophon, and Herodotus; in English he read a number of histories, and more than one treatise on government. It is pleasant to be able to add that he was also allowed to read *Robinson Crusoe*, the *Arabian Nights* and the novels of Maria Edgeworth. At the age of eight he began to learn Latin; when he was twelve his studies embraced also Logic (Aristotle and Hobbes) and Political Economy (Ricardo and Adam Smith). Every day the boy walked with his father, and had to answer a series of searching questions on the day's work.

This early training stamped Mill for life in his father's image: but, in youth at least, he was capable of a freedom of thought and an ardour of feeling that were never within the reach of James Mill. When he was sixteen John Stuart Mill first read an account of the French Revolution and was overwhelmed with enthusiasm for the spirit of liberty and equality that touched France in those years. His greatest ambition for some years was to play the part of a Girondin in an English Convention. At the time of his first meeting with Carlyle Mill was twentyfive years old; like Carlyle he was corresponding with d'Eichthal, and disposed to think highly of the St. Simonians.

Between the rational mind of Mill and the intuitive one of Carlyle there was in truth little common ground: but to Carlyle certainly, to Mill more doubtfully, this fact was hidden. At their first or second meeting the two men talked four hours. Carlyle was delighted. Mill, he told Jane, was a young man she could love, and in a few lines Mill was memorably put down on paper:

> A slender, rather tall and elegant youth, with small clear roman-nosed face, two small earnestly-smiling eyes; modest, remarkably gifted with precision of utterance; enthusiastic, yet lucid, calm; not a great, yet distinctly a gifted and amiable youth.

It was to be regretted, Carlyle found on a little further acquaintance, that Mill could not "*laugh* with any compass": Carlyle's own laugh was an immense, body-shaking feat and he tended to deprecate any of lesser scale. He noted also that Mill was "too fond of demonstrating everything" so that if he got up to heaven "he would be hardly content till he had made out how it all was". But still, his opinion of Mill was favourable almost without qualification: and through Mill he met a number of young diplomats, Members of Parliament and such, who paid some attention as he expounded to them the "Signs of the Times".

Such was his situation when Jane arrived in London after a twentyfour hour sea journey to Liverpool during which she had been sick the whole time. She came by coach to the Angel, where Carlyle and Doctor John awaited her. They had ready at John Carlyle's lodgings, where Carlyle had taken a room, a dinner of chops and rice pudding. Few of Jane's journeys were free from disastrous after-effects, and on this occasion she was ill for two days with one of the mysterious headaches that recurred regularly throughout her life. Moreover she discovered bugs in this, as in many of the other lodgings in which she stayed during her life. John Carlyle had been in the same lodgings for many weeks. Was he, one wonders, immune to the bugs, or indifferent to them? Or were they a product of her imagination? In any case, as soon as she was well Jane went out with her husband to look for new lodgings, and found pleasant accommodation in Ampton Street, off Mecklenburgh Square. The house, Jane noted, was the only clean one she had seen since she left Scotland.

A bad start, one might think, to her visit: but behind Jane's demure observation made to her Liverpool cousin Helen Welsh that she liked London very well, lay a deep realization that this was her natural home. She loved it all: the friends they saw, from the Montagus and Stracheys to Jeffrey, Mill, Charles Buller and Allan Cunningham; the opportunities for gossip; a visit to the theatre where "the Ladies . . . surprised me by their almost universal ugliness", and one to a lunatic asylum which was so delightful that she thought any sane person would like to gain admission there; and the occasional pleasant surprises, like the day when Carlyle was out, and she had to entertain the St. Simonian Gustave d'Eichthal. Even the disagreeable moments had in them a spice of something like pleasure: when Charles Lamb dipped his spoon into her porridge to see what it was like, her retort was sufficiently crushing.

Among the few occasions that gave Jane no pleasure were the visits they paid to Irving. The rocket of his fame had passed its peak, and in descending showed no scintillations. At the conference of which Irving had spoken to Carlyle on his last visit to Scotland those present, swayed by Irving's eloquence, had agreed that the end of the world and the second coming of Christ were near at hand; a second conference fixed the year of the world's end as 1847, and it was agreed also that signs of the approaching judgement should be looked for by the revival of such spiritual manifestations as the gifts of healing, of prophecy, and of speaking with unknown tongues. Irving and his followers felt little surprise, therefore, when two young women in Scotland, living fifteen miles apart from each other, were reported to have been blessed with the gift of tongues. The cases were investigated, and approved genuine: Mary Campbell, one of the young women, began to preach and prophesy before crowded meetings, and was brought to London. The gift seemed endemic: within a few months the wife of one of the investigators spoke three sentences in an unknown tongue and another woman sang in it; soon afterwards several other members of Irving's congregation began to speak in unknown tongues and to prophesy in English. Since such spontaneous utterances naturally could not be restrained to times or places, they caused much scandal; at the time of the Carlyles' stay in London Irving's fashionable congregation had fallen away, and his fame was turning to notoriety.

Irving himself was as charming, frank and open-hearted as ever, although his hair was now grizzled and he showed signs of weariness. When Carlyle attended a service at Irving's church he was touched by the piteous look, imploring belief, cast him by the preacher. On this occasion there were no manifestations: but when Carlyle and Jane went to see Irving one day there was a shriek at the top of the house, and Irving exclaimed: "There is one prophesying; come and hear her."

> We hesitated to go, but he forced us up into a back room, and there we could hear the wretched creature raving like one possessed: *hoo*ing and *ha*ing, and talking *as* sensibly as one would do with a pint of brandy in his stomach, till after some ten minutes she seemed to grow tired and become silent.

Jane was so upset by this incident that she nearly fainted: Carlyle told Irving that the gift of tongues came from Bedlam. Irving defended himself mildly, but with an approach to tears: it was notable that the preacher himself had not yet been marked with the gift.

While they were in London James Carlyle died quite suddenly. He had been losing strength for the past two years, and when he caught a cold, which presently developed into pneumonia, had little power of resistance. Carlyle was deeply moved by the event, and wrote long letters of consolation to his mother and to Doctor John. He found much ease of mind in writing the long memoir of his father already referred to, which was completed in a few days. This would at any time have been a remarkable document; the fact that it was written within a few days of James Carlyle's death renders its desperate attempt at objectivity the more extraordinary. On the way back to Craigenputtock Carlyle heard of Goethe's death, and felt as if he had lost a second father.

*   *   *   *   *

During the months in London Carlyle had written two brilliant articles: one on John Wilson Croker's edition of Boswell's *Life of Johnson*, which had already been anathematised from a different point of view by Macaulay, and the other, "Characteristics", a restatement of the views in his "Signs of the Times". In the guise of an article on metaphysics, Carlyle got in some trenchant strokes at such enemies as book reviewers and utilitarian philosophers, with their "perpetual dream . . . of Paradises, and some luxurious Lubberland, where the brooks should run wine, and the trees bend with ready-baked viands." Macvey Napier, who printed "Characteristics" in the *Edinburgh*, said doubtfully that he did not understand the essay, but that it had the stamp of genius, and the little circle of Carlyle's admirers in London read it with pleasure: but it is not likely that other editors were encouraged to look for contributions from a man who increased the difficulty of his thought by the wilful eccentricity (as it must have seemed to them) of its expression. The article that he wrote after returning to Scotland, on the *Corn-Law Rhymes* of the Sheffield iron-worker Ebenezer Elliot, must have alienated them further; for here Carlyle expressed altogether heretical views both about the condition of poetry at that time, and about the potentialities for poetry in the working-class writer. "It used to be said that lions do not paint, that poor men do not write; but the case is altering now"; and the essayist went on to suggest that "it is actually, in these strange days, no special misfortune to be trained up among the Uneducated classes, and not among the Educated; but rather of two misfortunes the smaller".

Such sentiments could be no recommendation; and when in 1833 *Sartor Resartus* was at last printed serially in *Fraser's Magazine*, and the author rewarded at specially reduced rates, the name of Carlyle reached its commercial nadir. The book was received, James Fraser told Carlyle, "with the most unqualified disapproval"; he lost subscribers and, like other editors, fought shy of accepting any further contributions. In 1833 Carlyle published the article on the Corn-Law rhymes, a short article on History, and two long semi-biographical pieces, one on Diderot and the other on Count Cagliostro; in the following three years he published nothing at all apart from a very short piece on Edward Irving. During these unproductive years the Carlyles left Craigenputtock, and came to live in London.

Perhaps neither of them felt Craigenputtock to be thoroughly delightful, after their glimpse of London life. Carlyle kept up a correspondence with Mill which reveals his restless feeling that life was passing him by, that the possibilities for some kind of decisive action in his personality were unfulfilled. He tried still at times to persuade himself that his existence among whinstone mountains and peat bog, peopled with oxen, grouse and sheep, was ideal for a philosopher: but he was eager to have news of events in London, and more than once expressed the view that "it is not good for me to stay much longer in the Nithsdale Peat-desert". The same note appears in letters to Doctor John, who was trailing round Italy with the Countess of Clare, and complaining occasionally of the solitary nature of his life. Craigenputtock, Carlyle surprisingly remarked to John, was actually one of the worst abodes for him in the whole wide world; and he wrote of the delights of visiting Edinburgh "to *live* for twelve weeks, with eyes and ears open".

His letters to Mill are bursting with questions, suggestions, ideas. Shall we not, he asks, have "*our own* Periodical Pulpit, and *exclude* the Philistine therefrom?" Or should they—this was a question that always fascinated Carlyle—"burst out into quite another sort of activity", and abandon literature and speculation altogether? Mill sent books for the work Carlyle was doing on Cagliostro, and contemplating on the French Revolution: but one catches, even at this distance of time, the alarm that must have shown in those small earnestly-smiling eyes at reading Carlyle's view of him as a mystic, the fear that this vociferous exclamatory enthusiast for a New Era might swallow up logical Mill altogether. When, however, Mill pointed out that there were many subjects on which they differed, Carlyle offered a characteristically enthusiastic assent which somehow swept away Mill's further suggestion that they were moving away from each other; when Mill thought that, upon the whole, it would be better for him not to visit Craigenputtock, Carlyle showed himself a little hurt. "There is inconceivable virtue in Silence, yet often also in wise communing of man with man. If you know any heart that can understand you, that has suffered the like of what you suffer, to that heart speak . . . I prescribe not as physician; but warn you that if you hide yourself in August, it will be *very difficult* to find an excuse that can pass here."

The cautious Mill was not altogether encouraged by this, nor by Carlyle's exhortation in another letter to "Come . . . and let us get fairly acquainted with you . . . You are worth getting acquainted with, I think; and as for me you know that at bottom I am a very inoffensive sort of fellow." After all, Mill did not come; in his place there arrived an equally earnest young American, to whom Mill had given a letter of introduction, writing at the same time to tell Carlyle that the young man was "not a very hopeful subject."

The name of the young man was Ralph Waldo Emerson. He was an eager and devout young Unitarian, who had broken off his connection with the Second Church, and as it turned out his career as a minister, in consequence of a difference of opinion concerning the rite of the Lord's Supper. This act, and the sudden death of his young wife, had completely unsettled Emerson, and in an attempt to raise his spirits he made a trip to Europe.

In America Emerson had been much impressed by the work of the "Germanic new-light writer" and had enquired his name: the short list of writers he wanted to see in Europe included Coleridge, Wordsworth, Landor, De Quincey—and Carlyle. These giants he approached in a spirit of earnest, but not uncritical, reverence. Emerson was courteously received by Landor in Italy, and noted with care the opinions he expressed on poetry, culture and history. He visited Coleridge, who burst into a great rhetorical declamation against Unitarianism; and the effect of Emerson's interposition that "whilst I highly valued all his explanations, I was bound to tell him that I was born and bred a Unitarian", was merely to make Coleridge say "I supposed so", and continue his attack with greater violence. The visit, Emerson felt, was rather a spectacle than a conversation, and he regretted that the old man could not bend to a new companion.

From London Emerson went to Edinburgh. He had much difficulty in finding out where Carlyle lived, but at last hired a rusty old gig to "the house amid desolate heathery hills, where the lonely scholar nourished his mighty heart." He had not been expected, but he was most hospitably received; the gig was sent back to Edinburgh, and told to return the next day. Emerson felt something of the unwilling fascination accorded to Carlyle by Jeffrey and Mill: the fascination held by the bold for the cautious, by the intuitive and dogmatic for the logical and timid. And Carlyle (as, Emerson noted, his wife called him, accenting the first syllable), free of the restraints of convention, could be—as he was on this occasion—an informal and delightful host. Emerson was charmed by his northern accent, and by the conversational idiom which called *Blackwood's* the *sand magazine* and *Fraser's* the *mud magazine*: and by the way in which, when Emerson urged the genius of one writer or another, Carlyle would praise the immense talent and intelligence of his pig. Carlyle's talk, moving briskly from pauperism to the immortality of the soul, from the puffing of books to the pleasures of London muffins, was one of the three things that most impressed Emerson in Europe; although the force of this tribute is perhaps lessened by the knowledge that the other two were a bust of Clytie rising from the Lotus in the Townley Art Gallery and the discovery of a man in Edinburgh who appeared to him to have something of the spirit of Dante. A day or two after leaving Craigenputtock Emerson visited Wordsworth, and was distressed to learn that the poet thought Carlyle wrote most obscurely, and was sometimes insane.

Such a pleasant visit as this pointed very sharply the chances open in London for Carlyle to gather round him a mystical school and to utter that mysterious and elusive word which, as he put down in his journal, would thrill the inmost soul of man when properly spoken. There was, too, the fact that although Jane said nothing, he was aware that after these years of isolation she longed for society. She was fond of quoting wryly, at this time, a remark made in a complimentary tone to Carlyle: "Mrs. Carlyle has the remains of a fine woman." "Think of that now!" she wrote to Bess Stodart, "at thirty to pass for a remains!" The winter of 1833 was savage: trees were uprooted, slates blown off; and for both Carlyle and his wife the time cannot have been a happy one. In some melancholy verses, written, probably by Jane, "To a Swallow Building under our Eaves", and dated "The Desert, 1834", the feeling of the Carlyles about Craigenputtock at this time is made plain. The verses quoted are the first two, and the last:

Thou too hast travelled, little fluttering thing,
Hast seen the world, and now thy weary wing
   Thou too must rest.
But much, my little Bird, couldst thou but tell,
I'd give to know why here thou lik'st so well
   To build thy nest.

For thou hast passed fair places in thy flight;
A world lay all beneath thee where to light;
   And strange thy taste!
Of all the varied scenes that met thine eye,
Of all the spots for building 'neath the sky,
   To choose this waste! . . .

God speed thee, pretty Bird! May thy small nest
With little ones all in good time be blest!
   I love thee much!
For well thou managest that life of thine,
While I!—O ask not what I do with mine!
   Would it were such!

These dark days had some dubious alleviations: Carlyle's friend William Graham came over and stayed for two days (but it was "amid bad weather, and rather wearisome conversation"); his disciple Glen, who had descended to harmless lunacy, was boarded at a neighbouring farm, and Carlyle went over and read Homer with him; he was given the freedom of a fine private library within riding distance of Craigenputtock. But still Carlyle hoped, and almost longed, for the life of a city: and in January 1834 he made a last attempt to obtain an official post through Jeffrey. The attempt failed: and in its failure severed the intimacy between the two men.

When Carlyle had been making his unsuccessful attempts to find a publisher for *Sartor* he thought that Jeffrey was upon the whole not very anxious to help him: and since the tone and matter of the book attacked the little lawyer's most closely-held views he had no reason beyond natural benevolence for urging its publication. Jeffrey was now a man of political importance, and his tolerance of Carlyle was approaching its end. Although he continued to write letters to Jane addressed to "My dear Infant", and felt the fascination of Carlyle whenever they met, he more or less ensured Carlyle's exclusion from the *Edinburgh* by writing to Macvey Napier that—as he had written long ago of Wordsworth—"Carlyle will not do". On his side, Carlyle had mentioned the ominous word *Gigmanic* in connection with Jeffrey. It was under these unfavourable stars that Carlyle saw in the newspaper that a new professorship of Astronomy was to be established in Edinburgh, and wrote to Jeffrey. Had not the Lord-Advocate said repeatedly that Carlyle should call on him at any time "whenever you think I can do you, or anybody you care about, any good"? Was it not plain that, if the appointment was not actually in his keeping, his good word would be highly influential? The more that Carlyle thought of the project the more he liked it: his qualifications were reasonable enough, and in any case the position was more or less a sinecure. He cannot have expected a refusal even to recommend him: but he got one. By return of post Jeffrey wrote that Carlyle had not the least chance of getting the Chair of Astronomy, and that it would be useless for him to make application. He went on to say that the tone of Carlyle's writings was "arrogant, vituperative, obscure, anti-national and inconclusive", and added in terms that in a man less mild than Jeffrey might have been thought threatening, "As you begin to experience the effects, you may perhaps give more credit to my testimony than you used to do". This—and there is much more of it—is the exasperation of the turning worm, of the weak man provoked beyond endurance; few men would have responded to it as Carlyle did, with good-humoured thanks to Jeffrey at least for his swift despatch of false hopes, and with a note to his brother John that he felt it wholesome to have his vanity humbled from time to time. Ever afterwards, however, what Carlyle called the "friendly or effusive strain" of their correspondence was missing, and before long the "theoretic flourishes of epistolary trumpeting" between the two men ceased altogether, although Jeffrey continued for some years to correspond with Jane.

With this last hope of an official position gone, the move to London was settled, and in May Carlyle set out to look for a house to rent. In the coach on the road he gravely saluted a Trades Union procession, and his salute was as gravely returned. After some searching in Kensington, Bayswater and Chelsea he settled on Number 5, Great Cheyne Row, "a right old strong roomy brick house, built new one hundred and thirty years ago". The house had three storeys, and at the end of it was a narrow strip of garden. They had, naturally, some doubts—

Carlyle about Chelsea as a place to live in, and Jane about the possibility of bugs in the wainscoting—but the low rental of £35 a year decided them to take it. On the 10th of June, 1834, on a damp and cloudy day, Carlyle, with Jane and their maid Bessy Barnet, drove from Ampton Street to Chelsea. As they crossed Belgrave Square Chico, the little canary bird brought by Jane from Craigenputtock, burst out singing.

CHAPTER TEN

THE FRENCH REVOLUTION

The chief desire of my mind has again become to *write* a masterpiece, let it be acknowledged as such or not acknowledged. . . . At this moment I write only in *treble*, of a situation, of a set of feelings that longs to express itself in the voice of thunder.

THOMAS CARLYLE: Journal, 1833.

Carlyle's writings make on me the impression of the sound of a single hatchet in the aboriginal forests of North America.

MONCKTON MILNES in his Notebook.

THE LITTLE BIRD SANG. We see the early years at Cheyne Row very much in the light of the letters Jane wrote to her friends and relatives in Scotland; letters as witty, as humorous, and as neatly intelligent as any in the English language. No pretentiousness remained unquizzed by her keen eye, no detail of domestic life was too trivial for her to turn it to comedy. What did it matter that they were setting up house with no more than £200 in hand, and the blackest financial prospect? "I declare to you", she wrote to John Carlyle, "I can never get myself worked up into proper anxiety about how body and soul are to be kept together. . . . I have always a sort of lurking assurance that if one's bread ceases it will be possible to live on pie-crust".

In the meantime bread was not lacking: and there was much to be done, and more to be observed. There was the extraordinary improvidence of the English, as shown by the way in which they flung platefuls of crusts into the ashpits. There were the activities of Mrs. Leigh Hunt who lived nearby and sent over almost daily to borrow tumblers, teacups, porridge, tea, and even a brass fender: and who, when Jane said that she had been painting, was much cast down to hear that it was a wardrobe and not a portrait. There were astonishing reports on clothes to be made to Carlyle's mother:

The diameter of the fashionable ladies at present is about three yards; their bustles (false bottoms) are the size of an ordinary sheep's fleece.

Her thrifty soul was maddened by the waste all around her. "When we dine out, to see as much money expended on a dessert of fruit (for no use but to give people a colic) as would keep us in necessaries for two or three weeks!"

One day her old suitor George Rennie called. He had been living in India for ten years, and was now a rich man. Jane noted maliciously that he was the sort of person with whom one discussed, with pseudo-seriousness, the condition of art in England. On first seeing him, it is true, she had been "within an ace of fainting": but further acquaintance showed, alas, that he lived in the wretchedest atmosphere of gigmanity. "Though he has come home with more thousands of pounds than we are ever likely to have hundreds, or even scores, the sight of him did not make me doubt the wisdom of my preference", Jane wrote to Carlyle's mother. "Indeed, I continue quite content with my bargain; I could wish him a little less *yellow*, and a little more *peaceable*; but that is all."

Peace had deserted Carlyle: he had at last begun to work on that study of the French Revolution which had been for so long fermenting in his mind. Years later he said that he would not have known what to make of the world but for the French Revolution: and the remark indicates the mood in which he studied all history. He tried to grasp the meaning of every event before putting pen to paper: and to grasp the meaning meant, for Carlyle, to see that event in its full historical, moral and religious significance. He was never interested in an academic approach to history: rather, he wished to interpret all history and all literature as a kind of vast religious poem. The doubts Mill felt in writing about the Revolution because in doing so he would feel bound to reveal his own lack of faith quite passed by Carlyle; but his own dubieties, though vague, were even more disturbing. Visiting the British Museum twice a week to search in the great, and at that time uncatalogued, collection of contemporary printed matter, or sitting at home surrounded by the boxes of books lent him by Mill, he found the subject "Gloomy, huge, of almost boundless meaning; but obscure, dubious—all too deep for me; will and must *do my best*." He noted too that "gleams . . . of a work of art hover past me; as if this should be a *work of art*. Poor me!"

With these doubts went a passion for verifiable fact, which haunted Carlyle all his life: he might have been a wonderful reporter. He bombarded Doctor John, now attending his

Countess in Paris, with requests for such things as a pianoforte score of Ça-ira, and asked him to look in the Rue du Faubourg Saint-Antoine and see if the Tree of Liberty planted there in 1790 was still growing. Nevertheless, at last he began to write regularly, from breakfast at nine until two o'clock; walking from two till four; and after dinner either reading or strolling with Jane by the river, watching the white-shirted Cockneys in their green canoes, or the old pensioners smoking. He much enjoyed walking the London streets in a new hat, a new brown cloth coat with fur at the neck, and a new dark rifle-green frock coat. ("Really a most smart man", he told his mother.) And gradually the work got done, not quickly indeed, but more or less to its writer's satisfaction. It would be a very queer book, he thought, but a tolerable one.

It was not perhaps to be expected that many visitors should be encouraged at a time when Carlyle noted in his journal that for five days he had spoken to no one but Jane, and that he sat at his desk, "mood tragical, gloomy, as of one forsaken, who had nothing left him *but to get through his task and die.*" Both Carlyle and Jane, however, were inclined to a certain extravagance of statement: visitors were more frequent than such words imply. Mill came round every Sunday afternoon, to walk with Carlyle and to discuss the Revolution, its history and its meaning. Leigh Hunt, at this time editor of *The Examiner*, came round three or four times a week, talked, sang, played the piano, and ate sometimes a plate of porridge with sugar: once Jane was so delighted to see Hunt that she jumped up and kissed him, and he wrote on the spot the anthology piece, "Jenny kissed me". Many other political Radicals visited the Carlyles, from John Sterling, a young Church of England clergyman whose father edited *The Times*, and who was at once dazzled and horrified by *Sartor*, to the burly, brilliant, flippant Charles Buller, now a Radical Member of Parliament; and including between such opposites reformers of several shades. The beliefs of these reformers were very various: but they were united in feeling a certain distrust mingled with their admiration of Carlyle. Thus when Sir William Molesworth, a wealthy young man who defended in the House of Commons the cause of the six labourers later known as the Tolpuddle Martyrs, put up £4,000 to start a Radical review, Carlyle hoped that he might be appointed editor: but even Mill, great as was his admiration for Carlyle, did not dare to

suggest that the editorship of a review should be entrusted
to a thinker so unsafely heterodox. Many men of letters
thought, like Wordsworth, that Carlyle was half insane; others
were determined to ignore him. When he received from James
Fraser some copies of *Sartor* made by stitching magazine
sheets together, he sent them to six literary men in Edinburgh.
Not one of them acknowledged its receipt. Carlyle on his side
had a contempt for most of the London Radicals at least equal
to their distrust of him. Some of them, like Hunt and Buller,
seemed to him amiable, but regrettably flippant; and those,
like Mill, whose seriousness was undoubted, lacked the hearty
and forthright enthusiasm that was so marked a feature of his
own nature. Among all these Radicals he often longed for
Irving: but Irving had reached the end of his story.

Two years before the Carlyles came to London Irving had
at last been dismissed from his church for a refusal to forbid
prophetic utterances during services. He retained his following
for a time, preaching sermons in a picture gallery in Newman
Street, where seven seats on a raised platform were allotted to
the prophets. These sermons were interrupted by manifestations, "the prophets speaking as utterance came upon them",
as a contemporary pamphlet puts it. It came upon them
rather often: when Irving was preaching on "Reconciliation
to God" he was rarely allowed to speak more than a few
sentences, and sometimes spoke only a few words, without
inspired interruption. When John Cardale, a respectable
solicitor, felt himself called upon to become the first apostle of
the Catholic Apostolic Church, Irving's power over his followers, and perhaps his belief in his own divine mission, began to
fail. He was expelled, as was inevitable, from the ministry and
membership of the Church of Scotland—the court that expelled
him meeting in Annan; and although he was ordained as chief
angel of the new Church, power in it passed quickly to, in a
worldly sense, more skilful hands. Irving was never moved to
prophesy, nor did he ever feel called upon to proclaim himself
an apostle.

The Carlyles followed this disastrous progress with sympathy
and wonder. Their meetings with Irving in these latter days
were few. When Carlyle came down to look for a house—and
found, eventually, Cheyne Walk—a black-clad figure started
from a seat in Kensington Gardens and clutched his hand;
with a shock he recognized Irving. His old friend looked like

death rather than life, Carlyle wrote to Jane, "pale and yet flushed, a flaccid, boiled appearance". In later recollection he filled out the picture of an old-looking grey-haired man, whose face was wrinkled and whose temples were marked with the peculiar white of age. Irving had abated nothing in friendliness; and "one short peal of his old Annandale laugh went through me with the wofullest tone". Soon afterwards Carlyle visited Irving and his wife at Newman Street. Irving lay on a sofa, and complained of biliousness and a pain in his ribs; his wife, also miserable and haggard, sat at his feet and watched Carlyle, whose influence on her husband she distrusted because of his impiety. Disturbed by his friend's evident decline Carlyle appealed to the preacher's friends and relatives to save him; but in vain. When Irving was ordered by the prophets of his church to preach the new doctrine in Scotland he went without hesitation. On a damp dim day he ambled up Cheyne Row on a bay horse, and spent a quarter of an hour with the Carlyles. He looked at the pretty little sitting room Jane had made and said, with a touch of his old rhetoric, "You are like an Eve, and make a little Paradise wherever you are!" Carlyle followed him to the door, held the bridle of his horse while he mounted, and watched him ride up Cheyne Row. They never saw him again. Worn out and utterly disheartened, Irving died in Glasgow in December 1834; almost his last act was to write a letter to his congregation full of questionings and doubts about the gift of tongues.

So passed Edward Irving, a man of talent, and even of wild genius, as we use such words, showing in his life, doubtless, as many morals as there are interpreters to read them: and to a twentieth century rationalist conveying no lesson more clearly than that genius of this kind is nothing, and the form in which it is manifested all. Carlyle wrote a short and moving eulogy of his dead friend, and an attack on the vices of the society that had killed him. Jane's epitaph was shorter, but at least as true. "If he had married me", she said, "there would have been no gift of tongues."

*   *   *   *   *

"Is it not strange", Jane wrote to Bess Stodart in Edinburgh, "that I should have an everlasting sound in my ears, of men, women, children, omnibuses, carriages, glass coaches, street coaches, waggons, carts, dogcarts, steeple bells, door bells, gentlemen-raps, twopenny post-raps, footmen-showers-of-raps, of the whole devil to pay, as if plague, pestilence, famine, battle, murder, sudden death, and wee Eppie Daidle were broken loose to make me diversion? And where is the stillness, the eternal sameness, of the last six years? Echo answers, at Craigenputtock! There let them 'dwell with Melancholy' and old Nancy Macqueen; for this stirring life is more to my mind, and has besides a beneficial effect on my bowels."

Such were the delights of London: and yet life was never perfectly happy for the Carlyles, for it was true, as Jane often said, that they had a skin too few for ordinary living. When their maid poured boiling water on to Jane's foot she became totally lame for weeks, and had to be carried upstairs and downstairs by Carlyle. Carlyle himself, although he refused without second thought a position on *The Times* offered him through John Sterling, nevertheless wrote bitterly in his Journal that it was twentythree months since he had earned a penny by the craft of literature; on finishing the first book of *The French Revolution* he noted simply: "Soul and body both very *sick*." Yet Carlyle and Jean were capable, as they now showed, of facing with fortitude a true disaster.

One person only beside Carlyle and Jane was trusted with the growing manuscript: John Stuart Mill. When the first book was finished Mill took it away to re-read and make notes. At this time Mill, to the surprise and distress of his friends, was constantly in the company of Harriet Taylor, the wife of a brisk and bustling Unitarian tradesman. Mrs. Taylor found her respectable husband dull: and although Mill might have been considered by some as not precisely sparkling company, he was sufficient of a Radical lion to be worth ensnaring. Carlyle put it with picturesque malice: "Mill who, up to that time, had never so much as looked a female creature, not even a cow, in the face, found himself opposite those great dark eyes, that were flashing unutterable things." She wrapped him up, Carlyle went on, like a cocoon: and although it was politely assumed that their relations were platonic, she separated from her husband rather than give up her friendship with Mill who regarded her, as he said once, just as he would have regarded a man who had the same fine qualities of mind. It has never been firmly settled whether the manuscript passed from Mill's hands to those of Mrs. Taylor: whether it was Mill or Mrs. Taylor who put it down upon a table one night before going to bed; whether it was Mill's or Mrs. Taylor's servant

who, in the morning, used what she thought were sheets of
waste paper to light a fire. In any case, almost the whole of the
manuscript was burned.

This was the news that Mill brought when, pale and un-
responsive, the very picture of despair, he appeared one afternoon at the Carlyles' front door, leaving Mrs. Taylor outside in
a cab. "Gracious Providence, he has gone off with Mrs.
Taylor", Jane cried. She left the room and Carlyle led Mill to a
seat, and learned that his manuscript had been destroyed;
Mill, in the telling, did not say whether it had passed from his
own hands. He had come as much for consolation as for anything else, and he stayed for several hours while the Carlyles
did their best to soothe his tortured feelings. When at last he had
gone Carlyle said to Jane: "Well, Mill, poor fellow, is terribly
cut up; we must endeavour to hide from him how very serious
this business is to us." The immediate shock was thus happily
survived: but during the night Carlyle felt sharp pains, as of
something cutting or grasping him round the heart, and
dreamt of his dead father and sister, "alive; yet all defaced with
the sleepy stagnancy, swollen hebetude of the grave, and again
dying in some strange rude country." On the next day he
wrote a generous letter suggesting that Mill's sorrow must be
greater than his own, and adding gallantly that he had ordered
a *Biographie Universelle* and a better sort of paper on which to
start rewriting. The loss of the manuscript, however, left the
Carlyles in a really desperate financial position: and Carlyle
agreed to accept a sum of money from Mill in compensation
partly for this reason, partly—we may readily believe—out of a
delicate feeling that such a gift would help to salve Mill's
distress. Mill offered £200 of which Carlyle accepted half, the
sum he calculated the writing to have cost him. He was
troubled by the fear that acceptance of the gift, although it was
reasonable, might also be gigmanic. But at last the thing was
settled: and then there was simply the rewriting to be done.

If the first writing had been a struggle, the second was a
task to which Carlyle found himself hardly equal. It was all
very well for him to tell his mother that the finger of Providence
had pointed at him, or to his brother that he felt like a schoolboy who had found his laboriously-written copy torn by his
master with the words, "No, boy, thou must go and write it
better." So far from writing it better, he found it hard to write it
at all; and for almost the whole of the rest of the time that he

was engaged on the book he was in atrocious spirits. At times he spoke of the whole thing as a mass of unformed rubbish, and thought of burning it himself; at others he thought that there was in it "a genuine picture or two". He became so absorbed in the task that he saw the Revolution and its aftermath everywhere: when he paid a visit to friends he discerned that through the thin cobwebs of laughter and conversation "Death and Eternity sat glaring". He who had spoken so contemptuously of the effects of art worried continually about the possible affectations of his style, and observed with much insight: "On the whole, I am rather stupid; or rather I am not stupid (for I feel a fierce glare of insight in me into many things); not stupid,—but I have *no sleight of hand*. A raw untrained savage; for every trained civilised workman *has* that sleight, and is a bred workman by having it: the bricklayer with his trowel, the painter with his brush, the writer with his pen". His indigestion returned in full force, and he was unable to sleep; he grew thinner and yellower; friends generally found him miserable when they came round in the evening, but as the hours passed he brightened and softened and became amiable.

What, in the meantime, did Jane do? She painted and rearranged, and she learnt Italian. When Carlyle paid a short visit to Scotland she advised him not to take castor oil, but chicken broth; when he returned, half-mad from battling with porters and cabmen, she brought him a large glass of sherry before giving him news or asking him questions. She made an attempt to, as she put it, "annihilate my I-ety": that part of her which, when she saw too much attention paid to her husband, called out like a little child in *Wilhelm Meister*: "I too am here." We may be glad that her I-ety was never annihilated: but some of her acquaintances found her sharpness very trying. "Do you know, Mrs. Carlyle, you would be a vast deal more amiable, if you were not so damnably clever!", Edward Sterling, the rough bluff editor of *The Times* who was a frequent visitor at the house, said to her.

Through her wit there runs always a line of malice, even in relation to her much-loved and revered Carlyle. "My husband is anything but well, nor likely to be better till he have finished his *French Revolution*," she wrote to her cousin Helen Welsh, and added: "I myself have been abominably all winter, though not writing, so far as I know, for the press." She was not an easy woman to live with, any more than Carlyle was an easy man: and when in 1836 she set off to pay a visit to her mother, it is likely that some disagreement between husband and wife was joined to her dislike of London in the summer, to prompt her going. At Templand things were no better than in London. She and her mother always acted as irritants upon each other, and now she found that Mrs. Welsh gave her the right things at the wrong times, the wrong things at the right times; moreover, she developed cramp, and was unable to sleep. In Carlyle's letters to her while she was on this visit there is a certain admonitory tone. He adjured her not to harden her heart but to soften it, not to be faithless but believing. "Do not fling life away as insupportable, despicable, but let us work it out and rest it out together like a true two."

After a stay of two months she was very happy to return home, and to see Carlyle's face, set off by a broad-brimmed white hat, peering in unexpectedly at the door of a crowded omnibus, "like the Peri, who, at the Gate of Heaven, stood disconsolate." On her return she expressed what she often thought, that although many people loved her far better than she deserved in their fashion, "his fashion is so different from all those, and seems alone to suit the crotchety creature that I am." And at last, to her relief, the book was done: Carlyle read her the last sentences with their blazing vision of a beneficial destruction of all cant and hypocrisy:

RESPECTABILITY, with all her collected Gigs inflamed for funeral pyre, wailing, leaves the earth: not to return save under new Avatar. Imposture how it burns, through generations: how it is burnt up; for a time. The World is black ashes;—which, ah, when will they grow green? The Images all run into amorphous Corinthian brass; all Dwellings of men destroyed; the very mountains peeled and riven, the valleys black and dead: it is an empty World! . . . For it is the End of the dominion of IMPOSTURE (which is Darkness and opaque Fire-damp); and the burning up, with unquenchable fire, of all the Gigs that are in the Earth.

He said to her: "I know not whether this book is worth anything, nor what the world will do with it, or misdo, or entirely forbear to do (as is likeliest), but this I could tell the world: You have not had for a hundred years any book that came more direct and flamingly sincere from the heart of a living man." He might have added, it occurred to him afterwards: "My poor little Jeannie and me, hasn't it nearly killed us both?"

*   *   *   *   *

The French Revolution was received much more warmly than its author had expected. Dickens carried a copy of it about with him everywhere; Thackeray wrote a handsome review of it in *The Times*; Southey praised it highly to Carlyle's face, wrote to one friend that he would probably read it six times, and to another that it was "a book like which there was nothing in our language before nor is likely to be again." Emerson thought it a wonderful book which would last a very long time, and assured Carlyle of its good reception in America, where *Sartor* had sold more than a thousand copies. Mill summed up this favourable view when he said that the sub-title of the book should not be "A History" but "A Poem". Jeffrey observed cautiously that it was a book which "cannot be read anywhere, without leaving the impression that the author (whatever else may be thought of him) is a man of genius and originality, and capable of still greater things than he has done even here."

To the other side such orthodox Whigs as Macaulay and Brougham recognized Carlyle as a man of dangerous and sinister talent, and disapproved wholly of his zest for violence; while Wordsworth wrote a sonnet against the book and thought it a pity that Carlyle and Emerson, who he joined together as "Philosophers who have taken a language which they suppose to be English for their vehicle" could not be "left exclusively to their appropriate reward—mutual admiration". The hostile view, however, was swamped by the chorus of praise for this, the first book on which Carlyle's name had actually appeared. Within a few months of its publication he found himself respected, and even famous, in the literary world of the day. Jane expressed a fear to John Sterling that she might be torn to pieces by her husband's feminine admirers, whom she ironically listed: deaf Harriet Martineau who "(presented) him with her ear-trumpet with a pretty blushing air of coquetry"; a Mrs. Pierce Butler who bolted in and out of the house with riding habit, cap and whip, "but no shadow of a horse, only a carriage, the whip I suppose being to whip the cushions with, for the purpose of keeping her hand in practice"; and a large soft vacant young American beauty who declared herself his ardent admirer and called out quite passionately at parting: "Oh, Mr. Carlyle, I want to see you to talk a long long time about—*Sartor*". Was it not curious, Jane added, that her husband's writings should be completely understood and adequately appreciated only by women and mad people?

The circle of friends and acquaintances that the book gained for the Carlyles was hardly as limited as Jane's irony made out. Tories like Southey admired the book's freedom from any doctrinaire viewpoint, and were surprised to find on meeting with Carlyle that he agreed with them on many points; English Radicals were pleased by an eloquence which they took to be exerted in support of their cause; and a number of exiled revolutionaries like Mazzini and Godefroi Cavaignac became constant visitors at Cheyne Row.

Today, more than a hundred years after its publication, we come to *The French Revolution* with a sense of its merits and deficiencies wholly different from that of Carlyle's own age. His single-handed battling with the slippery spirit of fact, here and in later books, means little to us in a time when historical documentation can be carried out by a whole corps of assistants equipped with card-indexes; his treatment of characters with whom he felt little sympathy, like Robespierre and Saint-Just, is marred by inaccuracies of omission, his estimate of such a man as Mirabeau is hardly tenable in the light of modern scholarship. More serious than these defects is the inadequacy of Carlyle's treatment of the sources of the Revolution. Beginning with the death of Louis XV, ending with the appointment of Buonaparte as General in 1795, his narrative rarely looks back or forward beyond those years: a limitation that gives force and compactness to his story, but imposes upon him the necessity of dealing with the Revolution in terms of individuals rather than of events. Carlyle was not unaware that the Revolution had its economic and industrial background; he saw that it marked the end of feudalism in France; but the whole pattern of his thought made it impossible for him to grant such considerations prime importance.

The struggle that worked in him between the Calvinism of his upbringing and the desire for social improvement through violent overthrow of the existing order had come to a solution that could have been reached only by a British thinker, and only in the nineteenth century. Social improvement there must be, and it could be obtained only by revolutionary means: so far Carlyle was a Radical far to the left of those with whom he associated, in his contempt for Parliamentary counting of heads, and in his zest for violence. "There is no period to be met with in which the general Twenty-five Millions of France suffered *less* than in the period which they name *Reign of Terror*", he wrote. He combined this extremism with the belief that the people needed a leader shaped in the form of his father's stern Calvinist God. Since the Revolution was an event ordained by the creator, its meaning in world history must plainly be as portent of a new world-society; and this could be achieved only through the beneficent influence of an acknowledged leader, who should obviously be the wisest, the most heroic and the most farseeing figure in French society.

It is difficult for anyone writing today to avoid identifying these ideas with the doctrines of German Fascism: and in fact Carlyle's writings were to have considerable influence on the development of right wing forces in Germany, and his idea of the iron-willed heroic saviour to obtain much sympathy in that country. But in considering Carlyle, fairly enough, as a precursor of Fascism, we should remember the libertarian strain that existed side by side with his desire for the stern God-father-dictator: and we should remember also that the wildest thoughts of the nineteenth century could not imagine in detail what was coming in the twentieth. The men to whom Carlyle found himself drawn throughout his lifetime were, in general, the most generous spirits of the age: and it was among such men that he looked for the hero through whom human history might realize a new dignity and magnificence. To the French Revolution he gave enthusiastic acceptance as a step forward towards this new society; and the enduring value his book holds is not as orthodox history, nor even as poem, but as a violent human drama interpreted by a great literary artist, rising into a paean of praise as the life-giving forces in society sweep away the detritus of the past and look forward hopefully into the future. It is a poor heart that can read the more im-passioned scenes of this drama without emotion: the establish-ment of the Third Estate, the taking of the Bastille, the march of women on Versailles, all the stress and fury of the Revolu-tion's last years. In this great picture of an old society falling apart and a new one coming to birth author and subject seem rarely and perfectly fused: the result is a vision of the Revolu-tion which is, of its kind, a masterpiece of literary art.

The French Revolution is the triumphant, and almost the only complete, justification of Carlyle's style: the effect, as Coleridge remarked on another occasion, is that of reading a story by flashes of lightning. In these flashes we see pictures, incomparably vivid, of people and events viewed by a mind at once compassionate and condemnatory, humorous, sorrowful, dry and gay. There are a thousand such pictures of comedy as that of Loménie de Brienne, who had felt all his life "a kind of predestination for the highest offices", and at last became Prime Minister: "Unhappy only that it took such talent and industry to *gain* the place; that to *qualify* for it hardly any talent or industry was left disposable". Or pictures at once dramatic and sinister, as of the Duc d'Orléans, later to be Philippe Egalite, sitting at a Royal Session:

> The rubicund moon-head goes wagging; darker beams the copper-visage, like unscoured copper; in the glazed eye is disquietude; he rolls uneasy in his seat as if he meant something. Amid unutterable satiety, has sudden new appetite, for new forbidden fruit, been vouchsafed him? Disgust and edacity; laziness that cannot rest; futile ambition, revenge, non-admiralship:—O, within that carbuncled skin what a confusion of confusions sits bottled!

He can body out a situation in one brilliant metaphor: "Insurrectionary Chaos lies slumbering round the Palace, like Ocean round a Diving Bell"; or in an ironic aside: "Were Louis wise, he would this day abdicate.—Is it not strange so few Kings abdicate; and none yet heard of has been known to commit suicide?"

But what, above all, Carlyle has to offer us, beyond his irony and pawky humour, beyond his electrifying pictures of Mirabeau, Danton, the sea-green incorruptible Robespierre and the rest; beyond that strange power to realize the paper doings of the past as concrete and living reality which is evident here, even more than in his other work: is the prophetic spirit of an idealism which as yet was still bright, untarnished by the smuts and blotches to be marked on it by time, disappointment and ill-health. In prose which, of its kind, has few rivals for intensity and power, he put down again and again his passionate moral vision of the world in such reflections as this one on the calling together of the three Estates:

Yes, friends, ye may sit and look: bodily or in thought, all France, and all Europe, may sit and look; for it is a day like few others. Oh, one might weep like Xerxes:—So many serried rows sit perched there; like winged creatures, alighted out of Heaven: all these, and so many more that follow them, shall have wholly fled aloft again, vanishing into the blue Deep; and the memory of this day still be fresh. It is the baptism-day of Democracy; sick Time has given it birth, the numbered months being run. The extreme-unction day of Feudalism! A superannuated System of Society, decrepit with toils (for has it not done much; produced *you*, and what ye have and know!)—and with thefts and brawls, named glorious-victories; and with profligacies, sensualities, and on the whole with dotage and senility,—is now to die: and so, with death-throes and birth-throes, a new one is to be born. What a work, O Earth and Heavens, what a work! Battles and bloodshed, September Massacres, Bridges of Lodi, retreats of Moscow, Waterloos, Peterloos, Tenpound Franchises, Tarbarrels and Guillotines; —and from this present date, if one might prophesy, some two centuries of it still to fight! Two centuries; hardly less; before Democracy go through its due, most baleful, stages of *Quack*ocracy; and a pestilential World be burnt up, and have begun to grow green and young again.

Add these attributes of Carlyle together: irony and compassion, indignation and continual humour, the mantle of an Old Testament prophet worn by a man with the visual sense of a great painter: and he had, certainly, some ground for the haunting fear that he might have produced, against his Calvinistic inclination, a work of art.

CHAPTER ELEVEN

THE PROPHET ACKNOWLEDGED

"After all", said Darwin the other day, "what the deuce
is Carlyle's religion, or has he any?" I shook my head, and
assured him I knew no more than himself.

JANE WELSH CARLYLE to Thomas Carlyle, 1838.

THE RECEPTION OF *The French Revolution* was gratifying,
but had little immediate effect in improving the Carlyles'
financial position; and before the book's publication he had
arranged, largely through the goodwill of Harriet Martineau,
to give a course of six lectures on German literature. The
prospectus announced a formidable programme which included addresses on the Teutonic people and the German
language, the Reformation, Luther, the Master Singers, the
Resuscitation of German Literature, the Characteristics of
New-German Literature, and the Drama: the whole to be
wound up by remarks on Results and Anticipations. Obviously
no concessions were made, or even thought of, to a general
human belief that the ideal lecture is one which can be heard
with the eyes open and the mind closed: yet the tickets, at a
guinea for the course of six lectures, sold well, and the audience
was both large and fashionable.

We have seen the agitation of Carlyle when, in his ripe age,
he was submitted to the minor trials of Edinburgh: this first
public ordeal, it may easily be imagined, was much worse. He
insisted resolutely on speaking extempore; and on the excuse
(for one can hardly regard it as anything else) that he was
reading the proofs of *The French Revolution* he made practically
no preparation. Something in him demanded that he should
face an audience unprepared, that his talks should be, as it
were, a contest of wills. For weeks before the lectures he
trembled to the bone to think of them; he complained of his
health; he compared himself to a man flung overboard to
swim or drown; he prayed that he might maintain an unfevered
heart, and—perhaps unnecessarily—that he might be kept
from the madness of popularity. A friend expressed a fear that
he would address the audience as "Gentlemen and Ladies";

F

Jane thought it more likely that he would call them, in her grandfather's style, "Fool creatures come here for diversion". She had, certainly, the impression that although the lectures might, as advertised, begin precisely at 3 o'clock if she put all the clocks and watches in the house half an hour fast, it was almost impossible that they should end precisely at their due time of 4 unless, just as the clock struck, a lighted cigar could suddenly appear on the table for Carlyle to smoke. She was ill during most of the winter with coughs and colds that could not be shaken off; and Carlyle, as he sat among his books and papers, was distressed by the sad cough on the other side of the wall. By the time that the lectures came to be delivered she felt better, but still her agitation was such that she did not attend the first of them; she went to the others, and mixed Carlyle a dose of brandy and water such as, many years later, she gave him for the occasion in Edinburgh.

Carlyle did not, after all, say "Gentlemen and Ladies", and if he went on after 4 o'clock it was with the consent of his audience. It is even possible that the success of the lectures was due in part to the nervousness of the lecturer, the battle he so plainly fought to ejaculate the thoughts within him. His eyes were downcast to the desk in front of him, at which his fingers nervously picked; his speech was even more disjointed than usual and he looked, in Harriet Martineau's words, as yellow as a guinea.

Few people like listening to a man for whom public speaking is obviously a refined kind of torture; it is remarkable that the size of the audience should have increased during the course of lectures, and still more that Carlyle should have given three more courses in successive years, always to appreciative upper class audiences. In 1838 he gave twelve lectures on European literature from the Greeks, through Roman, Spanish, German, Italian, French and English writers. When, in the year following, he spoke on the "Revolutions of Modern Europe", the whole street was blocked with carriages, and the lectures were highly successful, although Carlyle thought the one on the French Revolution very bad and noted that his audience, "mainly Tory, could not be expected to sympathise." The last set of lectures, and the only ones to be preserved between covers were delivered in 1840 on the theme of Heroes. The choice of Heroes appears curious, including as it does Odin, Mahomet, Dante, Shakespeare, Luther, Knox, Rousseau, Burns, Johnson,

Napoleon and Cromwell: and the lectures, when read, are among the less impressive, and least consistent, of Carlyle's written and spoken utterances. These four courses showed a profit of several hundred pounds. After 1840 Carlyle was never again in urgent need of money, and it was rarely thereafter that he could be lured even to the briefest public speech.

Delivery of the talks became no easier for him during the four courses: on the eve of the Heroes and Hero-Worship series he described himself as feeling like a man going to be hanged. Sometimes he lost self-consciousness, and on one morning he spoke for twenty minutes over his allotted hour without reference to notes; he could even, at such moments, sweep away his audience with the eloquence and fervour of a man who manifestly believed in the vital importance of the message he was struggling to communicate. At these times, when colour was in his cheeks and fire in his voice and a fine light shone down on him from above, he seemed to his wife a surprisingly beautiful man. But this was a partial view: other observers noticed the Annandale accent, harsh to southern ears, into the broadest variety of which he often unconsciously dropped; the sudden distortion of his features, as if he had been suddenly seized by a paroxysm of pain, when he groped for a point; the graceless gesticulation.

Assuredly it was not the style of the speaker that sustained his audience through these four courses of lectures: nor were his listeners partisan Radicals prepared to forgive oratorical deficiencies in one who uttered political truths. They included those most opposed to Carlyle politically, like the Whig Chancellor Lord Brougham or the Prussian diplomat Bunsen, aristocrats like the Marchioness of Lansdowne, men about town like young Monckton Milnes and actors like Macready. These outnumbered the sprinkling of Radicals who, in any event, did not feel able to endorse much of what Carlyle had to say. The Tory Bunsen noted with some enjoyment at one of the lectures on Revolutions that most of the audience were sadly startled by what they heard: but on another occasion Mill stood up and cried "No", when Carlyle declared Mahomet's Heaven and Hell and Day of Judgement a more valuable view of the world than that implied by Bentham's Utilitarianism. The lecturer went on as though he had not heard: but that cry of protest, wrung from a friend and sympathiser, had its symptomatic importance.

The reason for the success of the lectures, as one looks back on contemporary accounts of them, lay in the feelings of those who heard them that they were listening to a prophet; a man with a message to deliver that might alter the whole shape of the world. There was a sense in which the mission of Carlyle, as he conceived it, much resembled that of his friend Irving. A hesitant orator instead of a fluent one, with graceless instead of flowing gestures, he yet felt the same certainty of oncoming human doom—in Carlyle's case a doom of directly social, in Irving's of supernatural, origin—which might be checked by human determination to walk in the path of righteousness. Mid-nineteenth century society was peculiarly susceptible to such ideas: upon many of its most talented and most sensitive representatives lay a burden of guilt derived from the generally deepening social conscience about living conditions, which found issue in arguments about the literal truth of the Bible or delicate questioning of certain aspects of domestic political policy. To such men and women, now and thereafter, Carlyle spoke with the authority of a prophet. What policies did the prophet advocate? That was not easy to find out. What, as Charles Darwin's elder brother Erasmus asked, was his religion? What, even, were the politics of this man whose self-confessed Sansculottism was so often appreciated by Tories? Was he working for a violent overthrow of society? To read the more fervent parts of *The French Revolution* one might suppose so. Then what was he doing extolling the virtues of a New Aristocracy, led by a Hero from one of his own lectures, as the hope of the world? And what, most potent question of all, had he to offer in the way of a practical programme, distinct from virtuous moral precepts, to those who followed him?

Few of these questions were asked, or were asked so pointedly, in Carlyle's lifetime: certainly not in these early days of his fame when the blue eyes blazed, and the broad Scotch voice poured out a torrent of scornful metaphor about the stupidity of the nation's political leaders and the dullness of its in-tellectuals. Years later Arthur Hugh Clough expressed the feelings of many disciples besides himself when he wrote to Emerson: "Think where we are. Carlyle has led us out into the desert, and he has left us there". In the future lay some dis-illusionment. In the present the prophet made converts.

The converts were many. They were drawn almost equally by a conviction of Carlyle's greatness, and by Jane's charm.

We have already seen Harriet Martineau, that earnest econ-
omist and considerable lioness of her time and place, poking
forward her ear-trumpet. She came often to Chelsea and she
brought her friends, who were among the most earnest improvers of an earnest and improving age. "Her love is great",
Carlyle wrote. "Nay, in fact it is too great; the host of illustrious
obscure mortals whom she produces on you, of Preachers,
Pamphleteers, Antislavers, Able Editors, and other Atlases
bearing (unknown to us) the world on their shoulders, is
absolutely more than enough." Harriet sometimes shook her
head over Carlyle. One day he "made a great laugh" at
scientists; on another he replied to her insistence on knowing
whether he believed in immortality by saying that he did not
care whether there was another life or not. There were com-
pensations, however: a two hour talk with Jane, looking very
pretty in a black velvet dress, "about divers domestic doings of
literary people, which seem really almost to justify the scandal
with which literary life is assailed"; and even in Carlyle
himself, when she was not asking probing questions about
immortality, Harriet discerned a deep tenderness, a sympathy
with all suffering, lying below the surface abruptness and
ferocity. She would perhaps have been surprised by his verdict
on her in which, after praising her sharp eye, her self-possession
and her frankness, he added: "Her very considerable talent
would have made her a quite shining Matron of some big
Female Establishment, but was totally inadequate to grapple
with deep spiritual and social questions."

Carlyle's literary admirers were found among young men:
the most notable of them were Dickens, Tennyson and Browning; the most fervent was John Sterling. Dickens's admiration
for Carlyle as writer and thinker was almost unbounded;
Carlyle's for Dickens, on the other hand, was very limited.
He read *Pickwick* on Charles Buller's recommendation, and
observed that "thinner wash, with perceptible vestige of a
flavour in it here and there, was never offered to the human
palate." How explain that he had sat almost a whole day
reading it? Dickens himself, on the other hand, proved distinctly
agreeable when met at Lady Holland's: "Clear blue, intelligent
eyes, eyebrows that he arches amazingly, large protrusive
rather loose mouth, a face of most extreme *mobility*, which he
shuttles about—eyebrows, eyes, mouth and all—in a very
singular manner while speaking." Thackeray, he thought, had

much more literary talent: but Carlyle could never consider novels as anything but rather regrettable trivialities, and therefore did not make a very great distinction between the two. Dickens, he said with some condescension, was the only man of the time whose writings had genuine cheerfulness.

For Tennyson, whom he found one day talking to Jane in the back garden, he had a warmer feeling. Carlyle generally thought better of big men than of little ones, and Tennyson was a big man—"a large-featured, dim-eyed, bronze-coloured, shaggy headed man is Alfred"; he liked smokers and Tennyson was "one of the powerfullest *smokers* I have ever worked along with". Tennyson was also, of course, a poet; and although as Carlyle grew older he became more and more inclined to place the making of verses with the writing of fiction as a trivial occupation in a serious age, he induced Monckton Milnes to use influence in obtaining a Civil List Pension for Tennyson.

It has been remarked that Tennyson was almost the only poet of Carlyle's acquaintance whom he did not advise to write in prose: but in view of Carlyle's declining opinion of poetry this was perhaps not entirely a compliment. Browning, when he sent *Sordello* and *Pippa Passes* to Cheyne Row received the friendliest, if not the most acceptable, kind of admonition: he had, Carlyle observed, a rare gift, poetical, pictorial or intellectual, which he was perhaps *not* at present on the best way to unfolding. Would it not be a good thing if his next work were written in prose? "One must first make a *true* intellectual representation of a thing, before any poetic interest that is true will supervene", he wrote with something less than perfect clarity. "All *cartoons* are geometrical withal; and cannot be made till we have fully learnt to make mere *diagrams* well." John Sterling, son of that editor of *The Times* who was responsible for its receiving the appellation of the Thunderer, was of all these friends the one for whom Carlyle had most personal feeling. A Church of England clergyman troubled by doubts, the author of a didactic novel in which Carlyle and Goethe appeared as characters, and the most minor of minor poets, this gentle and charming man was marked for an early death from consumption almost from the time that the Carlyles first knew him. With Jane he exchanged flirtatious letters, with Carlyle desperate arguments about questions of style and ethics, while his hold upon life grew weaker.

Monckton Milnes, young, bland, influential and witty, was

brought to Chelsea by Charles Buller. He came often, and was responsible for introducing Carlyle to much literary upper-class society. At dinner Carlyle met Hallam and Gladstone, without striking any particular conversational sparks from them; at one of Samuel Rogers's famous breakfasts he met Macaulay, often bracketed with Carlyle as one of the bright young (or at least not old) stars of English literature. Macaulay, who had just returned from India, monopolized the conversation at this particular breakfast. Milnes followed Carlyle into the street afterwards, and expressed his regret that Macaulay had talked so much. Carlyle threw up his hands in mock astonishment. "What!" he said. "Was that the Right Honourable Tom? I had no idea that it was the Right Honourable Tom. Ah, well, I understand the Right Honourable Tom now." Of Rogers himself Carlyle gave one of the curt, brilliant sketches that make memorable so many of his letters:

A half-frozen old sardonic Whig-Gentleman: no hair at all, but one of the whitest bare scalps, blue eyes, shrewd, sad and cruel; toothless horse-shoe mouth drawn up to the very nose: slow-croaking, sarcastic insight, perfect breeding;—state-rooms where you are welcomed even with flummery; internally a Bluebeard's chamber, where none but the proprietor enters.

It was at Rogers's breakfast table that one of the now-forgotten lion cubs of the day, a French Royalist named Rio who had opposed Napoleon but disliked the Bourbons, listened to Macaulay and Hallam talking against each other for an hour with what seemed to him frightful volubility; they would have been distressed almost equally had they known that M. Rio thought them both Conservative historians, of different shades. There was, however, Rio noted in his diary, another point of view in England, represented by the Scotchman Carlyle. Rio could not help admiring *The French Revolution*; but the indulgent view of the Reign of Terror taken by the author filled the Royalist Frenchman with a hatred which seemed to him unalterable. He was astonished to find, on meeting Carlyle through the ubiquitous Milnes, that he was "a friendly and pleasant man of the right sort" instead of "a republican *savage*", and that in many matters touching politics and religion they were in perfect agreement. Could this, then, be the man who was friendly with people of the most sub-versive opinions? Apparently it could. "He had me dining at his house", Rio wrote, "in the company of Godefroi Cavaignac first of all, and then the appalling Mazzini himself."

Godefroi Cavaignac was a republican, elder brother of that General Cavaignac who was for a short time after the 1848 Revolution President of the French Republic. He was, Jane said, "a French republican of the right thorough-going sort, who has had the glory of meriting to be imprisoned and nearly losing his head; a man with that sort of dark half-savage beauty with which one paints a fallen angel." Jane, perhaps with some small spark of malice, asked Rio if he knew Cavaignac, and—if she is to be taken literally—some lively dialogue followed:

"Ah, who does *not* know Cavaignac by name. But I, you know, am a victim of *his* party, as *he* is a victim of Louis Philippe. Does Cavaignac come here?"

"Yes, we have known him long."

"Good gracious! How strange it would be for us to meet in the same room! How I should like it!"

"Well, he is to dine here on Monday."

"I will come; good gracious, it will be so strange."

Rio, Jane observed, seemed charmed by the prospect; but almost before he was out of the door Carlyle asked what she could be thinking of to bring together two men so utterly opposed to each other. Jane added a beefsteak pie to the leg of mutton she had originally arranged for Cavaignac and his friend Latrade, and hoped for the best. The best, however, was not to be:

Rio appeared on the scene at half-past three, as if he could not have enough of it. Latrade came as the clock struck four. But Cavaignac—Alas! Two of his friends were on terms about blowing each other's brains out, and Cavaignac has gone to bring them to reason; and not till they were brought to reason would he arrive to eat his dinner. . . . So, one half hour being gone, and still no appearance of him, I was on the point of suggesting that we should wait no longer, when a carriage drove up and deposited Mrs. Macready and Macready's sister. Was ever beefsteak pie in such a cruel predicament? There was no help, however, but to be amiable. . . . An hour and a half after the dinner had been all ready we proceeded to eat it—Rio, Latrade, and we. And when it was just going off the table cold, Cavaignac came, his hands full of papers and his head full of the Devil knows what; but not one reasonable word would he speak the whole night. Rio said nothing to his dispraise, but I am sure he thought in his own mind "Good Gracious! I had better never be in the same room with him again!"

Visitors to Cheyne Row were both mixed and cosmopolitan: and all offered entertainment to a household that had at this time, certainly, nothing gigmanic about it: where one maid fetched up two additional cups for tea at night, enquiring with surprise "Was there to be no gentlemen?"; and another lay one day dead drunk upon the floor in a welter of broken crockery and then, in a condition of more active drunkenness, had to be kept bolted in the back kitchen where she sat "all coiled up and fuffing like a young tiger about to spring"; where the dandy Count D'Orsay might call unexpectedly, and confront Carlyle in his grey plaid suit with a sky-blue cravat, yards of gold chain, white gloves and a velvet-lined greatcoat; where revolutionary exiles drank tea with intellectual aristocrats, earnest freethinkers clashed with Radical-minded clergymen, and professional politicians might meet practising poets.

Occasionally a small dinner party was given, and on one occasion Jane, as Carlyle wrote to his mother, "audaciously got up a thing called a soiree . . . That is to say a Party of Persons who have little to do except wander through a room or rooms, and hustle and simmer about, all talking to one another as they best can." It went off, Carlyle said, successfully, but as he smoked a pipe at midnight he prayed that it might be long before they saw the like again; and one may be sure that the prayers were not silent, nor spoken while he was alone.

The most notable among the many revolutionary exiles who visited Cheyne Row was introduced by the square, honest Unitarian husband of Mill's friend Harriet Taylor. He was a man a little under medium height, and of exceptional beauty: his olive complexion set off the perfect regularity of his features, his expression was open and of singular sweetness, his dark eyes flashed with bright natural gaiety. This was Joseph Mazzini, now in his early thirties, and already a legendary figure in his native country, where his Young Italy movement had petered out in the first of the many abortive or partly-successful risings with which he was to be associated. At the time of his first meeting with the Carlyles, Mazzini had been in exile for three years. He had come to England from Switzerland, and was deeply unhappy in a country that he found both harsh and strange. The life of a political exile is generally a sad one. Mazzini had little money, and what he had was shared with those even poorer than himself; he dropped into the hands of money-lenders who lent him money at thirty, forty or a hundred per cent interest. Living chiefly on potatoes and rice, unable to borrow books, speaking at first only a few words of English, Mazzini felt life and opportunity passing by. Could he have looked into the future, he would have seen disappointment and frustration enough ahead for his dreams of transforming Italy into a great unified republic composed of citizens moved by the purest moral and religious feelings: but his fear at this time was simply that he would not be privileged to play a part in the great national revolution which he thought might be achieved by secret and conspiratorial means. "Pray for me", he wrote to a friend, "That, before I die, I may be good for something." At other times he had the impression that he must be immortal, or else he would have died of physical misery and mental anguish.

In later years, when he was far removed from the republican sympathies of these days, Carlyle wrote with unusual inaccuracy that he talked with Mazzini "one or twice", but that they "soon tired of one another." In fact the Italian was for several years one of the most frequent visitors at Cheyne Row. At first rather silent, speaking mostly in French from distrust of his increasingly fluent but always erratic English, Mazzini grew into the affections of both Carlyle and Jane. Carlyle recognized a character of true saintliness, a life utterly dedicated to the creation of Italian unity: and for such a dedication he had never anything but the deepest respect, although he was at last separated from Mazzini by a deep gulf of speech and feeling. And in Jane Mazzini wakened, more even than the fallen angel Cavaignac, the reserves of romantic feeling that lay generally suppressed beneath her characteristic sharp shrewdness. She was delighted by his beauty, charmed by the wild grandeur of his revolutionary intransigence; among the coterie phrases from Schiller, Goethe, Byron and other writers, friends and relations in which her letters abound, are many from Mazzini's dashing Italian English. "Upon *my* honour", "Thanks God", "The cares of bread", "Put on my bonnet", and half a dozen others, occur again and again. She wrote little notes in Italian to Mazzini's mother in Genoa, and went so far as to send a brooch with a lock of her own hair and a lock of Mazzini's intertwined. The brooch was, perhaps, capable of misinterpretation; and Mazzini wrote hastily to his mother that he loved Signora Carlyle "like a brother". It was through Jane Carlyle that Mazzini moved to a house in King's Road, only a few minutes' walk from Cheyne Row, where the rural quiet of the neighbourhood delighted him; and for eight years, until the Revolution of 1848 took him back to Italy, he dined with the Carlyles one day a week. On other days Carlyle might call and invite Mazzini to walk with him; or Jane send a note asking him to accompany her to town on a visit to St. Paul's or to shop or to see friends. At times Mazzini found the Carlyles' concern that he should meet people almost embarrassing.

In many matters Carlyle and Mazzini agreed perfectly. Both admired Dante and Goethe, both disliked and distrusted the current doctrine of Utilitarianism. They shared a belief in a vaguely enunciated religious faith; and both believed that work was a good thing, almost independent of its object. But for Carlyle the faith to which Mazzini held throughout his lifetime, of the regeneration of Italy through a spontaneous national uprising, was moonshine. From a practical point of view he thought that such an uprising was unlikely to succeed; and it is true that there was an element of the ridiculous both in the schemes that Mazzini projected and in those he carried out. His attempt to provoke a rising through the agency of two young Venetian nobles named Bandiera failed ludicrously when a police spy persuaded them to assist an imaginary rising in Calabria; later he was involved in an even more hopeless plot in Genoa. He was a victim of the worst error of revolutionary politicians: that of converting dreams into facts. On one occasion he became very excited in Jane's presence about the prospect of invading Italy by balloon. It was goodbye then, she said, to her share in the expedition. Mazzini professed himself astonished. Was there not something suitable for her in descending as it were out of Heaven to redeem a suffering people? All this was said, Jane noted, "With eyes flashing hope, faith, and generous self-devotion! . . . is it not almost a desecration, a crime ever to *jest* with that man? He lives, moves and has his being in *truth*, and take him out of that, he is as credulous and ignorant as a two-year-old child."

Carlyle too found something childlike and touching in Mazzini's credulity: but that did not prevent him from attacking what he called revolutionary pipedreams. At this time, when he was becoming widely known as a magnificent talker of the monologuic kind, he first began to praise strongly the virtues of Silence. Certain words or phrases inadvertently mentioned by visitors would particularly prompt his passionate praise of Silence, carried on perhaps through an oration of half an hour's length; those who tried to interrupt him were borne down by a shower of metaphorical disclaimers uttered in a manner half-humorous and yet with some immense and furious explosion manifestly not far distant. Thus on one visit of Mazzini's a visitor who was incautious enough to suggest that "After all, the first thing to do is to ensure the happiness of the people", received a full blast of Carlylean rhetoric. "A torrent of invective, thunder following on lightning" battered the unfortunate visitor who, like the clergyman verbally executed by Doctor Johnson, remains nameless. At last, "more dead than alive", he rose to go, accompanied to the door by Jane who murmured soothing words. The torrent was diverted to Mazzini. Happiness, happiness, the sage cried as he strode up and down the room shaking his mane of hair like a caged lion, the fools ought to be chained up. Only work was good, only work, intellectual or manual, brought peace to the human soul. Work and silence, he said, were the cardinal virtues of humanity. Silence, silence! And not only men, but nations too should be silent until the voice of genius spoke for them. Was not Italy, however divided, oppressed, humiliated, great in the possession of Dante? And now, pointing himself directly at Mazzini, with a devastating drop into practical commonsense, Carlyle added: "You, you have not succeeded yet, because you have talked too much: the fundamental preparation is wanting!"

Mazzini was able to smile, and reflect that Carlyle "loved silence somewhat platonically". In the early days of their friendship he tried to argue; gradually, he realized that it is not possible to argue with a prophet. It is not certain whether he ever made the distinction uttered by Jane, after an evening when Carlyle had been attacking with especial ferocity Mazzini's "rose-water imbecilities": "These are but opinions to Carlyle; but to Mazzini, who has given his all, and helped to bring his friends to the scaffold in pursuit of such subjects, it is a matter of life and death."

It is not easy to record such occasions without leaving an impression disagreeable to those who have no need to express the emotions which they do not feel, and who assess the activities of their fellow human beings with all the percipience and passion of sheep. To such, a man like Carlyle must appear a simple curmudgeon. But for those who knew him a personal, and even a general, generosity shone through the invective. Mazzini, after all, was not deterred by these verbal storms from paying his weekly visit; and although Carlyle castigated Mazzini in private for his part in the Bandiera episode he wrote an indignant letter to *The Times* when it was revealed that the British Government had been opening the exile's correspondence and passing on the contents to his enemies in Italy. Mazzini, much touched, called the tribute "noble", and the word does not seem misplaced:

I have had the honour to know Mr. Mazzini for a series of years; and, whatever I may think of his practical insight and skill in worldly affairs, I can with great freedom testify to all men that he, if I have ever seen one such, is a man of genius and virtue, a man of sterling veracity, humanity, and nobleness of mind; one of those rare men, numerable, unfortunately, but as units in this world, who are worthy to be called martyr souls; who, in silence, piously in their daily life, understand and practice what is meant by that.

Carlyle's private testimony to Mazzini was equally notable. When the Piedmontese Minister in Britain spoke slightingly of the Italian exile Carlyle responded angrily: "Sir, you do not know Mazzini at all, not at all"; and left the house.

* * * * *

Mazzini was merely the most notable of the many poor and idealistic republican exiles from various countries taken by Jane under a surprisingly tender wing. Their tragi-comic lives were a compound of unrealized hopes, wildly gallant and absurd behaviour, ridiculous turns of speech and deeply-rooted personal unhappiness. There was Count Pepoli, Italian exile and dilettante, who had married Jane's elderly friend Elizabeth Fergus of Kirkcaldy; there was Garnier, "big German refugee, dusty, smoky, scarred with duel-cuts", who died fighting in Baden in 1848; there was a fattish German young man of good family named Plattnauer; there were others. The course of their lives in exile, watched by a shrewd eye and felt by a tender spirit, can be seen clearly in Jane's correspondence during these years. Efforts to help them had no lasting success. Garnier, settled in a quiet clerkship through Carlyle's agency, abandoned this position after a year or two, and became temporarily a little mad. He entered Jane's presence in Cheyne Row one day with rolling eyes, face, hands and clothes in the last stage of dirtiness and open shirt revealing, in Jane's parody of Mazzini's phrase, "What shall I say? strange things, upon *my* honour!" After telling her that he had discovered a nest of murderers in the court where he lived, *"of whom his landlord was the chief"*, Garnier said tenderly that she looked a little pale. After half an hour of this talk he held out his hand to her on departure, turning his head in the opposite direction. She rashly took his hand; and for a minute he exerted the most agonising pressure. When she held up her swollen hand he looked at it "with a devilish satisfaction" and said kindly, "Oh you are hurt—well I am sorry—but *it was necessary.*"

Plattnauer's madness was of a more serious kind. He was incarcerated in a curious asylum at Ham Common, from which Jane got him transferred into the hands of a mental specialist. Soon he was pronounced fit to be taken out by a friend: but Plattnauer had no friends. Carlyle, consulted, said gallantly: "He must come *here* for a while till he sees what is to be done next." Installed at Cheyne Row, however, Plattnauer proved not to be by any means perfectly sane; he required constant care and attention, and when Jane talked to other people for any length of time was almost beside himself with rage. Visitors were frightened of him, not without reason; he told Jane how strong had been the temptation to seize the poker and dash out the brains of a little man from Aberdeen. At last he left, not restored to perfect mental health; within a few months he had forced his way into Buckingham Palace and when asked his business said that the Queen was about to be confined, and had sent for him. This exploit caused his expulsion from England for some time; a year or two later he wrote to Jane that he would on no account agree to be Emperor of Germany unless "we all 'consent to accompany him' ". The letter, Jane added, was a beautiful one, and made her wonder whether a slight dash of insanity might not be a gain to some natures.

Many Americans found their way to Cheyne Row, for in America the prophet had been acknowledged with the publication of *Sartor*; and his reputation increased yearly, thanks largely to the loving care of Emerson, who arranged the terms of publication, and rendered accounts faithfully. From Emerson in America came the first money Carlyle received for *The French Revolution*; a draft for £50 which Jane sent on to Carlyle at Scotsbrig with tears in her eyes.

The friendship between Emerson and Carlyle prospered at a distance: in the voluminous record of their correspondence, we can sense early that much personal contact might lead to discord. Emerson's thinking, like Mill's, was thin and abstract; and, unlike Mill, he at first altogether misunderstood the cast of Carlyle's mind. It is doubtful if Carlyle was encouraged in his occasional speculations about visiting America by Emerson's desire that he should edit a periodical called *The Transcendentalist* or *The Spiritual Inquirer*; or that he was much moved by the words of a clergyman named Frothingham, solemnly put down by Emerson; "You cannot express in terms too extravagant my desire that he should come"; or that he was anything but repelled by the exhortation to "bring a letter from a Scottish Calvinist to a Calvinist here, and your fortune is made". How little Emerson was temperamentally fitted to appreciate Carlyle is shown by his early comment on the method of *Sartor Resartus*: "The form, which my defective apprehension for a joke makes me not appreciate, I leave to your merry discretion."

In the meantime the Americans, prompted by admiration or mere curiosity, came. They were received amiably, but generally with no great respect. The elegant George Ticknor, who noted that Carlyle's manners were not polished, was recommended by Carlyle to Monckton Milnes as a bore of the first magnitude. Bronson Alcott, thought by Emerson to be a great and majestic soul, was able to convert Tennyson temporarily to his own belief in vegetarianism, but was not pleased by the ridicule of Carlyle and Browning. "When shall I see you again?" Carlyle asked of Alcott after one such visit, and received the reply: "Never, I guess." At one time fourteen Americans came within a fortnight, including "a precious specimen of the regular Yankee" who paid a visit when both Carlyle and Jane were out, installed himself in the library, sat at Carlyle's desk, and wrote him a letter. When Jane came in he

subjected her to a series of questions about Carlyle's habits;
her brief answers "seemed to patter óff the rhinoceros-hide of
him as though they had been sugar-plums."

The Chelsea view of Margaret Fuller, one-time editor of
The Dial, was at first more favourable. "A strange lilting lean
old maid, not half such a bore as I expected", Carlyle wrote to
Emerson. Miss Fuller on her side was carried away by the
rich flow of speech, and the great full sentences sung like
ballads; his wit was "enough to kill one with laughing." But
alas, on a further view it appeared that Carlýle talked too
much, and that it was impossible to interrupt him. "If
you get a chance to remonstrate a moment, he raises his
voice and bears you down." Her appreciation of his conversational power, and its nature, is probably as good as any
we have:

Accustomed to the infinite wit and exuberant richness of
his writings, his talk is still an amazement scarcely to be
faced with steady eyes. He does not converse; only harangues.
This is not in the least from unwillingness to allow freedom
to others. On the contrary, no man would more enjoy a
manly resistance to his thought. But it is the impulse of a
mind accustomed to follow out its own impulse as the hawk
its prey, and which knows not how to stop in the chase.
Carlyle, indeed, is arrogant and overbearing; but in his
arrogance there is no littleness—no self-love. It is the heroic
arrogance of some old Scandinavian conqueror; it is his
nature, and the untameable impulse that has given him
power to crush the dragons. You do not love him perhaps,
nor revere; and perhaps, also, he would only laugh at you if
you did; but you like him heartily, and like to see him the
powerful smith, the Siegfried, melting all the old iron in his
furnace till it glows to a sunset red, and burns you, if you
senselessly go too near. He seems to me quite isolated—
lonely as the desert—*yet never* was a man more fitted to prize
a man, could he find one to match his mood. He finds them,
but only in the past.

He sings, rather than talks. He pours upon you a kind of
satirical, heroical, critical poem, with regular cadences. . . .
For the highest kinds of poetry he has no sense. His talk on
that subject is delightfully and gorgeously absurd. He sometimes stops a minute to laugh at it himself, then begins again

with fresh vigour. His talk, like his books, is full of pictures; his critical strokes masterly.

It was upon such an evening of conversation that Margaret Fuller said: "I accept the Universe", and Carlyle commented: "Egad, you'd better."

It is easy to estimate unfairly the confusion of ideas that inhabited in the late eighteen thirties and the early forties the restless mind of Carlyle: to deprecate the sound and fury, to shake a liberal head over his contempt for the blessed balance maintained by Parliamentary faction, to wrinkle distastefully a hedonistic nose at the sentiment of a man who praised the moral value of work; and to forget the generous indignation at sight of human misery, the pity for those who suffered and the detestation of those who exploited them, the desire to see human dignity achieved through the elimination of want and the spread of universal education, that was the motive force of Carlyle's actions now and for years to come. Yet the story of Carlyle's development has some lessons to teach those who still, in our own age, believe that human motives are simple and have their result in actions that can be judged quite easily as right or wrong; that the will of a people is expressed more exactly by a political party employing the tyranny of Act of Parliament than by a single man employing the tyranny of open force; that democracy and dictatorship are concepts which have no more in common than that they begin with the same letter of the alphabet.

Among the various sticks of dynamite that rattled together in Carlyle's mind, waiting only some appropriate emotional fuse to bring them to explosive expression, was what he called the Condition-of-England question. The eighteen thirties began with a Reform Bill which utilitarian philosophers applauded as the herald of improved economic conditions, which evidently must mean an increase of human happiness. But the thirties saw also the first growth of Trade Unions: the Grand National Moral Union of the Productive Classes for Establishing a New Moral World, founded in 1833 under the influence of Robert Owen, was believed to have had at one time more than a million members: it was crushed ruthlessly by the Reform Bill Government from which liberal-minded Utilitarians had hoped so much. The prosecution of the Tolpuddle Martyrs was succeeded by an attack of

well-organized employers in the building, hosiery and clothing
trades upon the principle of unionism. The Grand National
collapsed. It was succeeded by the London Working Men's
Association, which drew up a Charter with six suggested
reforms—manhood suffrage, election by ballot, annual parlia-
ments, equal electoral districts, payment of M.P.s and abolition
of the property qualification for Parliament. Acceptance of these
points would have meant a complete overthrow of the ruling
class in the state. In February 1839 a convention of 53 delegates
chosen mainly from industrial centres met to prepare a monster
petition to Parliament for the Charter's acceptance. The
petition, containing 2,283,000 signatures, was duly presented.
There was, of course, no faintest chance of its acceptance:
when did a ruling class sign its own death warrant? A motion
that the Charter should be considered was defeated in Parliament by 235 votes to 46. The Chartists planned, but abandoned,
a National Holiday or General Strike; the Government, acting
vigorously, arrested Chartists for sedition, unlawful meetings,
unlawful possession of arms; a rising in Wales was suppressed,
and some Chartists tried, and imprisoned or transported. The
Government triumphantly claimed the movement's destruction: in fact it had been only checked.

Such an atmosphere was one which Carlyle, however little
he would have admitted it, found congenial. The swirl and
clash of great masses of men, the prospect of social destruction
and rebirth, held a lasting fascination for him. He would have
agreed with the Russian terrorist Zhelyabov: "History moves
too slowly. It needs a push". He noted approvingly, when he
attended a Radical meeting presided over by Charles Buller a
little before the birth of Chartism, the presence of: "Two
thousand most grim looking fellows, in bitter earnest! To rule
10 millions of such by the drill sergeant scheme may be work for
Wellington, such as he has not tried yet. Peace be with him!
If he want *war*, I can promise him plenty of that too; and prettier
men have lost their head ere now in such a cause.—For me, I
declare I can see nothing but *destruction to the whole concern*."

In the winter of 1839 Carlyle wrote in four or five weeks a
short book on Chartism. It is typical of him that he wanted to
see the piece published in the Tory *Quarterly Review*: but its
editor, J. G. Lockhart, said that he did not dare to publish it.
Chartism was seen also by Mill who, a little unexpectedly,
thought it "a glorious piece of work", and was anxious to

publish it in the last number of his Radical periodical, *The Westminster Review*. Carlyle, however, still smarted under the fact that *The Westminster Review* had turned down his suggestion to write on the "Condition-of-England question" two years earlier. He decided to publish *Chartism* separately as a book; and the first edition of a thousand copies was sold in a week. His publisher also put out a new edition of *Wilhelm Meister*, and a little later of his collected articles and reviews. From America Emerson welcomed *Chartism*, and went into his usual kind and painstaking elaboration of printing costs and likely reward.

Chartism is among the most brilliant and percipient of Carlyle's works. In it he points out that the movement, under other names or in other forms, was not to be suppressed: that it was symptomatic of a profound discontent stirring in the English working classes which would certainly not be ended by using words like mad, nefarious and incendiary. His attack on the Reformed Parliament which refused to debate the "Condition-of-England question" but found time to debate the Queen's Bedchamber question, the Game Laws, the Usury Laws, Smithfield cattle and dog carts, is carried on with a high-spirited irony that makes it good reading even today, when Chartism is a mere fragment of history. *Laissez faire* and Radical politicians suffered equally under the tongue-lash of this Tory Radical and authoritarian Anarchist who whipped both for failing to understand that Chartism was "*our* French Revolution" which might, if guided correctly, be transacted by argument and not by blows, but which could neither be suppressed nor ignored. The upper class also did not escape. What had they, the natural protectors of the great dumb suffering masses, done for them? Provided soup kitchens and improved prison discipline, attended charity balls and devised the treadmill. And all this in the name of nothing better than the protection of private property, the preservation of game.

The attack is that of a man sincerely concerned for the welfare of the poor: yet its positive suggestions are not startling. Education and emigration: those were the words Carlyle opposed to *laissez faire* or Malthusian economists. Would it not be astonishing, he wrote, if "some fit official person" announced "that after thirteen centuries of waiting, he the official person, and England with him, was minded now to have the mystery of the Alphabetic Letters imparted to all human souls in this realm?" Would not such an announcement sweep the country? And what opportunities existed yet for mankind in a world where Canadian forests stood unfelled, American prairies unbroken, where nine-tenths of the planet was crying: *Come and till me, come and reap me!*; where idle English ships could take a new population to new shores. Could one, in such a world, hear without anger Malthusian cant of a necessary reduction of population, or still worse read the suggestion of a pseudonymous Chartist named Marcus that all children of working people after the third should be disposed of painlessly?

Beyond all this, however, Carlyle found in Chartism the desire of the mass for a leader. The most valuable right possessed by the ignorant man, surely, was that of being guided by the wise. Were not such sacred rights and duties, on the part of leader and led, the very meaning of freedom? More and more, as the years passed, his investigations of human society were to be conducted from such a point of view.

CHAPTER TWELVE

HOME AND AWAY

He is much too grand for everyday life. A sphinx does not fit in comfortably to our parlour-life arrangements, but seen from a proper point of view it is a supernaturally grand thing! You must feel proud of belonging to him, after all, and he deserves to have you.

GERALDINE JEWSBURY to Jane Welsh Carlyle, 1843.

PERSONAL HAPPINESS IS largely a matter of temperament. Animals, no doubt, are happy, except when they are being hunted by human beings; so, we have been given to understand, are many peasants; so certainly, very often, are people whose external circumstances seem to give positively no justification for the cheerfulness with which they greet the assaults of each new day. Carlyle's temperament was not that of a happy man, although he was able to endure misfortune with great fortitude. Living in London, and famous, he was no happier than he had been living at Craigenputtock, and neglected.

It was something, no doubt, that Doctor Arnold of Rugby should express his admiration of the wisdom and eloquence he found in *The French Revolution*, and his desire to meet its author; that a weaver from Paisley should find Carlyle's voice that of a spiritual father, and a young Quakeress express her admiration of his style and urge him with her whole soul to go on and prosper. Something no doubt it was to be a spiritual father, as time went on, to many young men and women: so that at last he had a letter specially printed and sent it off to those who applied for advice in their life and their reading. Something, but not much: often in his letters, and almost always in the notes put down in his journal, Carlyle bemoaned his life in terms not free from self-pity nor from self-reproach. Did he go to receptions, and see lords and lions at Lady Holland's? He had no sooner left such a party, which he attended with every appearance of enjoyment, than he wrote: "No health lies for me in that for body or for soul. Welfare, at least the absence of *ill* fare and semi-delirium, is possible for me in solitude only."

At other times he thought of "flaming about over both hemi-spheres" with his lectures, so that he could "earn the smallest peculium of annuity, whereon to retire into some hut by the seashore, and there lie quiet till my hour come." Solitude, like silence, he loved somewhat platonically: generally he was pleased to come back from it into society.

Happiness, then, eluded Carlyle in the days of his fame; and it was nervous gaiety, rather than serene contentment, that sustained Jane. Harriet Martineau wrote that Jane had eight bouts of influenza yearly: and although this was an exaggera-tion it is true that she suffered from frequent colds throughout the winter, and that at night such sounds as the wailing of a dog or the crowing of a cock murdered her sleep. On one occasion when Carlyle was away and the house was being repainted, she carefully closed the doors and opened her bedroom window so that the smell of paint should not give her a headache; then it occurred to her that with the windows open and ladders lying handy outside, a burglar might easily enter her room; and she was unable to sleep until she had laid a dagger and a large police rattle on the spare pillow. Like Carlyle, Jane suffered severely from constipation—largely, no doubt, because of the quantities of starchy food that they both ate (we remember that she thought fruit good for nothing but to give people colic); and the continual purges that she took had a bad effect upon her constitution. In 1840 they agreed that she should have a separate bedroom, and thereafter they did not sleep in the same room. Like Carlyle, Jane had no inclination to minimise her sufferings, and sometimes when he put his head round the door in the morning to ask how she had slept, she would say that she had got up thirty times in the night, or that she had never closed her eyes. Carlyle expressed no doubt of these stories, which he was able to match with troubles of his own: but Doctor John, whose bedside manner appears to have been the reverse of soothing, was less credulous. "It cannot be true", he told her, "for if it were true you would not be alive."

Doctor John, and the rest of the Carlyle family, have been absent from these pages for some time; they were not so absent from Carlyle's life and correspondence. The Doctor's round moonface was seen at Cheyne Row as often as the Countess of Clare came to England: and at times Carlyle meditated such projects as a "walk across the world", knapsack on back, to see his brother in Rome. "There is nothing *lost*, nothing impossible, if a man will but bestir himself", he wrote; but of course he did not go. At another time he thought of paying his brother a visit in Paris, and at another still the Doctor sent him thirty pounds to defray the expense of a visit to him in Germany. "Jane says rather, I *ought* to go, and stir myself up"; but again he did not go. Carlyle rarely admitted to himself his brother's high talent for idleness, but when they were together for any length of time he could not avoid a measure of irritation with one who became yearly more and more content with the uneventful course in which his life was cast; in correspondence with his brother Carlyle could still envisage the ideal Doctor John, a man truly and passionately devoted to medicine, who might yet make a stir in the world. No such illusions were possible after a day or so of the Doctor in the all-too-solid flesh. In general Carlyle bore patiently with his favourite brother: but when the Doctor, as climax to some often-repeated criticisms, said that Carlyle had formed a wrong judgement of the aristocracy because he had lacked the Doctor's opportunity of observing them, he received a scathing retort: "No! perhaps not Sir, I was never attached to any Noblewoman or noble woman—in capacity of flunkey or in any menial capacity whatever!!" The penitent Doctor—though one may feel that penitence would equally have become Carlyle—sent to Cheyne Row a length of tweed for his brother, and for Jane oranges, figs, French plums and a ham from Fortnum and Mason.

Relations with Scotsbrig were unmarred by such small asperities. The correspondence between Carlyle and his mother is touching in its tenderness on his side, and in her endeavour to understand and take pride in her son's achievement. Carlyle gave her the little items of news that he thought would please and amuse her, and often sent her money. When he had cashed a draft from America he sent her "five off the fore-end of it: the 'kitlin ought to bring the auld cat a mouse' in such a case as that,—an American mouse!" She was still inclined, when telling him of a hard winter, to add that the weather was nevertheless better than that deserved by a sinful generation, with which God in His mercy had never dealt as they deserved; but she had become, as nearly as possible, reconciled to the religious unorthodoxy of her eldest son. She looked eagerly for all the news she could get of him, and wept when she read the account of his lectures in *The Times*.

Between the old woman and Jane relations were never quite easy. Jane, in general so regular a correspondent, wrote few letters to Margaret Carlyle; and those she did write have an uneasy sprightliness about them, as though she realized that her wit, when applied to her husband, was a quality that the stern old Puritan at Scotsbrig would not appreciate. In copying out the letter addressed by the young Quakeress to Carlyle she added her own characteristic comment: "Pretty fairish for a prim Quakeress, don't you think? Just fancy her speaking all these transcendental flatteries from under a little starched cap and drab-coloured bonnet! I wonder how old she is; and if she is, or has been, or expects to be married. Don't you?" It is probable that Margaret Carlyle found such wonderings lacking in reverence, both to God and to her son.

London was made more pleasant to Carlyle by the gift of a horse from a linen manufacturer in Leeds. On this horse, named Citoyenne, he rode around the outskirts of the city almost daily, with much enjoyment of regions "green, frondent, fertile, entirely subdued to man". He preferred, nevertheless, regions unsubdued, and positively luxuriated in his yearly visits to Scotland, which were generally undertaken alone. After finishing *The French Revolution* he visited Scotsbrig, while Jane went to stay with Edward Sterling and his wife at Great Malvern. The correspondence they exchanged was typical of much to come later. Scotsbrig's old grey walls seemed to Carlyle a fast-departing vision; he would not, he observed, be long behind it. His brother Alick was opening a shop in Ecclefechan, a prospect which Carlyle regarded, rightly, as forlorn. He hoped that she was enjoying Malvern. Jane, however, had left Malvern for Clifton, where things were by no means well. Every day she rose with a headache; her nights were unspeakable; Nature, not unsophisticated, but "beautiful Nature which man has *exploited*, as a Reviewer does a work of genius", she found to be an intolerable bore. It was in vain that old Sterling, the Whirlwind as she sometimes called him, approached at intervals the door of the room within which she lay prostrate with headache to ask "if I believed that he was *exceedingly* sorry"; she could answer nothing more than "Yes, yes!" She had cried over his letter for two or three hours. She wanted to kiss him into something like cheerfulness: and yet "the probabilities are that, *with the best intentions*, I should have quarrelled with you rather." She longed to be home: "O my

Darling, we will surely be better, both of us, *there* again; effervescing even:—don't you think so?"

When travelling and the paying of visits involves such mental and physical anguish, it might be thought the part of common-sense to stay at home. At home, however, effervescence by its nature did not last: both Carlyle and Jane, after some seasons in London, found an occasional holiday not only from the city, but from each other, essential. Separated from each other by some hundreds of miles their love was perfect and their mutual understanding flawless; but neither of them had a nervous system able to endure without irritation daily contact with another human being. In 1838 he paid a lengthy visit to Scotland, where he bathed daily in the sea, often before breakfast, and was in good health; while Jane did not suffer a headache for three weeks. The following year they went together to stay with Mrs. Welsh at Templand, and in April 1841 Carlyle paid the first of several visits to Monckton Milnes's house at Fryston, going on from there to visit his mother. The previous winter had been a more than usually disturbing time for both of them. Carlyle, who was stirred by deep feelings of guilt when not working, and profoundly certain of the wretched character of his labour when he was, found the process of gestation in which a new book was taking shape in his mind the most painful of all. During this winter he read a quantity of books on Cromwell and the Puritan Revolution, with many complaints of their and his own dullness: and when in the course of this reading he was troubled by a feverish cold and received summons to serve on a jury, the household at Cheyne Row became markedly unpeaceable.

After sitting for two days on a case which was adjourned unfinished, Carlyle expressed to an official his absolute determination to refuse further service, saying: "You may fine me, you may kill me; but that box I will not enter any more." To save him further annoyance Jane burnt the next summons sent without mentioning it to him. After proposing to swear him off on the ground that "no man in his mad state is capable of seeing into the merits of any case", she wrote that he "would go, cursing from his heart the administration of British justice." The case was distinguished by the presence of a recalcitrant juryman who, when the others were agreed, said placidly that he had sat out three juries, and began to eat sandwiches and read a novel. The other jurymen were indignant but Carlyle, observing that the man's head was egg-shaped, "like a ball of putty dropped from a height", advised flattery. When the sandwiches were finished Carlyle sat by the juryman's side and congratulated him on being a man of decision and courage, regretting at the same time that he was resolved to involve his own side in further costs; for it was plain that a man of his resolution would not be found on another jury, so that his side was sure to lose. The other jurymen joined Carlyle, and after an hour's coaxing the obstructor allowed himself to be persuaded. Carlyle arrived home that night roaring so loudly with laughter that Jane thought the troubles of jury-service had affected his mind.

Jubilation at such rare triumphs of tact was dearly bought: the less happy features of the jury affair bulked large in Carlyle's mind for some time after. In the spring he spent several days in the Isle of Wight with Doctor John, at Easter he was with Milnes, and then he went on to Scotsbrig. Jane, delighted to be alone, spent her days stretched on the sofa reading, or not reading, books from the circulating library. His return to London was brief: even private objurgations of himself as a despicable mortal who should know what he wanted to do and then go and do it in silence, did not have the desired effect of setting him to work on Cromwell. He returned to Scotsbrig, and took a cottage on the seashore at Newby, near Annan, where Jane joined him for the summer, together with a maid who was to cook for them. Jane came up from London, staying a night or two at Liverpool on the way, he met her at Annan, and they drove to Mrs. Welsh's house at Templand. But at Templand some of the Liverpool Welshes were staying; Carlyle and his wife had to sleep not merely in the same room, but in the same bed. At 3 o'clock in the July dawn Carlyle, unable to sleep, rose and dressed, went to the stable, put his horse to the gig and rode off to finish his night's rest at Dumfries. From there he sent back a somewhat apologetic note asking her to "explain all my suddenness to your mother, to our kind friends." Such occasions always prompted him to take the most pessimistic view of marriage and the world, and in his note he said that he had "done little but think tragically about my poor lassie all day."

Under such ominous lights the holiday began. Carlyle bathed every day, and rode about the countryside, although he went to see none of his many friends in the district. He was absorbed by the utter loneliness of the scene, the everlasting roar of the loud winds, and the cosmic surge of the great Atlantic. He read Emerson's essays and found in them a tone of veracity, the rare and real utterance of a human soul. To America, he thought, Emerson might be a kind of New Era. He walked and brooded. The fruits of such a life, he noted, might be expected afterwards; and he delayed as long as possible on the way home, that those fruits might not be too quickly realized.

Jane made no secret of her dislike of Newby. "Another month of it and I must have lost my wits or taken to drinking", she wrote to her cousin Helen Welsh. She had been bored; she had been bitten by fleas; she was recovering only slowly from the "unimaginable horrors" of that ideal cottage by the seaside. Carlyle too, she thought, was somewhat chastened, for he spoke no longer of moving from Chelsea, but put down money for new carpets. The fruits, in fact, were those of the Dead Sea. Carlyle noted in his journal: "The adventure was full of confused pain, partly degrading, disgraceful; cost me in all, seemingly, some £70. We shall not all go back to Annandale for rustication in a hurry." Could he now write about Cromwell? He tried to do so, and destroyed what he wrote. "My thoughts lie around me all inarticulate, sour, fermenting, bottomless, like a hideous enormous bog." His ideas about life, and his own place in it, were in chaos. "But what is life, except the knitting up of incoherences into coherence?"

*   *   *   *   *

In writing about the lives of those who felt so deeply, and expressed their feelings and sufferings with such unreticent fluency, distortion cannot be avoided. It is necessary for the reader, as for the writer, to operate a more than usually elaborate system of checks and balances: to recognize, as husband and wife did, the element of comedy behind their joint explosions of irritability; to understand, as Jane understood, that her husband was neglectful in small matters but considerate in large ones; to realize with Carlyle the enduring affection behind his wife's sarcasm. In later years the colours of their lives were to darken, the sarcasms to become injurious instead of playful: but at this time their disagreements are still to be interpreted in comic, rather than tragic terms. The dark shades of Newby can be to some extent dispelled by considering

Carlyle's conduct on the death of Mrs. Welsh, and the entry of Geraldine Jewsbury into the life of Cheyne Row.

In February 1842 a letter from Templand brought the news that Mrs. Welsh had suffered some form of stroke. Jane set off immediately by train to her cousins in Liverpool, to learn when she arrived there that her mother was dead. She collapsed: and the affair of settling the estate had to be conducted by Carlyle. For two months he stayed in the house of memories at Templand, negotiating with farm agents and others about the settlement, and during the whole time he maintained a correspondence with Jane designed to keep up her spirits. Carlyle wanted to keep the house and garden and sublet the land, but Jane insisted that everything should be sold; he had the lease valued and sold it, and later disposed of all the household goods. On the day that they were sold he left his brother in charge and went to his mother-in-law's grave twenty miles away; on returning he was distressed to meet people carrying away furniture.

He seems to have written to Jane daily at this time, and to have dispelled as much as possible of the distress she felt. After her marriage Jane had never found it possible to stay long in the same house with her mother; now she lamented her own shortcomings with a facility natural to the children of that age. To Carlyle mournfulness of this kind seemed mere sentimentality, and we can gauge the effort with which, as he advised her to find work to occupy her mind, he wrote: "How often have I provokingly argued with you about all that! I will endeavour not to do so any more." Jane acknowledged the kindness of her friends and the great patience of her husband; but she remained sunk in a melancholy which was not shifted by the efforts of Mazzini to persuade her that her mother was not dead, "but knows all, and loves more, and watches and waits, intercedes and hovers over her child to help and strengthen her." It throws some light on Jane's religion, if not on her husband's, that Mazzini saw with pained surprise her complete disbelief in what he was saying.

It was in 1840 that Carlyle received a letter from an ardently intellectual young woman in her twenties named Geraldine Endsor Jewsbury, who was then living in Manchester, keeping house for her brother. It was to such young people as Geraldine, who were questioning the truth of Christianity and the whole nature of the world about them, that Carlyle's writings made particular appeal: a first reading of him overwhelmed her, purging her at once of Christian belief and of a romantic admiration for Shelley, bringing her—as she thought—to a realization of life's sternness and beauty. After some correspondence she paid a short visit to Cheyne Row, where the impression she made was very favourable. "One of the most interesting young women I have seen for years", Carlyle wrote. "Clear delicate sense and courage looking out of her small sylph-like figure." She was "seeking passionately for some Paradise to be gained by battle" and at this time, he regretted to find, was under such sinister influences as George Sand.

In person Geraldine was short and slight, with untidy reddish hair, and a face redeemed from plainness by a wide sensitive mouth, and the intense gaze of her near-sighted light brown eyes. Intensity was the keynote to her highly romantic nature. In several hysterical, but not untalented nor unreadable novels, she expressed her passionate need to be loved with a fervour that seemed not quite respectable in that day. She was intelligent, enthusiastic, generous and absurd. She fell in love with almost every slightly personable man who talked to her politely; she fell in love also with Jane Welsh Carlyle.

From the time of their meeting until their correspondence was terminated by death, a regular stream of letters flowed between Geraldine and Jane; letters which, they solemnly agreed, should be destroyed. Geraldine kept her promise, destroying Jane's letters in her own last illness: but Jane, with the reluctance both she and Carlyle felt ever to get rid of any piece of correspondence, did not destroy Geraldine's. The one side of this remarkable correspondence that remains shows that her relations with Geraldine gave full play to the masculine streak in Jane's character, so thoroughly suppressed in her life with Carlyle. Geraldine asked nothing more than to be allowed to worship; within a few months of their first meeting she was writing that she thought of Jane as Catholics think of their saints, that she loved her and tried to imitate her. "I have found you, and now I wonder how I ever lived without you", she wrote. "I don't feel towards you as if you were a woman." The masochism that emerges in the most casual consideration of her life and works is evident. "I would put my hands under your feet to keep you from a minute's pain." There can be little doubt that her passion took no overt physical form: at the same time that she called Jane her lover Geraldine described her affair with a man who "rushed down from the other side of the room, and fell down, selon des regles, at my feet, begging that I would try to care for him again." All of her real and imaginary romances (and they were many) were confided to Jane.

What were the feelings of the masculine partner in this queer emotional tangle? It is always pleasant to be idolized, particularly when, as in Jane's case, you see your husband planted by well-wishers upon an imaginary pedestal: yet Jane was too shrewd, too intelligent, too fond of hard sense, not to be aware of Gerldine's absurdity. She liked Geraldine, she was amused by her, she even admired her: but she also found Geraldine an intolerable nuisance. It is easy to imagine the surprise with which Jane heard Carlyle suggest one day that she should invite Geraldine to stay with them. As she stared at him in astonishment, he expressed increasing enthusiasm for the idea. Might she not, Jane suggested, be *dreadfully wearing*? Carlyle in reply was a little indignant that she should object to doing Geraldine a kindness: surely it would be a kindness to ask the poor girl to come and stay at Cheyne Row? The suggestion was enough to keep Jane awake half the night. In a long letter to her favourite cousin, young Jeannie Welsh, she weighed the benefits of a visit for Geraldine with certain doubts. "Tho' I am not jealous of my husband (pray read all this unto yourself and burn the letter) tho' I have not only his habit of preference for me over all other women (and *habits* are much stronger in him than *passions*) but also his indifference to *all* women *as women* to secure me against jealousy—still young women who have in them, as Geraldine has, with all her good and great qualities, a born *spirit of intrigue* are perilous sort of inmates for a married pair to invite." At last, however, she decided to invite Geraldine "*in a sort of a way*" to come "*for two or three weeks.*"

Invited thus dubiously, Geraldine paid a disastrous visit. She made attempts to charm, among others, Mazzini, Erasmus Darwin and Doctor John, who all professed a kind of sacred horror for her. On Sundays she came down in the morning with "*a bare neck*—and a black satin gown—or coloured silk!—all wasted, I assure you." She maddened Carlyle (who proved happily "absolutely *unreducible*") by stretching herself on the hearth rug at his feet and sleeping there. His opinion of her changed rapidly. "That girl", he said, "is an absolute fool—

and it is a mercy for her she is so ill-looking". Soon after her
arrival he began to sit upstairs in the evenings as well as in the
mornings; and Jane gave increasingly sharp replies to her
flatteries and caresses. Geraldine had altogether a poor time of
it: in the mornings she had nothing to do but scribble letters
on her knees, and in the evenings she slept. Surely, Jane
thought, she could not be enjoying herself? Surely she would
go home? But when at the end of the three weeks an invitation
came for her to stay with a friend in St. John's Wood she said
simply that she would be very happy to stop at Cheyne Row
until they asked her to go. Asked, explicitly, to go she could
hardly be, although her presence became every day harder to
bear, and even her evening sleep was at last cause for annoyance. After five weeks Geraldine went, in a flood of tears, and
even with mild hysterics: "on our side (the parting) was
transacted with dry eyes, with a composure of soul impassive
even for the claims of sympathy". The evening after she had
gone Carlyle said to Jane: "Oh my dear what a blessing it is to
be able to sit here in peace without having that dreadful young
woman *gazing* at me!"

Geraldine, then, had departed: departed, one might think,
for good. Within a few months, however, all was forgiven if
not forgotten, and the exchange of correspondence was as
regular as ever. There was, indeed, no quarrelling with
Geraldine. Who else would think, as she did, of rubbing her
friend's feet before she had been in the house five minutes?
("I am sure your feet have not got well rubbed since I did it
myself last year"). Who else wrote novels of reckless genius
"which even the freest spirits among us (must) call 'coming it
too strong' "? Who else would have "offered herself on paper"
to a man who wrote to reproach her for the indecency of her
writing? Who else would have escaped from that offer by
beginning an affair with a French Egyptian who was an
ardent St. Simonian? It was impossible to be angry with
Geraldine for long: and Jane even thought, at one time, of
marrying her off to Doctor John. It seemed for a little while
that the plan might be successful, but Geraldine exploited her
presumed advantage much too far. She asked to be taken to
plays, and other entertainments that cost money; it was too
much for Doctor John. "His incipient sentiment was too
weakly for bearing up against constant demands on his purse",
Jane wrote.

Geraldine, whose activities often shocked others, was capable of being shocked herself. She seemed, Jane wrote to her cousin Jeannie, "horribly jealous—nay, almost 'scandalized' ", about the frequent visits paid by Carlyle to the house of Lady Harriet Baring. And Mrs. Carlyle? "For my part I am singularly inaccessible to jealousy, and am pleased rather that he has found *one* agreeable house to which he likes to go."

CHAPTER THIRTEEN

THE NEW ARISTOCRACY

> I was taken to the opera . . . with Lady Harriet Baring—
> my *debut* in fashionable life—and a very fatiguing piece of
> pleasure it was, which left a headache and all uncomfort-
> ableness which I have not got rid of till this hour. Carlyle
> too was at the Opera, God help us!—went to ride in the
> Park at the fashionable hour then returned and dressed for
> the Opera!! Nobody knows what he can do till he tries! or
> rather till a Lady Harriet tries!!
>
> JANE WELSH CARLYLE to her
> Uncle John Welsh, 28 June 1845.

EARLY IN THE March of 1839 Carlyle attended a dinner
at Bath House, Piccadilly; Lord Ashburton was the host, and
the hostess was the wife of Lord Ashburton's son, Lady Harriet
Baring. Lady Harriet was an intellectual of her day and circle:
six years younger than Jane Carlyle, she was already a famous
hostess with an assured social position. Her appearance might
be called matronly or statuesque, according to the friendliness
or otherwise of the commentator: but there could be no doubt
of the formidable power of her personality.

She was imperious as by social right. The daughter of the
sixth Earl of Sandwich, she was proud of her lineage, and
inclined to be contemptuous of mere wealth; in youth she was
inquisitive, impertinent, moderately unconventional. After she
had married the shy, amiable and extremely rich Bingham
Baring, she snubbed her husband's relations. Was Lady
Harriet, then, a rebel against the standards of her society?
Not at all: her rebellion, such as it was, remained the wholly
personal annoyance of a woman who felt her speech and
activities restricted by the iron casing of class. When she shocked
friends by saying that she was in favour of polygamy, she meant
that she would like to go out and leave the other wife at home;
when she fretted at aspects of the social conventions to which in
general she firmly adhered, it was because some restriction
had been placed upon her own activity. She was intelligent,
and valued intelligence in others, but she was in no sense a
political Radical. She was conscious, one feels, of her own

G

benevolent attention to the lions she collected round her; lions who were expected to roar, yet not to roar over-loudly. One of these lions, introduced by Monckton Milnes and highly recommended by Charles Buller, was Carlyle; and with this lion, one highly valued apparently by the *cognoscenti*, Lady Harriet talked for an hour. Carlyle was impressed. She was, he wrote to his mother, "one of the cleverest creatures I have met with, full of mirth and spirit,—not very beautiful to look upon."

Such was the first meeting: and for some three years the acquaintance was not enlarged. When it was, Lady Harriet appears to have pursued Carlyle; she wrote to him that she was ill, that she was not allowed to go out in the evenings, that there was almost nobody in the world she liked to talk with so much as Carlyle. It would be a work of charity and piety for him to come and see her. "When a handsome, clever, and reputedly *most haughty* woman appeals to the *charity* and *piety* of a simple man like Carlyle you may be sure she will not appeal in vain", wrote Jane. So Carlyle went to the big ugly yellow house in Piccadilly that was the Barings' London home. If Jane had known how many times he was to walk from Chelsea to Piccadilly she would not have written in this letter so lightly of "Lady Harriet Baring's love-making to my husband."

The first meeting between the two women was arranged by the kind offices of Mrs. Buller; at tea one day Jane inspected Lady Harriet, and upon the whole liked her. She noted some brusqueness of manner, but none of the impertinence or hauteur of which she had been told. "She is unquestionably very clever—just the *wittiest* woman I have seen—but with many aristocratic prejudices—which I wonder *Carlyle* should have got over so completely as he seems to have done—in a word I take her to be a very lovable spoilt child of Fortune—that a little *whipping*, judiciously administered, would have made into a first rate woman." What, Jane wondered, had Lady Harriet thought of *her*?

Something, plainly, to judge from the "prodigious looks" with which she was surveyed from time to time. Something: but, we can guess, not very much. Jane was in her own world accepted as a very witty woman; at Cheyne Row, among the exiles and the Americans and the young admirers, she played the lioness to perfection, sometimes at the expense of the lion. Listening in silence to Carlyle's monologues she would murmur at the end of them: "My dear, your tea is getting quite cold;

that is the way with reformers." Such small ironies flowered within her own charmed circle, by her own warm fireside: they withered, or went unspoken, in that more rarefied upper class air which Lady Harriet habitually breathed, and which her robust conversational talent was accustomed to rule.

This contrast in their talents had a certain relation to their appearances. Lady Harriet, although she lacked beauty, possessed a fine beefy magnificence and power. Jane, on the other hand, had lost the freshness of her youth, and looked smaller and more fragile with the passing years. The portraits of her painted by the Italian exile Gambardella in 1843 and by Lawrence in 1849 show a face increasingly pinched and drawn; her complexion had become decidedly sallow, and only the dark, burning eyes, full of malice, irony, tenderness and sorrow, recalled the spirited young woman who had married Carlyle. In any contest with Lady Harriet she would fight, it was plain, upon the defensive, conscious that the younger woman possessed the advantage of serene and natural self-confidence.

One speaks too soon, however, of a contest: it had not come to that. There is no reason to think that Jane was at first displeased by her husband's predilection for Lady Harriet's company. Little notes went back and forth: amiably imperious, we cannot doubt, on Lady Harriet's side, and on Carlyle's composed in that vein of uneasy gallantry which was, upon the whole, his least happy form of literary expression. "Sunday, yes, my Beneficent, it shall be then; the dark man shall again see the daughter of the sun, for a little while; and be illuminated, as if he were not dark!" Jane professed herself amused by the obedience with which her husband obeyed Lady Harriet's commands; Lady Harriet, she said, was an arch coquette. John Mill, when he paid a visit to her, "appeared to be loving her very much"; to Mazzini she had expressed high commendation of George Sand and when prevented from speaking further to him, in Mazzini's words, "shook her head impatiently, which from a woman, especially in your England, was—what shall I say?—confidential, upon *my* honour."

Jane, too, was not immune from Lady Harriet's spell; she described her at various times as the cleverest, the most amusing and the most graceful woman she had ever met, and added wistfully: "I *could* love her immensely if she looked to care for it". Lady Harriet was always amiable, and even friendly to Jane: but somehow she never did care for it. In Lady Harriet's presence Jane seems often, in these early days of their acquaintance, to have felt herself provincial. Exultation is mingled with disturbance in the picture of the four days spent by her at the Barings' villa at Addiscombe, while Carlyle was away in Scotland. She was, of course, unable to sleep: "in the whole *three* nights I lay in bed at Addiscombe I slept just *one hour and forty minutes* by my watch!" The house was full of fine people, who were incessantly and intolerably witty; only Lord Ashburton seemed prepared to behave like a reasonable human being, only in Lord Ashburton's presence was she able to talk. That, decidedly, was not pleasant: and yet she had to admit that Lady Harriet was a woman of good sense and perfect breeding, gracious and not at all haughty. Lady Harriet was insistent that Jane, and Carlyle too, had promised to stay the whole winter at Bay House, Alverstoke, the Barings' seaside residence. Why was it that Jane had "an unconquerable persuasion that she does not and never can like me!"?

Carlyle, at Scotsbrig, was disturbed by plans of such magnitude. He wrote a deprecating letter to Lady Harriet, and a sharp one to Jane, to which she replied as sharply. " 'If I promised to spend the whole Winter with Lady Harriet'. Bah! When did you know me to do anything so green—so pea-green as *that*? *She told me* I had promised it formerly; that was all." In the end the Carlyles went for three weeks, and stayed for six. They did not exactly enjoy their visit, and yet they did not exactly regret it either. The life of the society presided over by Lady Harriet was based on leisure, and the full apparatus of Victorian luxury was in evidence. To Jane, accustomed to have it taken for granted that a house could be run with the aid of one maid-of-all-work, the surroundings were utterly strange. Here there were innumerable housemaids, a limitless number of manservants, an unending supply of food; no duty was imposed upon the guests but that of making brilliant conversation. Not serious conversation, as the Carlyles understood it, but talk that moved lightly, easily and with swift intelligence over the surface of the whole world; the talk of an upper class undisturbed by Carlylean rumblings of doom, curious about intellectual theories but in the end wholly satisfied with itself and its beliefs. Witty Lady Harriet was no Victorian bluestocking. "A few of my friends write, and the rest never open a book; none *read*", she said with the confidence of one who knows that she will not be taken quite seriously.

In such an atmosphere Jane's puritanical shrewdness rose to the surface. She was inclined to be suspicious and distrustful; and in consequence she seemed to dwindle to the rather ordinary little wife of a famous Scotchman. The wit at Lady Harriet's table was grand, like the company, whereas Jane's talent and company were homely. She did not enjoy her stay. Bay House, she admitted, was magnificent; Lady Harriet had an excellent heart, and was not a coquette at all; but the battledore and shuttlecock, the nonsense that was talked! "Nothing could exceed the sumptuosity of the whole thing, nor its uselessness." She was heartily glad to be back at Chelsea.

And what of Carlyle? This, surely, it may be thought, must have been the least congenial company in the world for the philosopher of work, the enemy of the idle aristocracy? Did he not compare these feasts of idleness and over-eating with the pitiful lives of the poor? He did not. There were grumbles about the state of Do-nothingism in which they were living, the rich food and the witty unfruitful talk. "The prospect of such a thing *for life* was absolutely equal to death. Meanwhile it cannot but be said to be pleasant enough, and perhaps not useless for a season." Mild words, these; Carlyle seems to have persuaded himself that the fragment of English society encountered at Lady Harriet's might contain the germ of that nation-saving aristocracy of which he now very often dreamed. They were idle, but they were intelligent; might they not be persuaded to self-saving, self-sacrificing activity? As for Lady Harriet, he positively refused to believe that she could like the idleness in which she lived. He was always urging upon her some useful and educational task, always attempting to "snatch her from the Phantasms" of the social life that was her whole existence. In Carlyle's relations with Lady Harriet there entered upon his side an element of snobbery. She appeared to him a perfect representative of the New Aristocracy for which he was looking: perfect, that is to say, if she could be induced to recognize the duties of her lot. She was, he said, "the daughter of an Ironside, fallen on shabby times": and even after her death he wrote, in an unintentionally comic phrase, of "her grand and noble endurance of want of work." The eye so quick to perceive cants and insincerities was dazzled indeed.

*   *   *   *   *

"When", wrote Carlyle to Mill in 1840, by way of an appreciation of the latter's essay on de Tocqueville, "will you write of the New Aristocracy we have to look for? That seems to me the question; all Democracy a mere transitory preparation for that." That did not seem to Mill at all the question; and the correspondence between these two men who had been so warmly friendly faltered and died. They had ceased to have many ideas in common, but the decisive agent in separating them was probably the lady called by Carlyle Mrs. Platonica Taylor. Both Carlyle and Jane were incurable and malicious gossips: and Mill, who cut himself off ruthlessly from his own family because of their opposition to Mrs. Taylor, is not likely to have spared the Carlyles. Mrs. Taylor (who may also have been annoyed by Carlyle's reluctance to act as trustee for her children) later referred to the Carlyles as "the gentility class —weak in moral . . . narrow in intellect, timid, infinitely conceited and gossiping"; Jane referred to Mrs. Taylor, after she had become Mrs. Mill, as a peculiarly affected and empty body.

Mrs. Taylor must, in any case, have thought it a duty to separate Mill from a man who had such strange ideas about a New Aristocracy; and most of Carlyle's Radical friends viewed with alarm the way in which his thoughts were tending. The "Condition-of-England question" had not been dispelled from Carlyle's mind by the writing of *Chartism*: and it revived with full force when in September, 1842, he set out from London to join Jane at Troston in Suffolk, where she was staying with the Bullers in the country parsonage of their son Reginald. During his stay in Suffolk he gathered a good deal of material for the book on Cromwell which still stayed unwritten: but he saw also with indignation the workhouse of St. Ives in Huntingdonshire, where able-bodied men sat with no work to do. He also made several visits to Bury St. Edmunds, and visited the ruins of the abbey.

Out of this visit was born *Past and Present*, a book written in some four or five months, with comparatively little pain to its author. The visit to the workhouse appears in the opening chapter, which treats with fine irony the fate of those in workhouses, "pleasantly so-named, because work cannot be done in them." From one point of view the book is a plea, as Carlyle intended it should be, for "the oppressed Poor against the idle Rich." What juster demand could the Governed make of the

Governing than that of a fair day's-wages for a fair day's-work? He praised the recent Manchester insurrection; he made a slashing attack on the Victorian shibboleth (which indeed was current until very recently) of over-production. "Too many shirts? Well, that is a novelty, in this intemperate Earth, with its nine-hundred millions of bare backs . . . Two million shirtless or ill-shirted workers sit enchanted in Work-house Bastilles, five million more (according to some) in Ugolino Hunger-cellars; and for remedy, you say,—what say you?—'Raise *our* rents!'—You continue addressing these poor shirt-spinners and over-producers in really a *too* triumphant manner!"

Such sentiments must have met with the approval of all contemporary Radicals: it was the solution suggested by Carlyle that they found shocking. There was no other remedy for the sad condition of England, he said, than—hero-worship. The worship of a true Hero was "the summary, ultimate essence, and supreme practical perfection of all manner of 'worship'"; it was "the soul of all social business among men"; it was "the topmost blessed practical apex of a whole world" which might include also a blessed Parliament and a "blessed Aristocracy of the Wisest". To point his moral Carlyle dredged the past, and came up with the chronicle of a monk of St. Edmundsbury called Jocelin of Brakelond, which he modernised and dramatised. The skill displayed in the recreation of monastic life and habits in the twelfth century is marvellous; and this life has its hero in Abbot Samson, who redeems the wretched condition of the monastery by his wise authority. The conclusion was obvious, and is pointed in the last section of the book. The modern world must get rid of Sir Jabesh Windbag the politician and of Pandarus Dogdraught, "the offal of Creation", and yet a member of the best clubs; and discover its hero. The worker must obey him; so must the aristocracy. If not, for the latter, "the voice of God from the whirlwind is very audible to me." In an enlightened society, however, the New Aristocracy would have a leading part to play.

Such is *Past and Present*, a strange, impressive and dangerous book. An interesting analysis of two copies of the manuscript, made recently by an American scholar, reveals how much Carlyle deliberately added of colour and rhetoric, how passages of preaching were interpolated, how punctuation was changed to strengthen and dramatize the sentences. There can rarely have been a writer who was more consciously an artist at the same time that he expressed contempt and distrust of art. The style is the man, doubtless: but such a style as Carlyle's is also, in a sense, always a lie. Carlyle's alterations had the effect, very strikingly, of making his writing more concrete, richer and more strange: he replaced general nouns by particular ones, and used modifiers to point a meaning or make it fully specific; his purple passages are covered with revisions which have the effect always of adding another twist of verbal excitement; and mixed with this effort always to strike a higher pitch of sarcastic indignation or rhapsodic praise is the addition of his characteristic archaisms and unidiomatic turns of speech, very often replacing standard English. Is there not something unacceptable, something false, in the deliberate construction of a style that proclaims, and gains its effect from, breathless ejaculative spontaneity? Is it not disturbing to see how much the conversational periods of an angry man were made, with fine art, in his study?

The reception of *Past and Present* was not warm: its fervour frightened Radicals, its sarcasm annoyed economists, its criticism of the existing state of affairs angered the ruling class. Like Carlyle's other works, however, it made disciples for him among young men at the Universities who were looking for a new way of life. There were other disciples: John Tyndall, it will be remembered, read it at Preston and became an adherent of Carlyle at once. Had the book been more simply written it might have made thousands of converts among the working class. From this point of view the most telling criticism of it, and incidentally of Carlyle's other propagandist writings, is that of Monckton Milnes: "It would be very dangerous if turned into the vernacular and generally read."

The way was clear now for Cromwell: but before dealing with the English dictator Carlyle wrote an essay about the Paraguayan Doctor Francia, a kind of curtain raiser which perhaps helped to settle his own attitude towards dictators. For Francia, as one who had helped to construct order out of chaos, Carlyle discovered much admiration: and he admired nothing more than Francia's way of dealing with plots, which he "pounced on . . . like a glede-falcon, like a fierce condor . . . struck beak and claws into the very heart of it, tore it into small fragments, and consumed it on the spot." That, Carlyle remarks, was Francia's way: and the zest with which he records it is significant.

The achievement of *Oliver Cromwell's Letters and Speeches With Elucidations*, published in 1845, is a considerable one. At the time that Carlyle wrote the accepted, and almost unquestioned, view of Cromwell was expressed in the Whig John Forster's remark that he "lived a hypocrite and died a traitor". To counter this view Carlyle turned his history into autobiographical form: digging through the mass of inaccuracies and prejudices about the Protector he came through to the original correspondence and used it to tell, by his own lights, Cromwell's story. The book consists therefore of Cromwellian letters and speeches, and Carlylean annotations and elucidations, together with such magnificent set pieces as the account of the battle of Naseby, the field of which he had visited in company with Arnold of Rugby. The value of *Cromwell* as pioneer work is now, very naturally, forgotten, but at the time the view of Cromwell's conduct which Carlyle took, and triumphantly supported with factual material, was thoroughly heretical. In the general appreciation of the book as a feat of historical research little regard was paid to Carlyle's enthusiasm for Cromwell simply as a dictator: *Cromwell*, to the surprise of both Carlyle and Jane was highly successful, even though some readers of it may, like Margaret Carlyle, have read the large type of Cromwell's speeches and ignored the rest. A second edition of the book was called for quickly, and then a third.

What subject could reasonably come after Cromwell? Carlyle thought of dealing with William the Conqueror. "Oh, for a day of Duke William again!" he said in conversation with Tennyson, who protested that the modern world was not the England of Duke William, nor even of Cromwell, but a totally new England quite unlike theirs. To Tennyson's arguments Carlyle merely repeated, "Oh, for a day of Duke William again!" When the poet mentioned William's cruelties Carlyle said that they were no doubt very sad, but that "somehow he conceived he had a right to do (them)—and upon the whole, he had!" The exasperated Tennyson said that the returning hero had better steer clear of him, "or he will feel my knife in his guts very soon." It was upon this or a similar occasion that Carlyle laughed and answered: "Eh, you're a wild man, Alfred!"

It was, upon the whole, a modern hero rather than an ancient one that Carlyle looked for, in what seemed to him England's desperate condition. In the House of Lords he heard old

Wellington speak, noted his "fine *aquiline* voice, quite like the face of him", and admired the soldierly, unrehetorical delivery of the man to whom he had promised, not so many years before, war and plenty of it if he were so unwise as to try to rule by "the drill sergeant method". Yet Wellington, however aquiline his voice, was now past hope as a saviour of England: and Carlyle looked elsewhere. When Peel abolished the Corn Laws Carlyle sent him a copy of *Cromwell* with a letter, subscribed "Your obliged fellow-citizen and obedient servant", expressing his admiration of the "great veracity *done* in Parliament, considerably our greatest for many years past—a strenuous, courageous and needful thing, to which all of us that so see it are bound to give our loyal recognition and furtherance." Peel had met Carlyle in the company of Monckton Milnes. His reply was polite but non-committal.

CHAPTER FOURTEEN

THE TURNING POINT

Meanwhile thanks for Mulock's book, which I read with immense interest. It is long since I fell in with a novel of this sort, all about love, and nothing else whatever. It quite reminds one of one's own love's young dream. I like it, and I like the poor girl who can still believe, or even 'believe that she believes', all that. God help her! She will sing to another tune if she go on living and writing for twenty years!

JANE WELSH CARLYLE to
John Forster, December 1849.

SLOWLY, AND TO ourselves imperceptibly, the pattern of life is formed. In the wearing process of day to day passion turns into habit, a mind once flexible becomes rigid, a system of ideas is transformed mysteriously into a collection of pre-judices. Looking back over the lives of the Carlyles we can trace the causes of the deepening disillusionment felt by Jane and the bewildered, at last savage, frustration of her husband: we can see the forces at work, in the years from 1846 to 1850, that settled for this man and woman whose skins were "too thin for the rough purposes of human life", the sorrows and bitterness of their old age.

When she was in her middle forties Jane Carlyle's delicately-balanced mental stability began to waver. In her letters written during those years we read more and more frequent accounts of agonized, sleepless nights caused by a barking dog or a crowing cock; of tartar emetic, castor oil, blue pills, opium and morphia; of five grains of mercury taken one night in mistake for half a grain; of nervous irritation, nausea and subsequent languor; of occasions when Doctor John sat at her bedside for hours, holding her down, and reading to her when she was quiet. Whether her condition was connected with the change of life, with sexual dissatisfaction, or whether it was more purely somatic, we have no means of knowing. The several doctors who attended her seem to have attempted no other treatment than that of drugs; with the exception of Doctor John, who at one time told Jane that her troubles were entirely imaginary, at another recommended that she should smoke an occasional cigar so long as she did not send the smoke through her nose, and at another still said that she should "make a point of getting out a little", so long as she stayed indoors while her cold lasted. Doctor John's general attitude as medical man was indicated by his advice to her on taking senna: "You had better take it—and then again perhaps you had better not."

In any case Jane's mental and physical condition did not preclude her from being witty in chosen company; it did not make her correspondence less shrewd and vivid; but it led her to occasional hysterical actions, such as her extraordinary behaviour at a temperance meeting when she clambered up to the platform, flung herself at the preacher's feet, and later, in tears, asked for one of the medals that were being handed out. Her condition also encouraged the development of a latent tendency to morbid jealousy. A strong element of jealous possessiveness is evident in Jane's attachment for several years to her young cousin Jeannie Welsh. In her relations with Geraldine Jewsbury it is plain that she took pleasure in provoking the "tiger-jealousy" of Geraldine, and in administering a sharp rebuke when Geraldine had "for a whole evening been making love before my face to *another* man". And jealousy of a different kind settled on her mind in connection with Carlyle and Lady Harriet Baring, or as she became in 1848 Lady Ashburton.

There can be no question that, in purely sexual terms, her jealousy was baseless; from what we know of Carlyle's character, and the glimpses we have of Lady Harriet's, anything else is unimaginable. It is probable that Jane had no fears about her husband's physical faithfulness: her reasons for jealousy were more complex, and were rooted in the change in Carlyle's behaviour brought about by the relationship. She was used to his bearishness, his occasional rudeness, his explosive bursts of speech, his condemnation of all social ceremony as cant; she had no objection to living in unfashionable Chelsea, and to managing a house with only one maid-servant; in an odd way she was proud of these things, as symbols of a virtuous way of life. Now it seemed that these rules were to be abrogated at Lady Harriet's word: to Bath House, to Addiscombe, to Alverstoke, to the great country house in Hampshire called The Grange, Carlyle went when he was bidden, generally with his wife but sometimes without her.

In a society which, surely, the philosopher would years ago have called gigmanic, he now moved serenely and with few signs of disapproval; with that society's hostess and bright star he maintained a very regular correspondence. Jane commented on this metamorphosis of her husband's behaviour with jealous irony: she was not able, nor perhaps would she have been interested, to trace in it the shift of his social hopes from Radicalism to the New Aristocracy; she understood little of the deep desire for some kind of personal political action now haunting him, as it haunted later the imaginations of Dickens and Ruskin.

The element of snobbery certainly existed in Carlyle's, and in Jane's, relations with Lady Harriet and her circle: yet it would be easy to overestimate that element while ignoring the degree to which Carlyle, who was in some ways exceedingly ingenuous, looked for some kind of concrete practical result from his encounters through Milnes and the Ashburtons with leading politicians of all parties. One small, almost symbolic, hint of what he hoped to achieve, may be found in the part he played in agitating for a London Library. Very largely through Carlyle's efforts an impressive collection of supporters was gathered together, including a number of influential noblemen and such literary men and politicians as Milnes, Bulwer, Gladstone, Charles Buller and John Forster; and in 1840 the London Library came into existence. The spread of education was only a small part of his concern for practical social action. To Thomas Ballantyne, once a Paisley weaver and now editor of a Radical paper in Lancashire, who asked for his support in a project to establish public parks he wrote that "I do sincerely hope you will get on with it—for the sake of the poor little sickly children, and the dusty, toilsome men, to whom, for a thousand years, generation after generation, it may be a blessing". He was irked, now and always, by the feelings of the things that might be done for the poor of Britain if only "brave men with hearts and heads" would "bestir themselves a very little"; and he came more and more to believe that the brave men were to be found in the company of Lady Harriet and that social reforms must be effected with the aid of those at the top, not the bottom, of society. He became also increasingly impatient with those who were concerned with the condition of the poor in other countries, telling "four rigid-looking elderly Quakeresses" who came to ask his support for the abolition of

negro slavery that "the *green* and *yellow* slaves, grown green with
sheer hunger in my own neighbourhood, are far more interesting to me." It was upon one such occasion that Carlyle told
John Sterling that he had determined to cast all tolerance to the
winds, and Sterling replied, "My dear fellow, I had no idea
you had any to cast."

As he looked round the world Carlyle became more and
more convinced that writing was a mere substitute for action;
after the completion of his book on Cromwell he wrote nothing
else. He noted instead what seemed to him the worsening state
of things everywhere. In a letter to his brother Alick, who had
at last emigrated to Canada with a capital of £500 provided
equally by Carlyle and Doctor John, he wrote of the potato
disease which was then ravaging Ireland in particular, but was
affecting in a lesser degree much of the rest of Europe; with
pity and restless scorn he looked at the crowds of Irish labourers
who had emigrated to Britain to help build the new Caledonian
Railway.

As always happened when he was idle, Carlyle became more
and more morose: half-unconsciously, he sought escape from
his sickly tart-tongued wife in the company of Lady Harriet
and her friends where he was not subjected to domestic ironies,
but welcomed simply as a great man. Fewer visitors came to
Cheyne Row. In the summer of 1846 affairs came to a crisis.
Jane went off to see her friends the Paulets at Seaforth, near
Liverpool: of their parting Carlyle wrote after she had gone
that "Certainly we never parted before in such a manner;
and all for—literally nothing." That the cause of their quarrel
was Carlyle's relation with Lady Harriet cannot be doubted;
and that it was about "literally nothing" may be true enough if
we take Carlyle's view of his own conduct. It appears that Jane
had asked him to break off an association which had become
intolerable to her, and that he had rejected the demand as
unreasonable.

In this extremity Jane seems to have contemplated separation from her husband. She wrote some letters to Mazzini,
which are lost; but two of his replies have been preserved, and
they make it plain that she had asked his advice on her course
of action. Mazzini adjured her to avoid selfish materialism and
recommended, with many vague moral admonitions, that she
should "by a calm, dispassionate, fair re-examination of the
past, send back to nothingness the ghosts and phantoms that

you have been conjuring up." The phantoms, however, could not be dismissed: they lost nothing of power from Jane's knowledge that she was to her husband, "in spite of the chimaeras and illusions . . . dearer to me than any earthly creature", as he assured her in sending a little card-case in remembrance of her birthday. He had sent a gift every year since the death of Jane's mother, and she suffered anguish when, on this day, a postal error made her think that no gift and no word had come from him. Had he decided not to write to her any more? Was he at Addiscombe, and forgetful? Or ill and unable to write? When, only a few hours later, she received the card-case, one feels a note of truth in her words: "Oh, my dear! I am not fit for living in the world with this organisation. I am as much broken to pieces by that little accident as if I had come through an attack of cholera or typhus fever."

She knew that her husband loved her, but the knowledge was not enough; within a day or two her thoughts were turning to the pleasures of death, and she was again writing to ask him to break off relations with Lady Harriet and her husband. He agreed to do so; he would not go to Addiscombe, "today nor tomorrow, nor indeed, for an indefinite, perhaps infinite, time to come." Yet at the same time he told Jane that he might perhaps join the Barings for a few days if they carried out a projected tour of Scotland. He had become "heartily weary of a relation grown so sad", and after reaching Scotsbrig he hoped that the bad weather would prevent the Barings from making their tour: but within a day or two he was writing to Lady Harriet that he would think nothing of a walk of twenty miles or more to see her, and a few days later that a note she had sent him was beautiful "in its words and in its silences." For some days after arriving at Scotsbrig he had no letter from Jane, and his plaintive protests show a state of mind not much more rational than hers. "It is not right, my poor dear Jeannie! it is not just nor according to *fact*. . . . To the deepest bottom of my heart that I can sound, I find far other feelings, far other humours and thoughts at present than belong to 'jealousy' on your part . . . Oh, my Jeannie! my own true Jeannie! bravest little life-companion hitherto, into what courses are we tending?" Nevertheless he met the Barings and stayed with them during five days of atrocious weather, during which Carlyle was depressed and Lady Harriet bad-tempered; only Bingham Baring maintained his almost invariable good humour. On returning to Scotsbrig Carlyle found a letter from Jane, which told him that the failure of their correspondence had been caused by a miscalculation of addresses on her part.

From Scotsbrig Carlyle went to Ireland, to see for himself the condition of the country; Jane after paying a visit to Manchester, where Geraldine treated her with much tact and sympathy, returned to Chelsea. We have a glimpse of her in Manchester as seen by the American actress Charlotte Cushman, which shows that Jane's troubled nerves had not affected her conversation:

> On Sunday Mrs. Carlyle came at one o'clock and stayed till eight. And such a day I have not known! Clever, witty, calm, cool, unsmiling, unsparing, a *raconteuse* unparalleled, a manner inimitable, a behaviour scrupulous, and a power invincible—a combination rare and strange exists in that plain, keen, unattractive, and yet unescapable woman.

*　*　*　*　*

There was something decisive about the events of this summer. Afterwards the Carlyles' social contact with the Barings was resumed. In October they visited the Grange together; early next year they went to Alverstoke; Jane accepted the existing relationship and, so far as we know, made no further attempt at a radical alteration of it. Carlyle on his side appears for a time to have intended to cease writing to Lady Harriet; instead he maintained the correspondence—but in secrecy. His letters to her are full of incoherent self-justification and self-accusation curiously mingled. At one moment he exhorts her to write, "but not to *me*—and *ignoring* this, never having *received* this!"; at another he tries to persuade himself that there is something divine in their friendship which "will live thro' all trials, and the earnest part of it will be a possession to us both for ever." The struggle had ended, one might say vulgarly, in a victory for Carlyle; and yet the victory had its terrible, unrealized cost. Nobody reading the letters of Carlyle and Jane as a whole could fail to appreciate the extraordinary understanding and sympathy that existed between them; nobody could fail to remark the decline of that sympathy from about this time onward. Jane's letters are still witty, and often charming; but the gaiety is now brittle, and the wit is frequently that of a woman painfully disillusioned about human motives. Carlyle has lost none of his humorous exaggerative genius but there is something lacking of the old zest and perfect intimacy in what he writes.

And the third member of this strange triangle? If it is difficult to understand exactly what Carlyle found so fascinating about Lady Harriet, it is almost impossible to interpret the attraction Carlyle held for her. For Carlyle was the pursued rather than the pursuer: one cannot doubt that any slackening of enthusiasm on her part would have produced an instant reaction on his side. Here again, the idea that Lady Harriet was a lion hunter who had trapped a desirable lion covers only a little of the truth. The link that bound these two was not one of physical attraction, nor did their minds move in the perfect accord that Carlyle's had done with Jane. The social gap between them represented utterly different modes of thinking and feeling. Yet Lady Harriet, writing of her "dear old Prophet Carlyle" asked "has one any right to more than one such friend in a lifetime?"; and for the sake of this friendship Carlyle became through the years more completely alienated in sympathy from Jane, and paid less and less regard to the sufferings that were no less real because their origin was neurotic. The mystery of Lady Harriet's friendship with Carlyle could be solved only by a deeper psychological interpretation than, on the evidence available, there is much ground for making. Such an interpretation would certainly take into account the fact that Bingham Baring's personality and career was quite manifestly subdued—very willingly on his part—to his wife's social success and reputation: and that this was not satisfactory, although it may have been perfectly congenial, to Lady Harriet. One of her casual remarks that has been preserved was that a certain man "looks all a woman wants—strength and cruelty". It is possible, at least, that she thought she discovered such qualities in the work and personality of Carlyle.

The sense of strain at Cheyne Row grew greater. Carlyle returned from a week's tour of Ireland in the company of two "Young Irelanders", Gavan Duffy and John Mitchel, more than ever convinced of imminent social disaster; at home he was savage to Mazzini, and paid with Jane a rather gloomy visit to the Grange. There were troubles with maidservants; the reformed drunkard Helen left to keep house for her brother, and her departure caused what Carlyle called "a sordid form of servile chaos" in the house. Helen was succeeded by a handsome and cultivated-looking girl from Edinburgh, who proved to have no capacity for work. Jane was struck down with influenza and spent three weeks in bed, being treated with tartar emetic and opium; the new maid, Isabella, was summarily dismissed by Carlyle. "My brief request to her was to disappear straightway, and in no region of God's universe, if she could avoid it, ever to let me behold her again." Isabella was replaced for a short time by an "old half-dead cook", and she by a little Cockney girl named Anne, who proved reasonably satisfactory.

There were other changes. Old Sterling died: a fortnight before his death, speechless from paralysis, he had himself driven to Cheyne Row although he knew Jane was not at home, and made signs as if he were leaving a message, pointing to his lips and then to the house, with tears running down his face. John Sterling, Carlyle's friend and a male confidant of Jane, had died a year or two earlier from tuberculosis, after a long illness; and the wife of old Sterling's second son, Anthony, developed a monomaniac belief that her husband was in love with Jane, and was ruining himself in giving her presents. Most of the foreign exiles ceased coming to the house, disturbed by Carlyle's illiberalism and ill-temper. In any case he saw few guests, for he adhered to a regular routine which kept him upstairs until 3 o'clock in the afternoon; then he walked or rode till five, when he took his place at the tea-table; later he adjourned to the kitchen with any other smokers, to blow the smoke from his churchwarden pipe up the chimney. The Duke of Saxe-Weimar paid Carlyle the compliment of an official visit at which Jane, after doing some careful dusting, giving the flowers clean water and making sure that the maid wore her best gown, went to Mrs. Buller's to be out of the way. When the Duke arrived Carlyle was "doing a Yankee" introduced by Emerson; the Yankee was summarily dismissed, although he showed an inclination to loiter, and the Duke stayed talking more than an hour. He was, Carlyle told Jane, very handsome, with beautiful blue eyes, extremely aristocratic looking, and the most dignified German he had ever seen. More dignified than Plattnauer? she asked maliciously. "Why—no—the indestructible dignity of Plattnauer *in all sorts of coats* is what one *never* sees the like of", Carlyle amiably replied.

Amiability was not his most obvious characteristic at the present time, although he remembered to buy Jane a New Year's gift and also a birthday present of a cameo brooch—

by which, typically, she was much upset. ("His gifts always distress me more than a scold from him would do"). He dined out a good deal, and expressed his views on virtue and wickedness more and more in the manner of one divinely informed. When Milnes, who took some pleasure in teasing Carlyle, suggested that good and evil were relative terms, he was directly contradicted: "We *do* know what is wickedness. *I* know wicked men; men whom *I would not live with*; men whom under some conceivable circumstances I should kill or they should kill me." The ingenious argument of a young man named Skirving about right and wrong was disposed of with the words: "I see what you are now—a damned impudent whelp of an Edinburgh advocate." At a breakfast party he engaged in violent argument with Macaulay about the merits of Oliver Cromwell's son Henry; on a visit to Manchester he became involved in a controversy with John Bright about the merits of railways and of negro slavery. And while he was spending time with the Barings or with Milnes or in other fashionable society, a sense of guilt made him complain of the idleness, folly and noise around him. He wrote to Jane, who was ill in Chelsea, from Lady Harriet's on an unintended note of comedy:

Ach Gott! Why do I complain to poor thee, confined to thy own bed at present? Well, I will not complain. Only, if *you* had been strong, I would have told you how very weak and wretched I was.

Into these troubled waters sailed, in October 1847, Emerson, come to England on a lecture tour. On landing at Southampton he received an enthusiastic invitation to stay in Cheyne Row. "Know then, my friend, that in verity, your Home while in England is here . . ." Carlyle's personal word of welcome, when Emerson arrived at 10 o'clock one night, had less of a flourish. "Well, here we are, shovelled together again", he said. They had not met since Emerson's visit to Craigenputtock nearly fifteen years before, when Carlyle had found Emerson one of the most lovable creatures he had ever looked upon, and Emerson thought Carlyle's conversation one of the three most remarkable things he had encountered in Europe. The years had changed them both. Carlyle was not prepared in these days to tolerate abstract arguments about ideal virtue, nor speculations on the immortality of the soul; he was not, in fact, much interested in argument of any kind, but only in the expression of his own thoughts in splendid monologues, half-comic and half-serious but wholly dogmatic. Such a mind was bound to find uncongenial the thin, high, perfect seriousness of Emerson; and Emerson was, in any case, no longer the humbly enquiring student of the world who had come to Craigen-puttock. He had his own not inconsiderable fame, his own habit of talking for the benefit of listeners; he, too, had some reputation as a prophet.

During the days when Carlyle was showing Emerson the sights of London the sages had the opportunity of observing each other, not altogether with approval. Emerson noted in his journal that the floods of Carlyle's talk were plentiful. "He says over and over, for months, for years, the same thing." His "hairy strength" was contemptuous of art, he punctuated every sentence with a scoffing laugh and some word such as "windbag" or "donkey", and a mild criticism of Cromwell made him turn upon Emerson "quite fiercely". The sage of Concord concluded that the sage of Chelsea was growing morbid, and found an expressive descriptive phrase for him: "An enormous trip-hammer with an Aeolian attachment."

Thus Emerson on Carlyle: what of Carlyle on Emerson? His chief complaint was the same as the American's: there was too much talk. "His sad Yankee rule seemed to be, that talk should go on incessantly except when sleep interrupted it: a frightful rule." There was no getting into any intimacy with him. A certain fastidiousness in his manner made no appeal to Carlyle; nor was his appearance wholly pleasing. "A delicate, but thin pinched triangular face, no lips, lean hook-nose; face of a *cock*: by none such was the Thames ever burnt!" After Emerson's departure Carlyle put down in his journal that there was no good to be got from the American, except through his "friendly looks and elevated exotic polite ways; and he would not let me sit silent for a minute." Such an encounter always encouraged his tendency to self-pity. "Lonelier man is not in this world that I know of . . ."

But the most vivid, and probably the most accurate, account of Emerson at Cheyne Row is Jane's. After praising his polite-ness and gentleness and the way in which "he *gives* under the most provoking contradictions, with the softness of a feather-bed", she added that he lacked "what the Yorkshire wool-cleaner called 'natur' ". He had "a sort of theoretic geniality" and was "the most elevated man I ever saw, but it is the elevation of a *reed*—run all to heighth without taking breadth along with it." Was it perhaps upon this occasion that Emerson, speaking of the certain ultimate triumph of good over evil, maintained that even in a brothel man's moral aspiration was still tending upwards? Jane's comments were caustic, and Emerson decided that, upon further acquaintance, he did not care for Mrs. Carlyle.

Emerson went off on his lecture tour; when he returned to London the Carlyles attended his talk on "Domestic Life", of which Carlyle in the lecturer's presence could find no greater praise than to say that it was "very Emersonian", while privately he remarked that it was intellectual moonshine. Arthur Hugh Clough, the young poet and disciple of Carlyle, was among the audience; he pointed out the prophet to a young man who on this occasion had no speech with Carlyle, but heard "his loud, kindly contemptuous laugh" at the lecture's end. The young man was at this time thirty years old and had, according to Geraldine Jewsbury, a strange elfin beauty; much later, his frankness as Carlyle's biographer was to cause a major literary storm. His name was James Anthony Froude.

CHAPTER FIFTEEN

1848 AND AFTER

Let the tail shift for itself; I will bury the head. And what's the
    Roman Republic to me, or I to the Roman Republic?
Why not fight?—In the first place, I haven't so much as a musket;
In the next, if I had, I shouldn't know how I should use it;
In the third, just at present I'm studying ancient marbles;
In the fourth, I consider I owe my life to my country;
In the fifth—I forget, but four good reasons are ample.
Meantime, pray let 'em fight and be killed. I delight in devotion.
So that I 'list not, hurrah for the glorious army of martyrs.

        ARTHUR HUGH CLOUGH: *Amours des Voyages.*

IN THE EARLY WEEKS of 1848 Carlyle put down in his
journal ideas for new books, all of them bearing on the sad
state of the world. One such was the "Exodus from Hounds-
ditch"—that is, from orthodox Judaic Christianity; this he
flinched from writing because of the great gap that would be
left in his own vague faith by the destruction of organized
religion at a time when there was nothing to replace it. Another
was a series of sketches on the miseries of Ireland, another still
a portrait of *The Scavenger Age*, implying that "sweeping *out the
gutter*" was "the indispensable beginning of all." Even in
contemplating a book about the life of his friend John Sterling,
Carlyle was concerned with the number of things that might be
taught "in the course of such a delineation."

Before any of these books had been begun there came on
February 24 news of Revolution in Paris, of Guizot's downfall
and the expulsion of Louis Philippe: this was followed by
revolts in other countries. In March Mazzini, in high spirits,
came to say goodbye to Jane, whose spirits were low. She could
not feel for Mazzini's distress at the likelihood of his being
allowed to return to Genoa in peace, instead of as the leader
of a conspiratorial rising. Within a year Mazzini was to be one
of the three triumvirs of the new Roman Republic; within
another, his plans defeated by Louis Napoleon, he was to be
back in England with a greyish beard ("You must recollect, my
Dear, that in the old times I needed always to have a barber to
shave me—and in the camp with Garibaldi, and flying for my

life, I could not of course take everywhere with me a barber!"
he explained to Jane). In England the revived Chartist movement spoke of using physical force to gain its ends.

Such a revolutionary ferment was what Carlyle had been
prophesying for years: was it not part of that process of sweeping
out the gutter which he had been contemplating as the subject
of a book? He did not feel quite with Leigh Hunt, who wrote
that "the state of things in France is DIVINE": but for a few
weeks he was enthusiastic. For the first time in his life he took
in a daily paper, *The Times*; Emerson noted the improvement
in his spirits. He spoke of starting his own magazine, because
the tone of some articles he had written was too strong even for
The Examiner; he looked forward to the possibility of a Chartist
Parliament. He made notes about another book on the inevitable triumph of democracy, the labour question, and the need
for wise government. "Notion of voting to all is delirium. Only
the vote of the wise is called for, of advantage even to the voter
himself." To half a dozen correspondents he fired off excited
letters. "This immense explosion of democracy in France, and
from end to end of Europe, is very remarkable and full of
interest . . . I call it very joyful; yet also unutterably sad."
Unutterably sad: that thought would hardly have entered the
mind of the Carlyle who, eleven years before, wrote *The
French Revolution*. This was a very different man: one whose loss
of faith in the usefulness of any revolutionary movement in his
time could never be adequately compensated by aristocratic
acknowledgement of his merits as writer and talker; yet a man
by now too far committed to the existing order of society, both
in his public and his private life, ever to find release in the
simple solvent of action.

No portrait painter was successful with Carlyle. The various
drawings done by Samuel Lawrence present a figure with a
curious likeness to Sir Laurence Olivier; the painting by John
Linnell in 1844 shows what is almost a dandy, cloak slung over
arm, hands carefully posed on stick, in a pose surely uncharacteristic. There is a photograph of the period, however,
which offers us a credible actor in the events of these years. The
features have become beakily assertive, and the whole face
seems shrunken; a heavy line runs from nose to mouth. The
long upper lip is pulled in to the point of invisibility, the lower
is thrust upwards and outwards above the disproportionately
long chin bedded in a butterfly collar. It is the face of a man

committed to rigidities of form and suppressions of feeling: it is not surprising that when we ask what part this man played in the revolutionary upturns of 1848 the answer should be that he played no part in them.

To such recent disciples as Froude and Arthur Hugh Clough the prophet offered no coherent word. Clough in 1848 gave up first his tutorship, and later his fellowship at Oriel: he went to Paris with Emerson, where he saw with sorrow the defeat of the working class by the bourgeoisie. In 1849 he went to Rome, where his visit coincided with the siege of the city by Louis Napoleon. Clough paid a visit to Mazzini who, a few weeks before the defeat of the Republic, was in good spirits; he heard the guns and saw the dead and wounded. The Roman population, Clough thought afterwards, had not fought *very* hard; the French had not behaved *very* barbarously. Clough, in spite of his Republican sympathies, could not bring himself to assist the revolutionary movement in any way; he wrote instead his long, amusing narrative poem *Amours des Voyages*, and after the fall of the Roman Republic wrote the hymn, "Say not the struggle nought availeth", which later was put to such curious uses.

In his unheroic attitude Clough was a precursor of many modern intellectuals; nevertheless, he was a good deal closer to participation in these events than the self-proclaimed devotee of action in Cheyne Row. Carlyle got no nearer to seeing a stick thrown in anger than when he ventured out to see the great Chartist uprising announced for April 10th. When he reached Cadogan Place it began to spit with rain, and he had no umbrella. At Burlington Arcade he decided to wait for a little, and when the shower became a downpour he hailed a Chelsea omnibus and went home. Such was Carlyle's appropriately ludicrous role in the ludicrous uprising; obligingly warned in advance, the ruling class had sworn in 150,000 special constables. Feargus O'Connor was warned that the procession would not be allowed to cross the Thames, and in fact it made no attempt to do so; the new monster Petition (which was found to contain 2 million instead of the boasted 5 million signatures, and to weigh $5\frac{1}{2}$ cwt instead of 5 tons) was taken to the House of Commons in three hansom cabs, and the "uprising" was over.

The absurdly ineffective nature of these activities bears no relation to the depth and seriousness of the feelings that went

to make them. The defeat of Chartism had its effect in setting
back organized working-class movements in England for nearly
half a century. Carlyle's knowledge of his own failure to act
caused him prolonged anguish of mind. From a distance
he envied the single-minded and simple stand of Mazzini
against the French. At breakfast-tables he was irritable; those
who asked his opinions on Chartism were likely to be subjected
to a violent, and not particularly intelligible, diatribe about the
villainous and cowardly conduct of Feargus O'Connor; he
went with Emerson to look at Stonehenge, and bade the
American farewell, remarking with comparative charity that
he was "a dignified, serene, and amiable man of a certain
indisputable natural faculty, whose friendliness to me in this
world has been great." He noted in his journal—he made
many such notes in his lifetime—that he had never until now
been so low, "utterly dumb this long while, barren, undecided,
wretched in mind." He made such furious objections to Jane
overlooking the proofs of Geraldine Jewsbury's second novel
on the ground of its probable obscenity that she hastily revoked
the permission she had given for its dedication to her. At a
dinner party given by Dickens, Carlyle answered the pressing
and continual questions of his host about his health in the
words of Mrs. Gummidge: "I know that I am a lone lorn
creetur', and not only that everythink goes contrairy with me,
but that I go contrairy with everybody." It was at this dinner
party that old Rogers, who had come to dislike both the
Carlyles for talking too much ("When that man's tongue stops
that woman's begins") asked Jane unamiably if her husband
was as much infatuated as ever with Lady Ashburton.

In May of this year Bingham Baring succeeded to his father's
title, and in September the Carlyles paid a visit of five weeks to
the Grange—a visit of which Carlyle noted, in spite of the
extreme friendliness shown them, "Feelings . . . altogether
unfortunate, generally painful, and requiring to be kept
silent." In November Charles Buller died from the after-effects
of an operation; and Carlyle, who had been able to forgive this
spoilt child of fortune even his irresponsible gaiety, wrote an
obituary notice very delicate in its tender sympathy. To the
easy charm of Charles Buller his contemporaries paid abundant
testimony; even Jane, though priding herself on her im-
munity from "the extravagant homage which he is used to
receive from all people, especially women", and believing that

she was "too wise a woman to be *Charlesed*", gave way when on a wet day he seized his gun and shot a hollyhock, which he presented to her, dripping wet, between finger and thumb. The portrait of Charles Buller by Duppa shows us a young man with an open expression, very thick curling lips and a dashing sensual handsomeness; it leaves unrendered, of necessity, the spontaneous graceful good nature that made this former pupil of Carlyle's "the most agreeable person alive". Old Buller had died a few months before Charles; Mrs. Buller declined visibly after her son's death, and died early in 1849. The Carlyles became aware, a little painfully, that they were growing old. In his journal Carlyle meditated on the futility of any attempt to write his life. "The *chief* elements of my little destiny have all along lain deep below view or surmise, and never will or can be known to any son of Adam." And Jane, reacting a little differently to the thought of age, wrote to her namesake, Carlyle's third sister, that although there was no change in her affection "There are other changes, which give me the look of a very cold and hard woman." Carlyle's account of her, she said, was never to be depended on, since "So long as I can stand on my legs, he never notices that anything ails me."

Some of Jane's activities in the later eighteen forties show an attempt to find some compensation for the gradual slackening of the perfect sympathy that had linked her with her husband. There is a richly comic, but also pathetic, account in one of her letters of a visit paid her by a six year old godchild, the daughter of the actor Macready. The letter describes in detail the troubles of having to dress the child's dolls, play horses with it, wash and comb it "and all that sort of thing", and—most difficult of all—to keep it out of Carlyle's way. At night it proved not at all easy to get the child's clothes off, and she could not be put in the spare room for fear that Carlyle, sleeping nearby, might be disturbed. Put down in Jane's own bed the little girl began to sing, and after an hour's conversation was left still wide awake; at midnight Jane went to bed, "but of course not to sleep: all night long she pitched into my breast with her active little heels—and when she awoke at seven and threw her arms about my neck calling out 'Oh I am so glad to be here!' I had not once closed my eyes, and in this state to have to wash and dress her and play at horses again! it was a strange and severe penalty for being a Godmother."

The godchild departed; but there came instead that tradi-
tional consolation of frustrated women, a dog. "My dear, it's
borne in upon my mind that I'm to have a dog", she said to
Carlyle, "with such a look and style" as he afterwards remembered; and the dog Nero was one of the chief solaces of her
existence for the next ten years. Nero slept in her bed; Nero,
concealed in a basket, accompanied her on railway journeys;
Nero showed great jealousy when Jane spoke a polite word to
the cat; Nero on one occasion, when Carlyle had talked of
needing a horse, came and scratched on his door bearing round
his neck an envelope enclosing the picture of a horse and a
cheque for fifty pounds, half its purchase money. Nero, from
Chelsea, wrote letters to T. Carlyle Esq. at The Grange,
Alresford, Hants; and Mrs. Carlyle from Addiscombe, wrote to
Master Nero at Chelsea letters which had their sharpness in
references to "The lady for whom I abandoned you—to whom
all family ties yield."

Nero was a consolation: and there were other consolations
as time went on for the loss of the Sterlings and the Bullers and
that little circle of Continental refugees whose exploits and
absurdities had so much delighted her. There was, of course,
always Geraldine to be confided in and bullied. There was
Doctor John, who shuttled to and fro between Scotsbrig and
London, busy with inaction. Towards the personality of the
Doctor, "accursed vegetable", as old Sterling had called him,
"not a man at all but a walking Cabbage", Jane had become
more nearly reconciled. Doctor John had been made more
endurable, for one thing, by his absorption in a translation of
Dante: a work on which he had been started by Carlyle's
observation that he was now too old for it. Doctor John actually
completed the translation of *The Inferno* which he sent out, as he
cautiously observed in his preface to it, "by way of experiment": but although the book was reasonably successful, the
effort of work and the strain of correcting proof sheets deterred
him from beginning to translate the *Purgatorio*. The translation
of *The Inferno* was absolutely the only work Doctor John did in
the last thirty years of his life. All his life he had intended to
do some work: but he was, in one of his phrases delightedly
adopted by Jane in her correspondence, "with the best intentions always unfortunate", and there was, after all, in another
of his favourite phrases, "no use at all in rebelling against
Providence."

Notable among her other friends of this time was the buzzingly pompous John Forster, who had busied himself with good offices related to Geraldine Jewsbury's works. When Forster failed in attentiveness he was pulled up briskly. "My dear Mr. Forster,—I died ten days ago and was buried at Kensal Green; at least you have no certainty to the contrary: what is the contrary?" There were young people to be seen, like Thackeray's daughters who came often to Cheyne Row, and were enchanted by the house, its mistress, dressed in velvet and point lace, and the hot cups of chocolate she prepared against their coming. And in 1849 Jane brought herself to the point of visiting Scotland again, for the first time since her mother's death, and renewing old friendships. At Haddington she looked at her father's tomb, scraping the moss off it with a button-hook; wandering through the churchyard she saw that the names missing from the signboards appeared on the tombstones; she remembered Edward Irving and the little girl who long ago had climbed over the churchyard wall. A cooper who did not recognize her remembered Miss Welsh, "the tastiest young lady in the whole place." In a letter to Carlyle that is like a long and brilliant essay—it occupies twenty pages of print— she poured out her memories of the past. "And it is only in the past that I can get up a sentiment for myself. The present Mrs. Carlyle is—what shall I say?—detestable, upon my honour."

*　　*　　*　　*　　*

This long letter was sent to Carlyle in Galway; in an attempt to stir himself to the point of writing he had paid a visit to Ireland, again in the company of Gavan Duffy. Four years earlier Duffy had come to Cheyne Row with two compatriots: there was considerable argument, and Jane took some note of the visitors. One of them, she thought, might prove an Irish Robespierre (in fact he became an advocate at the Indian Bar); of another she could recall nothing but that his nose bled from excitement; Duffy, the third, "quite took my husband's fancy, and mine also to a certain extent . . . With the coarsest of human faces, decidedly as like a horse's as a man's, he is one of the people that I should get to think beautiful, there is so much of the power both of intellect and passion in his physiognomy." In 1849 most of the young men in whose company Carlyle had made his earlier Irish visit were State prisoners or political refugees. The most notable of them, John Mitchel,

received a savage sentence of imprisonment for treason; Duffy
himself was arraigned on the same charge, but after ten months'
imprisonment, during which Carlyle wrote him several friendly
letters, escaped through the mishandling of the prosecution.
To Duffy Carlyle expressed his intention of paying another
visit to Ireland, to see in particular the famine areas; and after
some characteristic delays he boarded the Chelsea steamer on
Cadogan pier. The blessing of a journey by sea, he observed
to Duffy, was that he would be left entirely alone. "Alone, and
very miserable, it will beseem me to be, a good deal in this the
most original of my 'tours'." The concealed relish of this
passage is reminiscent of a note on another occasion, that he
was not yet sufficiently miserable to start writing.

Miserable Duffy did not find him. There is, indeed, a striking
difference between the gloomy tone of the reminiscences of his
journey which Carlyle wrote down, and those which were
published by Duffy. To Duffy who was his constant, and often
his only, companion for six weeks, he was never arrogant or
impatient and never expected to exercise the authority which
might have been thought the prerogative of one in his position,
in deciding the details of the journey; in general he was good-
natured, sympathetic, and seemed to be enjoying himself. By
the account given in Carlyle's reminiscences, however, the
journey was a prolonged agony, relieved only by his companion's amiability. In such contradictions lie the explanation,
upon a superficial level, of the opposing views about Carlyle
taken during his lifetime and shortly after his death. To Carlyle
the inner confusions of his mind, now far beyond any possible
reconciliation, were continually present; and whenever he had
time to do so he put them down on paper. To his friends these
confusions were not apparent; and some of them protested
indignantly that the man who put down these melancholy
reflections had been frequently the life and soul of the party.
In Ireland, there was indeed enough to depress any man of
sensibility. At Dublin Carlyle was fêted: but he found the in-
cessant nationalistic talk tedious. In the south Duffy's name
opened all doors, and Carlyle talked to priests and patriots,
Anglo-Irish gentry and Poor Law Inspectors; in none of them
did he find much hope for Ireland. He was, as usual, unable to
sleep. Through Killarney and Limerick, Clare and Mayo and
Sligo he passed with thoughts black as a thunder-cloud. At
Glendalough seven churches mouldered in ruins, and beggars

cried for alms; at Killarney there were 3,000 paupers in the workhouse. In Westport half the population were paupers, and crowds of paupers gathered round the priest in the street; here they were shown the mansion of a baronet who had ejected 320 persons within the last few months, and who spent in London an income of £30,000 a year drawn from his tenants.

So far Carlyle, in his reminiscences of a country where "you have beauty alternating with sordid disordered ugliness, abrupt as squares on a chessboard." When we turn to Duffy the picture is changed; the weather is fine, if sometimes sultry, with thunder-clouds rumbling only occasionally in the distance. The notes of their conversation, put down at the time by the young Irishman, have an agreeably Boswellian flavour. In carriages and in railway trains, in stage coaches and Irish cars, there were abundant opportunities for Duffy to question Carlyle about life and literature. The Irishman, a respectful but not an idolatrous observer, noted that Carlyle was not a bad mimic; his attempts at badinage were clumsy but he entered into them with such pleasure in his own absurdity that the farcical result was often more enjoyable than skilful acting. When moved by indignation or contempt he was apt to drop into broad Annandale speech.

Who, Duffy asked on the first day of their journey, was the best talker he had met in London?

When he met Wordsworth first, Carlyle replied, he had been assured that the poet was the best talker in England. It was disappointing, then, to find that he spoke continually of how far you could get carried out of London, on this side and on that, for sixpence; but still, it was a genuine expression of the man.

But, Duffy persisted, *was* Wordsworth the best talker in England?

Leigh Hunt would emit more pleasant, ingenious flashes in an hour than Wordsworth in a day, Carlyle answered; but in one case it was perfumed water, in the other deep, earnest, painful thought. There was only one exception to the pleasure one had in Wordsworth's conversation; that was when he spoke of poetry, and harangued about metres, cadences, rhythms and so forth. Then one could not be bothered to listen to him.

The slightly-shocked Duffy suggested that Wordsworth would naturally like to speak of the instrument through which he had wrought a revolution in English poetry. But Carlyle had now tired of this subject as, we gather, he frequently tired of Duffy's persistent questioning; and he launched into observations on the unimportance of Wordsworth's pastoral pipings, and expressed regret that this cold, hard, silent, practical man had not done some effectual work in the world.

Duffy had expected to hear, he said, of a softer and more sympathetic man. To this the reply was final.

"No, not at all; he was a man quite other than that; a man of an immense head and great jaws like a crocodile, cast in a mould designed for prodigious work."

Jeffrey, Carlyle said as an afterthought, had said more brilliant and interesting things than any man he had met, if one regarded talk simply as recreation.

This was only a beginning. Earnestly, throughout the whole tour, Duffy questioned Carlyle about literary men, Browning and Coleridge, Landor, Dickens, Thackeray, Sir James Stephen, Forster, Emerson, Buckle, Mazzini, and about the authorship of the letters of Junius. In Carlyle's replies we gather probably more of the spirit of his conversation (distinct from his monologues) than from any other single source. Dogmatically assertive, impatient of contradiction and yet capable of deprecating his own exaggerations with a strange and attractive humour; a painter of astonishing verbal pictures, able to strike off in a moment, from the vast resources of his metaphorical memory, a brilliant concrete image like that one of Wordsworth's great crocodile jaws; elaborating with richly grotesque absurdities one particular point in his subject's appearance or character. He praised Browning less as poet than as a possible writer of prose; we know what he thought of Coleridge, and that opinion was not raised by Duffy's insistence on reciting one of Coleridge's poems. Landor, alas, had fallen into an extravagant method of stating his opinions, but his merits as a writer had not been fully acknowledged. Dickens was a good, cheery little fellow, but his theory of life was quite wrong. He thought men ought to be buttered up, and the world made soft for them, and all sorts of fellows have turkey for their Christmas dinner. But he was worth something—worth a penny to read of an evening before going to bed. Thackeray had more reality in him, and would cut up into a dozen Dickenses.

Sometimes irritation got the better of Carlyle in dealing with

Duffy, as it did with Johnson in dealing with Boswell. When Duffy said that he thought the first volume of Buckle's *History* showed "prodigious reading and a remarkable power of generalisation", Carlyle admitted his ignorance of the book. Duffy insisted on the value of Buckle's work, and went so far as to outline his theories. There is a rumble of thunder in Carlyle's reply. "People kept asking him, 'Have you read Buckle's book?' but he answered that he had not, and was not at all likely to do so. He saw bits of it from time to time in reviews, and found nothing in them but shallow dogmatism and inordinate conceit. English literature had got into such a condition of falsity and exaggeration that one may doubt if we should ever again get a genuine book. Probably not." Duffy was not deterred by such setbacks; nor did he flinch when Carlyle, asked his opinion as to the identity of Junius, replied that in his opinion it did not matter a brass farthing to any human being who was the author of Junius. Duffy advanced arguments at length, and with enthusiasm, but "Carlyle made no answer, and proceeded to speak of other things."

Remembering the tour in his old age, after he had become respectable, been knighted and made Minister of Public Lands in Australia, Duffy thought that it was a wonderful thing for Carlyle to have chosen as his companion a man who was at the time a symbol of Irish opposition to English rule. It was, he said, "what nobody else who counted so much would ever have dreamed of doing. The Castle resented it. He showed me a letter of private remonstrance he received from the Lord Lieutenant, Clarendon." After leaving Duffy finished his tour with a visit to Lord George Hill, one of the Irish landlords who were attempting to improve their estates; here he renewed acquaintance with Plattnauer, now tolerably sane, and by the Carlyles' agency tutor to Lord George's children. Carlyle admired Lord George and called him a "beautiful soul", but thought little of his project for model farms and model tenants. It was, he said, the largest attempt yet seen by him at "the emancipation, all-for-liberty, abolition-of-capital-punishment, roast-goose-at-Christmas system. Alas, how can it prosper?" In August he left Ireland and went to Scotsbrig. Later he joined the Ashburtons at their Highland shooting box, Glen Truim, where he was as miserable as might be expected. He slept badly, an attempt to wash in a foot-pail brought on lumbago, there was hardly a reasonable word spoken each day. "It is, in fact, such a scene of *folly* as no sane man could wish to continue in or return to." But why was he there at all?

* * * * *

The trip to Ireland was the sparking point of a book: but not a book about Ireland. He remained friendly to Duffy, and wrote an article that appeared in Duffy's periodical, *The Nation*, but he wrote nothing at length about Ireland. Perhaps he felt that in doing so, in writing of the workhouses, the poverty, the people on Galway streets more debased than Swift's Yahoos, he must have spoken with the voice of that "speculative Radical, of the very darkest tinge", who had written *Sartor Resartus*. That voice was not to be heard again. Instead he wrote an "Occasional Discourse on the Nigger Question", followed by a series of eight articles published separately as they were written, and later collected together under the title of *Latter-Day Pamphlets*.

The value in the writings of such a visionary moralist as Carlyle depends first of all upon his capacity to apprehend the external events around him. A true visionary, a Boehme or a Blake, can afford to remain securely wrapped in the cocoon of his vision; he has no practical message to impart, but only a mystical experience to communicate. But such a writer as Carlyle, who pretends to lay down general principles of human conduct, and even puts forward specific proposals for social improvement, must begin from realities which we can accept. From the time of *Latter-Day Pamphlets* onwards, Carlyle's writings do not conform to this elementary principle. His mind is closed, henceforth, to facts which fail to accord with his preconceived opinions; he becomes less and less interested in the humanity, the well-being of which has always provided at least the starting point of his speculations, and more concerned with simple aggrandisement of the super-human hero. He is prepared to contradict eyewitnesses of events about which he has hardly read; corrected when he misquotes, he calmly repeats the original error. His writings gradually lose their hold on reality, and become more and more expressions of a pathological state of mind.

The background of the *Latter-Day Pamphlets* is one of personal and social frustration. These articles, which attempt an analysis of Britain's social troubles in terms much more specific than Carlyle had used before, and suggest actual remedies for the

H

ills described, make a curious and distorted approach to the social action from which he had flinched in the year of revolutions. Faithful to the heroic principle, he discovers in the pamphlets Britain's hero: none other than that gentlemanly figure, Sir Robert Peel. Not long before he began to write the pamphlets Carlyle had had some conversation with Peel at Bath House, and later had been invited to dine with the Prime Minister. Upon Peel's freshness, heartiness, and the vein "really of genuine broad drollery" in him Carlyle based the extravagant hope that this velvet-handed member of the upper middle class might be the dynamic hero for whom Britain was waiting: the Messiah who would reform Downing Street, reorganize the Foreign Office, the War Office and other departments of State, and would say to the great army of paupers: "Enlist, stand drill; become, from a nomadic Banditti of Idleness, soldiers of Industry!" In this great revision of society led by Peel, Carlyle seems to have envisioned himself playing some honourable part.

The form in which this idea is presented allows vent to the repressed sadism of Carlyle's nature; he had no longer anything new to say, but he could repeat his often-expressed ideas with the ugly violence of impotent anger. He had commented before, sharply and sensibly enough, upon charity that did not begin at home, but now he drew a fantastically inaccurate picture of the West Indian Negroes, "sitting yonder with their beautiful muzzles up to the ears in pumpkins, imbibing sweet pulps and juices; the grinder and incisor teeth ready for ever new work . . . while the sugar-crops rot round them uncut, because labour cannot be hired." What was the 'Nigger's' true wish? Not to eat pumpkins in idleness, we may be sure, but to be compelled to work: "The tacit prayer he makes (unconsciously he, poor blockhead), to you, and to me, and to all the world who are wiser than himself, is 'Compel me!!'" Not only the Negroes made this tacit prayer; so also did the prisoners in the model prison which Carlyle visited, where he found all the food "of excellence superlative", and saw a literary Chartist whose lot he considered superior to that of any Duke. "Which Duke . . . has cocoa, soup, meat, and food in general made ready, so fit for keeping him in health, in ability to do and to enjoy? Which Duke has a house so thoroughly clean, pure and airy; lives in an element so wholesome, and so perfectly adapted to the uses of soul and body?" In dozens of such passages, written with perfect seriousness, we see how utterly Carlyle has lost touch with realities of life and feeling. What would Carlyle's hero and saviour say to these "Devil's regiments of the line"? "Mark it, my diabolic friends, I mean to lay leather on the backs of you, collars round the necks of you; and will teach you, after the example of the gods, that this world is *not* your inheritance, or glad to see you in it." This, we may remember, was the man who in *Chartism* had attacked the rich for devising the treadmill and improving prison discipline.

It was in dealing with those who had been his friends and early admirers, however, that Carlyle was most savage: all the improvers and the intellectual Radicals, the rationalists and the over-pious Christians, all those whose sympathies and enthusiasms he had understood, but, through the rigid Calvinism of his upbringing, had not been able to share. What did they create but a "universal syllabub of philanthropic twaddle"? What were their beliefs but "the rotten carcass of Christianity", a "malodorous phosphorescence of *post-mortem* sentimentalism"? In a series of "Pig Propositions" which are certainly not without morbid power he parodied the philosophy of his friends:

1. The Universe, so far as sane conjecture can go, is an immeasurable swine's-trough, consisting of solid and liquid, and of other contrasts and kinds;—especially consisting of attainable and unattainable, the latter in immensely greater quantities for most pigs.

2. Moral evil is unattainability of Pig's-wash; moral good, attainability of ditto.

Yet when one has gone so far in dispraise of *Latter-Day Pamphlets*, there is still another word to be said. The problems adumbrated, rather than confronted, in them are those which most vitally concern us today: the power of the State, direction of labour, the use of coercion to obtain the better organization of society: and to hardly one of Carlyle's contemporaries did these seem to be serious problems at all. Most of the Victorian intellectuals, and the Edwardian social reformers who followed them, were practical men where Carlyle was wholly impractical. Yet which is nearer the world we live in today, the abstract attempts to define liberty of a John Stuart Mill or a H. G. Wells, or Carlyle's terse note: "For the rest, I never thought the 'rights of Negroes' worth much discussing, nor the rights of men in any form; the grand point, as I once said, is the *mights* of men,—what portion of their 'rights' they have a chance of getting sorted out, and realised, in this confused world''? And which, again, seems nearer the truth of the world we live in: a liberal and Fabian doctrine of gradual social evolution or Carlyle's catastrophic view that:

> Some remounting,—very temporary remounting,—of the old machine, under new colours and altered forms, will probably ensue soon in most countries . . . and everywhere the old daily life will try to begin again. But there is now no hope that such arrangements can be permanent; that they can be other than poor temporary makeshifts, which, if they try to fancy and make themselves permanent, will be displaced by new explosions, recurring more speedily than last time.

Have not these words some topical interest?

* * * * *

The reception of *Latter-Day Pamphlets* was almost wholly unfriendly. If anything had been needed to make Mill break finally with Carlyle this assault on most of his dearest beliefs would have done it; he attacked the first pamphlet vigorously on its appearance, and when next the two men met Mill deliberately averted his head. Among the reviews Mill's voice was one in a chorus of astonishment and indignation: *Punch*, the most friendly to Carlyle of the London periodicals, brought him up for trial on a charge of injuring his reputation. Mazzini was estranged, and such liberal friends as Forster were distressed and surprised.

Carlyle expressed his amusement at this reaction, and also said that he never read anything written about him in reviews; but there is little doubt that he was both surprised and disconcerted by the personal unfriendliness he had aroused. He had originally planned a series of twelve pamphlets, but stopped short at eight: the sudden death of Peel, through a fall from his horse, when the eighth pamphlet was being written, destroyed his illusions of any practical result coming from their publication. It is barely possible that if Peel had lived Carlyle might have entered Parliament as permanent official to Lord Ashburton in the Ministry of Education—Ashburton, as Bingham Baring, had been a member of Peel's administration in 1835.

We may be certain that he would not have stayed there long; nevertheless his disappointment at the failure of this first, and last, attempt to face the contemporary situation in practical terms, was still considerable. It is even possible that he might have been a success in this particular official position; for in his attitude towards libraries, and public education generally, he showed throughout his life great interest and tolerance. When he was examined in 1849 by the Commissioners appointed to enquire into the administration of the British Museum he suggested the provision of public libraries in every county, and stressed the importance of issuing a printed catalogue of the Museum's books, which at that time were in chaos. His evidence on the arrangement of books, the choice of books, and suitable reading conditions, is admirably concise and clear.

The death of Peel put an end to such possibilities, and left merely a cantankerous prophet fulminating against the society that, in a practical sense, had overlooked him. That is an unfriendly gloss: a friendly one is provided by Froude, who came to Cheyne Row at this time and listened to Carlyle talking about pamphlets which he had left unwritten. "The imagery, the wild play of humour, the immense knowledge always evident in the grotesque forms which it assumed, were in themselves so dazzling and so entertaining, that we lost the use of our own faculties till (the discourse) was over."

CHAPTER SIXTEEN

THE SOUNDPROOF ROOM

We have the misfortune to be people of weak health in this
house; bad sleepers in particular; and exceedingly sensible
in the night hours to disturbances from sound. On your
premises for some time past there is a Cock, by no means
particularly loud or discordant; whose crowing would of
course be indifferent or unsignificant to persons of sound
health and nerves; but, alas, it often enough keeps us un-
willingly awake here, and on the whole gives a degree of
annoyance which, except to the unhealthy, is not easily
conceivable.

If you would have the goodness to remove that small
animal or in any way render him inaudible from midnight
to breakfast time, such charity would work a notable relief
to certain persons here, and be thankfully acknowledged
by them as an act of good neighbourship.

THOMAS CARLYLE to G. Remington, 12 November 1852.

IT WAS IN 1853 that Carlyle set the builders to work upon
an extraordinary plan: the creation of a soundproof room on
the top of his house. Certain repairs and renovations had
already been carried out, including the enlargement of the
first floor library into a library and drawing-room combined;
and nothing less was now proposed than the addition of a new
storey to the house. The soundproof room was to cover the
whole top floor, and was to be rendered impervious to noise
by the construction of a second wall inside the outer one; the
lighting was to be by means of a large skylight.

The enterprise seems a desperate one: but the condition of
Carlyle was desperate also. Sounds of any kind in the night-
time had by now become insupportable to him. The cocks of
his neighbour Remington were suppressed to give him peace;
but equally loud birds replaced them in the gardens of other
neighbours. Organ grinders played under his windows; fire-
works occasionally disturbed him; the commonest of street
noises caused him intense distress. It was the cocks and parrots
of his next door neighbour Ronca that became (after the
suppression of Remington's birds) the chief cause of trouble;
and the cocks, Carlyle said, must be abolished, entirely silenced,

whether the new room was built or not. Should he shoot them, he asked Jane? "But I have no gun, should be unsafe for hitting, and indeed seldom see the wretched animals." One thing was certain, however: "the cocks must either withdraw or die."

It was under such stresses that the soundproof room was planned and built. An enthusiastic friend named John Chorley superintended the operation, running furiously up and down ladders to instruct the Irish labourers in their work. According to one account there was a strike of building workers at the time, so that inferior workmen were engaged: one of them, inferior or not, came crashing down into Carlyle's bedroom in a vortex of old laths, lime and dust, while another fell in Jane's room within a yard of her head. After a little Carlyle escaped to Addiscombe; when he returned the soundproof room had been built. It was pleasant, large, well-ventilated; the light in it was superb; but, alas, the cocks and macaw of Ronca were still plainly audible. The Carlyles escaped again, this time together, to the Grange: there Jane suggested that they should rent Ronca's house and let it stand empty and noiseless. "What is forty or fortyfive pounds a year, to saving one's life and sanity?" She returned to London accordingly, made a present of five pounds to Ronca and bound him legally "never to keep, or allow to be kept, fowls, or macaw, or other nuisance on their premises." The victory accomplished, she went to bed immediately with a nervous headache.

This is comedy: but the life in which such incidents assumed a large part was not at all comic. The three years since the completion of *Latter-Day Pamphlets* had seen the publication only of *The Life of John Sterling*: a book remarkable for the sympathy and tenderness which Carlyle found it in his heart to show the memory of his hesitant theological friend. Of Sterling we do not gather, as we do in reading contemporary accounts of Charles Buller, the impression of a greatly gifted mind, nor do his prose or poetic remains give assurance, or even promise, of high talent. Something in him more than discipleship, we must believe, attracted Carlyle; but what it was this lucent and delightful biography, brilliant particularly in its picture of old Edward Sterling and in the account of Coleridge at Highgate Hill, leaves still uncertain. *The Life of John Sterling* was written quickly and easily, and published in 1851. Since that time Carlyle had been meditating, and making researches for, a book about Frederick the Great.

The decision to deal with the life and times of such a subject was not made without much disturbance of mind: nor, during the thirteen years of working on this enterprise was he ever wholly reconciled to the subject itself, or to the fact that he was dealing with it. At certain moments he persuaded himself that Frederick was truly a type of hero—and he had ceased to be interested in anything but heroes. At others, the whole enterprise appeared absurd. Looking at the "fiercely shrivelled" plaster cast of Frederick's face he saw "The face of a lean lion, or else partly, alas! of a ditto *cat!* The lips are thin, and closed like pincers; a face that never yielded,—not the beautifullest kind of face". The see-saw of approval and distaste lasted for years: if one were to count up all the occasions in Carlyle's journals and letters when, within a few days, he expressed contradictory opinions about the worthiness of his subject, they would number certainly dozens, perhaps hundreds. The book became for him at once a refuge and a torment: buried in it he could forget the uneasy tangle of his married life, and was able to pay less and less attention to contemporary events; a torment because he was all the time aware that immersion in the affairs of Frederick was in an obscure way a betrayal of that Carlyle who had written *The French Revolution*, and who had wished nothing more than to be immersed in the destructive element of the age. As a protection against such thoughts he exploded more and more often in great bursts of irrational violence against the stupidity of his contemporaries, who failed to realize mankind's need for an autocratic ruler; as a cloak for his feelings of guilt about Jane he engaged in an examination of Frederick's life and thoughts admirable in its thoroughness but fantastic in its intensity: and all the while he cried out at the horrors of the task he had voluntarily undertaken and berated himself for self-pity.

In the late summer of 1852 he went to Germany for a visit which, to others, would have been a pleasure trip: but to Carlyle the thought of the project was frightful, and its execution hardly endurable. He was accompanied, from Rotterdam onwards, by Joseph Neuberg, a German of Jewish origin, who had written an enthusiastic letter to Carlyle as long ago as 1839, but was introduced to Cheyne Row by Emerson nine years later. Among other unamiable features that had developed in Carlyle's nature during the past few years was a detestation of most things Jewish, based originally perhaps on his distaste for Judaic Christianity, developed by the political success of Disraeli, and confirmed by what he heard of Jewish speculation and business acumen. Like many who dislike what they imagine to be the nature of Jews in general, however, Carlyle had no objection to them in particular; and Neuberg quickly became, and remained until his death in 1867 Carlyle's friend, assistant-researcher and volunteer amanuensis. Neuberg needed, and apparently possessed, great patience and tolerance: for on this German trip, which included visits to many large German cities and a stay of nine days in Berlin, Carlyle's spirits were very low. From Rotterdam, where snoring neighbours and "the most industrious *cocks* I ever heard" rendered sleep impossible, to his return seven weeks later, the whole thing was "a biliary adventure". He tried to console himself with the thought that it had also been an indispensable one.

At Bonn University they got a number of books to study, and Neuberg recommended a spa called Roland's Eck for a quiet night's rest: but from Roland's Eck, when reached, Carlyle turned with horror at its noisiness. Next day Neuberg found accommodation in a small village at the foot of the Sieben Gebirge mountains. "With shuddering reluctance", Carlyle consented to try it. The result was not happy. He slept in "a bed more like a butcher's tray or a big washing-tub than a bed, with pillows shaped like a wedge three feet broad, and a deep pit in the middle of the body." Outside there was street gossip until nearly midnight, peals of church bells, a watchman's horn, "and a general Sanhedrim apparently of all the cats and dogs of nature." Nevertheless he got three hours' sleep, smoked his pipe out of the window and, he assured Jane, "was not so unhappy at all". At Ems things were better, and he enjoyed and admired the Rhine; at Frankfurt he wrote his name in a book in Goethe's room, and at Eisenach climbed the short stair of worn stone leading to the room where Luther lived, and kissed the oak table where he had worked on his translation of the Bible. At Weimar he stood by the graves of Goethe and Schiller and dined at the Grand Ducal Palace. By this time he had "renounced the hope of any considerable sleep in Germany" and had abandoned the idea of serious work. Nevertheless he went on to see Lobositz, the first battlefield of Frederick in the Seven Years' War, and paid his visit to Berlin. There he was much lionized, although the Prussian historians and men of letters gave him no particular encouragement to write

Frederick's life. Nor did Carlyle, at the end of his visit, require much damping. "Every new German *Book* I read about him, my feeling is, All up with Fritz", he wrote to his sister. But this feeling was all one with his considered view of the visit. "It was a journey done as in some shirt of Nessus; misery and dyspeptic degradation, inflammation, and insomnia tracking every step of me . . . Neuberg, I ought to record here and everywhere, was the kindest, best-tempered, most assiduous of friends and helpers."

*   *   *   *   *

In one of her letters Jane told her cousin Helen Welsh, half-jokingly, the kind of woman Carlyle should have married: " 'A strong-minded woman' . . . with a perfectly sound liver, plenty of *solid fat*, and mirth and good-humour world without end." There was, however, "no altering of all that now—nothing to be done but make the best of it—which I candidly confess I am far from doing." She spoke a true word: for although one can only speculate as to what effect a placid and good-tempered woman might have had on Carlyle's temperament, there is no doubt that Jane's neurotic sensibility played a part in exaggerating his hypochondria. Perhaps it was less necessary for Carlyle to have a wife who consistently respected and understood his genius than one who occasionally reminded him that in the ordinary affairs of life he was entitled to no more, and no less, consideration than other men.

The years had not dealt lightly with Jane, mentally or physically. In the gaunt, sunken-cheeked woman with deepset anguished eyes who looks out at us from a photograph of this period, hardly anything is left of the vivacious Jeannie Welsh or of the softly pretty woman painted by Lawrence in 1838; and all the brilliant vivacity, the bright spirit, the gay intelligence, of Jeannie Welsh had somehow turned sour. She developed an intense interest in crimes of violence, and noted in her journal the cases of a workman suffocated in a sewer, of a boy killed by a waggon crashing over his head, and of a woman who drowned one of her children in the Thames; she obtained photographs of several murderers and pasted them into her album. Her interest in mad people had always been very marked; now she feared at times that she was losing her senses, and made Carlyle promise that, if ever she should do so, he would not send her away. The number of her pets multiplied, and to Nero was added at various times cats, canaries, hedgehogs and a leech.

The dissatisfaction she felt, unnameable and unassuageable, embraced every aspect of her life. If she was aware of Carlyle's shortcomings, she was as keenly conscious of her own. "God knows how gladly I would be sweet-tempered and cheerful-hearted, and all that sort of thing for your single sake, if my temper were not soured and my heart saddened beyond my own power to mend them", she wrote to him in 1850. Carlyle at this time was returning from a long visit to Scotland; he spent three days at Keswick and then went to stay with friends at Coniston. He was driven by the demon noise to return to Chelsea suddenly, and by express train. Jane was paying a visit to the Grange and was deeply distressed that, for the first time since their marriage, she was not at home to receive him. He would no doubt prefer solitude, she bitterly (and inaccurately) reflected, and if she returned home by the next train she would take away more from his comfort than she added to it. "Certainly, this is the best school that the like of me was ever put to for getting cured of every particle of the 'finer sensi-bilities'." Why should she stay at the Grange, where nobody cared for her, when at Cheyne Row there was still somebody who cared for her a little? The Ashburtons, of course, were not to blame: and yet it is plain that she wanted to blame them.

The visits to the Grange and Bath House, to Alverstoke and Addiscombe, had by no means ceased; nor should it be imagined that Jane was averse to accepting invitations. She could never quite bring herself to dislike, or do other than respect, Lady Harriet; and in general both she and Carlyle, neither of them easy guests, were treated with great courtesy and consideration: although it is true that there was an occasion when Lady Harriet decided that her guest was a hypo-chondriac, who must be treated by stern measures, and instructed the housemaid to take away the coals so that Jane could not light a fire in her bedroom, gave her hock for dinner (which Jane believed made her ill), and denied her the two glasses of Madeira which was the current prescription of Doctor John. Carlyle's secret correspondence with Lady Harriet continued: he wrote to her letters which, indeed, contain nothing more compromising, in a narrow sense, than ex-travagant and quite plainly unsensual comparisons and similes. She was a Beautiful Lady and he was the Beast, "the Beast

undeliverable?"; he confided in her, almost as much as in
Jane, his hopes and doubts in relation to Frederick; and he was
obliged to remind her, upon more than one occasion, that his
letters must be regarded as "not received". This cautious
deception sometimes had curious results: in the autumn of 1851,
when Carlyle had decided that it would be wise on Jane's
account not to accept a Christmas invitation to the Grange,
Jane told him that she had accepted on behalf of them both.
"I was obliged to *deny*, on the spur of the moment, that I
wished to go or could go, which indeed is not far from the
truth, so fatally am I situated just now. For reasons that my
noble Lady understands too well . . ." Jane, at the same time,
mentioning the invitation to Doctor John, wrote that "If I
refuse this time . . . she will quarrel with me outright . . . and
as quarrelling with her would involve quarrelling with Mr. C
also, it is not a thing to be done lightly."

The invitation was accepted; Jane went to the Grange early
in December, and Carlyle followed a few days later. On this
occasion Lady Harriet behaved with much tact, and the party
was a happy one. Jane helped Lady Harriet and her mother the
Countess of Sandwich to dress the dolls for the Christmas
tree. Presents were distributed from the tree, which was
decorated with such inscriptions as "God Save the Queen" and
"Long live Lord and Lady Ashburton", to fortyeight children
who came with their mothers. Lady Ashburton distributed the
presents, saying something witty with each; and when she
called "Thomas Carlyle—the Scholar", gave him a map of
the world in pieces, with the words, "*There* is a map of the
world for *you*—see that you put it all together and make the
pieces fit." Carlyle, Jane noted, looked as enchanted as any
little boy or girl among them. It was all very fine: but she
could not help reflecting that the fortyeight presents had cost
only two pounds twelve and sixpence, an exercise of economy
which seemed to her incomprehensible in somebody with an
income of £40,000 a year. "I should have liked each child to
have got at least *a frock* given it—when one was going to look
munificent. But everyone has his own notions on spending
money."

Apart from these joint visits to the Ashburtons the Carlyles
went away more and more frequently on visits, generally
separately. Carlyle paid a yearly visit to Scotsbrig, where at
long intervals he placed his order to an Ecclefechan tailor for

six pairs of trousers and three or four coats and vests; and these visits usually included several other calls paid as far away as South Wales, so that they involved his absence from Cheyne Row for several weeks. In 1851 he went for a few days to Paris with the Brownings: he was annoyed by French literary men and saddened by the French actors' "wretched mockeries upon marriage" and their "canine libertinage and soulless grinning over all that is beautiful and pious in human relations." Jane went to see Geraldine Jewsbury and her brother at Manchester, or the Paulets at Seaforth, or her cousins at Liverpool; and once she had conquered her aversion to visiting Scotland she went there again and again. Reading the accounts of the journeys made by these two uncommonly bad travellers one gets an impression of a man and a woman trying desperately to escape, not so much from each other as from the pattern of their own lives.

About such visits there was still some comedy. Doctor John, now in his early fifties, had after many hesitations married a widow (who after only a year of marriage died in childbirth, leaving him with three stepsons); and Jane paid them a visit at their home in Moffat. Here she was kept awake, she triumphantly told Carlyle, by—a hyaena—"yes, upon my honour". On her arrival a caravan of wild beasts was pitched in front of the house, and during the night it was her impression that the lion roared: but John said, "No, it was only the hyaena." On this visit she made the ascent of a precipitous hill called the Grey-Mare's Tail, accompanied by the Doctor. She had taken a double dose of morphia on the previous night, and when some way up was overcome by vertigo. The Doctor, who had reached the top of the hill, clambered down and reached her. "Don't give way to panic", he said. "I will stand between you and everything short of death." She aimed to reach the bed of a torrent, but he called out that if she got among the stones she would "roll to perdition". Thus encouraged, she reached the bottom of the hill, her face "purple all over, with a large black spot under each eye."

From Moffat Jane went to pay her first visit to Scotsbrig for many years; there was news that Carlyle's mother, now in her eighties and very feeble, was near to death. When she heard that Jane was coming, the indomitable old woman insisted on rising from her bed and being dressed, so that she could receive her daughter-in-law out of doors. Jane noted with pleasure that her mother-in-law "chewed some nice mutton-chop" and that her faculties were still perfectly clear. Soon after Jane's arrival Margaret Carlyle took to bed again, and lay in a cold deathlike coma that seemed to presage the end: but, miraculously, she recovered. Within a few days Jane was reporting to Carlyle that his mother had slept a fine natural *pluffing* sleep until one o'clock in the morning, when she woke and asked for porridge; then she slept till six, woke again and said that they should tell the doctor "no to come back the-day; for 'atwell she wasna needing him." Jane attributed the recovery partly to Mrs. Carlyle's abandonment of alcohol; on one day, John told her placidly, he had given his mother a bottle of Greek wine, a quarter of a bottle of a whisky 25 over proof, and a tumbler of porter. There was some argument between John and Jane, and as a result of it she left Scotsbrig suddenly.

She wept, she told her husband, all the way out of Scotland, as far as Carlisle, for love of her country and despair at the departed years. At Liverpool she was welcomed by her uncle and cousins, but was unable to sleep; at three in the morning she took two morphia pills, and spent the next day between retching and fainting. Here she received her birthday present from Carlyle, the rather curious gift of a coloured lithograph showing a wife shaving her husband; while holding his nose in her left hand and a razor in her right, she is chatting to a visitor. The endorsement read: "To my dear Jeannie, (14th July, 1853) from her ever-affectionate T. Carlyle (dealer in emblems)."

Such visits and such journeys imposed an almost intolerable strain upon her nervous system: which, soon after her return to Chelsea, was subjected to some shattering blows. Within a few days of coming back she heard from her cousin Helen of her uncle's death; a little more than two months later, just after her triumphant exorcism of the fowls, she received the news that Helen also was dead. Carlyle, who had shown a strange reluctance to visit his mother, suddenly decided just before Christmas to leave the festivities at the Grange and go to Scotsbrig: he arrived to find her manifestly near death. On Christmas Eve she was in pain, and John gave her half a dose of laudanum; she recognized her eldest son and bade him good night, saying "I'm muckle obleeged t'ye." Those were her last words. She died on Christmas Day.

So ended the year 1853, with Jane unhappy at Chelsea and Carlyle brooding at Scotsbrig, noting in his journal:

My dear old mother is gone from me, and in the winter of the year, confusedly under darkness of weather and of mind, the stern final epoch—*epoch of old age*—is beginning to unfold itself for me.

CHAPTER SEVENTEEN

THE EPOCH OF OLD AGE

Alone this evening. Lady A. in town again; and Mr. C.
of course at Bath House.
> When I think of what I is
> And what I used to was,
> I gin to think I've sold myself
> For very little cas.

JANE WELSH CARLYLE: Journal, 5 November 1855.

'Oh', he often said to me after she was gone, 'if I could
but see her for five minutes to assure her that I had really
cared for her throughout all that! But she never knew it, she
never knew it.'

J. A. FROUDE: Note in *Letters and
Memorials of Jane Welsh Carlyle.*

HE WAS A VERY famous man, respécted even by those
who differed from him utterly: and the reason for his fame lay
less in what he had written, much though that was regarded,
than in what he was. Fame, and comparative affluence, had
left his way of life in most things unaltered; he had no thought
of moving into fashionable London, or of wearing fashionable
clothes. A reproachful granite figure, he stood with finger
outstretched in scornful accusation of a society ready to confuse
spiritual health and material well-being; to such a society he
was a kind of compensation, a menacing yet somehow comfort-
ing assurance that a scale of moral values existed which could
be respected in words, even if it was ignored in practice.
Emerson noted acutely that society kept the prophet "like a
sort of portable cathedral-bell, which they like to produce in
companies where he is unknown, and set a-swinging." When the
bell deafeningly exhorted all those within hearing to leave their
false economic gods and worship at the true heroic shrine,
those who had set it swinging were delighted. By a few the
bell's clamour was taken seriously: but those who stopped their
ears to its sound were still pleased to know of its existence. By
his middle fifties Carlyle was a prophet with honour throughout the whole of Britain.

Such a position had the effect of making him exaggerate, unconsciously, a personality already sufficiently emphatic. The regular attendants at Cheyne Row were now mostly impressionable young men who had lost their way in the world, like the Manchester journalist Francis Espinasse or the young poet and Customs official William Allingham; with one or two exceptions, like Froude and Clough, their intellectual level was much below that of Carlyle's associates in the days when he had been writing *The French Revolution*. And it was impossible now to talk to the prophet upon anything like equal terms: he was determined to inform, instruct and enlighten. Herbert Spencer, after two or three visits, decided that there was little point in seeing Carlyle because it was impossible to reason with him. Carlyle's verdict on Spencer had perhaps more reference to their argument than to any factual assessment of Spencer's mind. "An immeasurable ass", he said tersely. Once, when bored by conversation with Espinasse, he gave the young man an account of the origin of the Arabic numerals from 2 to 9 "by the addition of strokes and curves to the perpendicular straight line which denotes the primitive numeral 1." If the company appeared dull he would recite "in impressive mono-tone" some favourite passage of poetry, sometimes with a word or phrase incorrect.

His remarks about art were now those of a self-satisfied Philistine. His earlier doubts about the validity of literary art, in the sense of a formal pattern consciously imposed upon material, had extended and changed. Now, at an intemperate moment, he said curtly to Espinasse that his attempts to popu-larize German literature had only increased contemporary confusion; it was not literature at all, he often implied and sometimes said, that was wanted. Towards the graphic arts he was more openly contemptuous. "Ah, well, I can make nothing of artists, nor of their work either", he said to William Bell Scott and the pre-Raphaelite Thomas Woolner. "Empty as other folks' kettles are, artists' kettles are emptier, and good for nothing but tying to the tails of mad dogs." This was said, again, at one of those moments when Carlyle had cast to the winds the tolerance which he did not possess: but at the best his view of art was now ordered wholly by its usefulness—a word which he interpreted in the most limited sense. He visited Holman Hunt's studio with Jane, and praised highly some of the pictures; but he burst into a rich flow of invective, very skilfully set down by Hunt, at sight of "The Light of the World", which he called "a poor misshaped presentation of the noblest, the brotherliest, and the most heroic-minded Being that ever walked God's earth." Hunt rashly tried to argue, but the broad Scotch voice rose almost to a scream and Jane, standing behind Carlyle, put up an emphatic finger and shook her head while the sage spoke in passionately vituperative tones of all paintings of Christ except those of Dürer.

Among the most faithful chroniclers of Carlyle's conversation at this time was William Knighton, an Anglo-Indian who for several months spent one evening a week at Cheyne Row: the Boswellian dialogues he set down in simple admiration disclose a mixture of peevishness and prejudice on the part of their subject, much advanced even since the tour in Ireland with Duffy. Words set down in print are, of course, misleading, especially in relation to such a man as Carlyle: they omit the occasional playful consciousness of absurdity, the rich enjoyment of his own rhetoric, the repetitions and exaggerations that made servants leave the room because they were unable to contain their laughter. Yet when we have made all the allowance we can for the Carlylean magic, the impression left by these informal conversations is still that of Thersites railing at a world which has not accepted his prescriptions for reform.

The most contemptible man of the day, Carlyle told Knighton, was a literary man; an honest shoeblack was to be preferred to him. The literary reviews had been busy with him, had they? "I never read them. I have the most utter contempt and abhorrence for the literary *canaille* of the day." There was no hope for literary men, there was no hope for the French, there was no hope even for the English unless they abandoned writing and talking, recognized that they were a superior race, and went back to *doing*. The best of England, better by far than the talkers and writers, was the aristocracy: but still there was little hope, in England or in Europe, in the United States or in Australia. The whole civilized world would be overcome by barbarians, as the Roman world had been; and this was a conclusion for which he showed some relish. "History does not exactly reproduce itself, but we want a superior race, to be got somewhere and somehow—a race of God-fearing, honest, sincere men."

Most of the great public enterprises of the day Carlyle interpreted as mere symbols of man's stupidity and the wrath to come. The 1851 exhibition he regarded as a well-got-up piece of nonsense; and to Herbert Spencer, in the midst of a long tirade against the "horrible, abominable state of things", he expressed his indignation at the exposure to the public of such disgusting brutes as the monkeys at the Zoological Gardens. He admired the Crystal Palace, however, saying that it "surpassed in beauty of effect and arrangement all the edifices I have ever seen or read of, except in the Arabian Tales." About this time he gave his support to a Peace Congress, with an expression of hope that they would "not too much extinguish the wrath that dwells, as a natural element, in all Adam's posterity." When the Crimean War came in 1854 he laid the blame for it, typically, on "the idle population of editors, &c."

In the eighteen fifties his appearance was much changed by the fact that he ceased to use a razor. This was the work of Lord Ashburton, who had extracted from Carlyle a promise that if he adopted a beard Carlyle would grow one also. Ashburton reinforced the reminder of his promise by taking away Carlyle's razors. Carlyle complained that he felt as if he had a gorse common on his chin, but soon became reconciled to the beard and moustaches that made him look, Jane said, like an escaped maniac. By ceasing to shave he believed that he saved half an hour a day, but according to her he simply spent this time "wandering about the house, bemoaning what's amiss in the Universe."

*　　*　　*　　*　　*

A more and more remarkable difference appears between the public and the private life of the Carlyles as the years go by. The figure presented by Carlyle to the great mass who did not know him, and even to many who did, was the simple one of a sage exuding, not sweetness perhaps, but a warm genial light: in writing to those, and they were many, who asked his advice on questions that ranged from the existence of hell to advice about books to read, he showed a judicial calm and kindness rarely apparent except on such occasions; in helping to preserve the London Library from an attempt by Gladstone to force through an unsuitable nominee of his own as secretary he showed a surprising skill in lobbying against Gladstone's candidate.

And Jane's correspondence lost nothing of its percipience and vigour: she could still enliven the trivial incidents of domestic days with a wit incomparable in its kind. She could still address to Carlyle the "Budget of a Femme Incomprise" in which, with mingled humour and sharpness, she described the difficulty she had in managing the house on the money given to her ("You don't understand why the allowance which sufficed in former years no longer suffices? That is what I would explain to the Noble Lord if he would but—what shall I say? —*keep his temper.*") Her narrative, punctuated by cries of "Question, question" and "Be brief", told in detail the story of a more expensive servant, the cost of having gas and water laid on, increased taxation and the rising cost of living ("Candles are *riz* . . . Bacon is 2d a pound dearer; soap ditto; potatoes, at the cheapest, a penny a pound, instead of three pounds for 2d. Who could imagine that at the year's end that makes a difference of 15s 6d on one's mere potatoes?") Beneath the humour of this long, curious document, bitterness is hidden, not very deep down: "You asked me at last money row, with withering sarcasm, 'had I the slightest idea what amount of money would *satisfy me*. Was I wanting £50 more; or forty, or thirty? Was there any conceivable sum of money that could put an end to my eternal botheration?' I will answer the question as if it had been asked practically and kindly." She ended by asking for an extra £29 a year, divided into quarterly payments. Where was the money to come from? Such a question was surely unnecessary, for Carlyle had some £2,000 lying in the bank at Dumfries; but she was determined not to be accused of increasing expenditure, and among other economies she suggested that he should give her no Christmas or New Year present, and that her dress allowance of £25 a year should be cut down to £15.

Carlyle recognized the humour of this budget. At the foot of the last page he wrote:

> Excellent, my dear Goody, thriftiest, wittiest, and cleverest of women. I will set thee up again to a certainty, and thy £30 more shall be granted, thy bits of debts paid, and thy will be done.

But is it possible that he was really unaware of his wife's increasing bitterness, of the desperate loneliness in the private life behind the public façade? That is hard to believe: yet all the evidence suggests that it was so. He did not even notice the worn, sad gaze that made Woolner unhappy to look at her, and induced another new acquaintance to declare that she had the patiently hopeless look of a mourner standing by an unclosed grave. When we look at the private thoughts of Carlyle and Jane, as they are put down in their journals, the picture is that of a controlled misery upon his side and a thwarted bitterness upon hers, which must make the primary emotion in thinking about them pity rather than blame. Only those insensitive of the love between them can imagine that he ever intended to wound her feelings by neglect; or that Jane was not well aware of the part her own sourness and poor spirits played in driving him away from her into the almost equally metaphorical arms of Frederick the Great and Lady Harriet.

Upstairs in the soundproof room Carlyle shut away not only sound, but as far as possible the whole uncomfortable world of reality. He laboured desperately to write; his ostensible subject was Frederick, his real one the dissatisfied endeavour to explain once more the whole unhappy world that had made him a Puritan, that had somehow damaged his relations with the woman he loved, that had made him long for the happiness his upbringing taught him to despise. Miserably he put down in his journal his feeling of loneliness; his mind turned continually to the past. "On the whole I have a strange interior *tomb* life, and dwell in secret among scenes and contemplations which I do not speak of to anybody." In dreams he sometimes saw waste and desolate scenes gathered from Craigenputtock, "but tenfold *intensated*"; at others nightmare shapes came round him, including Frederick the Great and other figures out of history. Lady Harriet also appeared, not horrible but "brightly beautiful, good and spirit-like, as you have always seemed to me".

For some months after his mother's death Carlyle paid very few visits; in 1855 he went to stay with Edward Fitzgerald in Suffolk, and was delighted by Aldeburgh. He asked Jane to come there, but she had made an expedition of her own to Brighton, and thence to the little village of Rottingdean. "Is it always as quiet as this?" she asked the maid at a hotel, who replied that it was almost too quiet. And here at Rottingdean was a small cottage, which she had "almost committed" herself to take for a year at £12, but hesitated for fear that he might not like it. She was perfectly right. They set out one morning to look at it, but turned back at London Bridge because it was a wet day. One feels that at this time it was enough that one of them should express a liking, for the other to reject it. The Ashburtons had offered Addiscombe to them for the remainder of the summer, and to Addiscombe they went, Carlyle on horseback and Jane by rail; but there, in spite of the dead silence, Jane could not sleep. She returned to London and came down only on odd days to Addiscombe: a little later Carlyle was writing to Lady Harriet that he had had "24 of the strangest beneficent Days here" and that he must have made tea fortyeight times in "your little fairy teapot (the red tile-china saucy little teapot)", and Jane was at work on a melancholy little journal of her own.

She designed this journal to be about "what Mr. Carlyle calls the facts of things", believing what he had taught her, that "Your journal all about feelings aggravates whatever is morbid in you." This philosophical introduction was cut short by Carlyle's return from Bath House:

That eternal Bath House. I wonder how many thousand miles Mr. C has walked between there and here, putting it all together; setting up always another milestone and another betwixt himself and me. Oh, good gracious! when I first noticed that heavy yellow house without knowing, or caring to know, who it belonged to, how far I was from dreaming that through years and years I should carry every stone's weight of it on my heart.

"About feelings already", she wryly noted, and indeed the journal is filled with the feelings which rarely, and perhaps never, found utterance. There are other things in the journal too—a brilliant description of her visit on Carlyle's behalf to the Tax Commissioners, and amusing remarks occasioned by such things as a burst cistern; but these are almost incidental to the curt unreasonable little notes of personal anguish, written often with high literary art, that spot almost every page. She wrote with bitterness of the trivial things that she had done a hundred times, and gladly, in the past:

The evening devoted to mending Mr. C's trowsers among other things! "Being an only child", I never "wished" to sew men's trowsers—no, never!

She expressed again her fear of madness:

They must be comfortable people who have leisure to think about going to Heaven! My most constant and pressing anxiety is to keep out of Bedlam! That's all!

Preparations for one of those visits to the Grange which she, like Carlyle, looked forward to, and back on, with mingled pleasure and distaste, appeared intolerable:

> To have to care for my dress at this time of day more than I ever did when young and pretty and happy (God bless me, to think that I was once all that!) on penalty of being regarded as a blot on the Grange gold and azure, is really too bad. *Ach Gott!* If we had been left in the sphere of life we belong to, how much better it would have been for us in many ways!

To grow old gracefully one must allow the past to remain buried, not rootling too often among old memories, nor looking too keenly at withered neck and wrinkled skin, nor comparing grim maturity with a sparkling youth that is generally half imaginary. This gift of forgetfulness Jane possessed even less than her husband: she might tell herself that looking back was not intended by nature or our eyes would not be set as they are in our faces; but she looked back just the same, and seeing what had been made of life by that spirited Jeannie Welsh whom Carlyle had called a genius, she could not forbear to weep. When Carlyle told her that he had met the unlikeliest man in London in the street, she named him instantly: George Rennie, returned from his post as Governor of the Falkland Islands. When she met this former lover her "bright, whole hearted impulsive youth seemed conjured back by his hearty embrace." But not for long. When Mrs. Rennie insisted that they should go to dine Jane remembered, among the clatter of knives and forks and the babble of conversation, that the gentlemanly iron grey man who offered her roast duck might have been her husband.

She was haunted by the past, afraid of the future, and constantly ill: yet it would be a mistake to accept her journal quite at its face value, or to forget such notes in it as: "Last week I was all for dying; this week all for Ball dresses." A mistake to forget, too, what was written by Geraldine Jewsbury, who had come in 1854 to live two streets away from Jane and was, in spite of all indiscretions, her greatest friend:

> Oh, my dear, if you and I are drowned, or die, what would become of us if any superior person were to go and write our 'life and errors'? what a precious mess a 'truthful person' would go and make of us, and how very different to what we really are or were.

That error of over-truthfulness one endeavours not to make: but was not Geraldine herself in error when she supposed the existence of some "reality" apart from the visible pattern of what we think and do?

* * * * *

While Jane wrote in her journal Carlyle worked upstairs, with ever-increasing self-absorption, at a task which became more difficult, obscure and unsatisfactory, the more it was prolonged. The trouble he almost always found in writing was caused less by anything inherently intractable in his subjects than by the complex personal pressures that operated as soon as he tried to write. From the appalling tangle of sometimes unuttered generosities and often unadmitted doubts in his own nature he tried, inevitably without complete success, to break free in literature. The history of Frederick the Great was not intrinsically more difficult to handle than that of Cromwell or of the French Revolution; but the dissatisfied and lonely, yet still burningly energetic, man of genius had to comprehend in it all his old Radical enthusiasm and his desire to express human history in terms of dictatorial heroes, his mingled eagerness for and revulsion from violent action, the appeal to a just, ruthless God and the occasional doubt that any such God existed, and all the personal sins of omission and commission that festered where they had been stuffed away at the back of his mind. It has been said that a novelist sufficiently percipient and sympathetic could recreate the whole history of mankind in a book which ostensibly described nothing more than a man walking down a street; for Carlyle, similarly, it became necessary to write a history of Europe in the eighteenth century, partly to explain Frederick, but chiefly to justify his own attitude to the world.

His habits of work were now those, as some would say, of a

business man; others would call them those of a compulsive neurotic: perhaps the two descriptions are not mutually exclusive. He rose at an hour that varied with his capacity for sleep, but was never later than seven. A sponge bath in his bedroom was followed by a walk: he was home for breakfast at eight. A smoke after breakfast, and then he repaired to the soundproof room, where he remained until 2 o'clock. The maid sometimes brought up a few spoonfuls of strong beef tea or milk pudding during the morning; later this was replaced by a morning cup of mixed coffee and castor oil. At 2 o'clock he took exercise, either walking, or riding on the bay horse Fritz, bought in 1850, which was his companion for several years. Dinner at 5 or 6 o'clock was followed by a short sleep, conversation with visitors, or reading. This pattern was invariable while the Carlyles were at Cheyne Row; it was broken, of course, when they paid visits. On the whole most men of letters would not call such a day an unduly hard one: if Carlyle cried out continually under such a régime, as he did, it was because of his conviction that this, like all other, literary work was in reality not worth doing.

He cried out certainly, loud and long: in his journals, in letters to his family and friends and Lady Harriet and, we may be sure, to Jane. He complained that Frederick was an unfortunate subject; he exhorted himself on numerous occasions to awake and arise, and then lamented that he had to do "most mournful, dreary, undoable work"; he was unable to find a genuine portrait, something upon which he much relied. At times he seemed to believe that there was something heroic in Frederick, but generally the elements of any kind of book on him seemed "scattered, disorganised, as if in a thick viscous chaotic ocean, ocean illimitable in all its three dimensions", and it was possible only to swim and sprawl towards an uncertain end.

In such swimming and sprawling he did not lack assistants. Joseph Neuberg worked indefatigably for years on the Frederick book, his chief function being to assuage Carlyle's ever-increasing thirst for verifiable historical facts. For three months Neuberg worked in the State-Paper Office extracting useful material; and for years he made excerpts and abstracts from all kinds of documents, checked and discovered dates, collated material, and summarized the eighteenth century German newspapers which Carlyle used as a comic chorus. Neuberg was the chief assistant, but not the only one. At the end of

1856 a young collector on the Chelsea steamers named Henry Larkin suggested that he should provide indexes for the collected edition of Carlyle's works then announced. The offer was accepted (it is an offer which, surely, throws a strange light upon the character of the man who made it); the indexes were pronounced masterly, and Larkin's aid was extended to the book on Frederick. Carlyle said later that he did "all manner of maps, indexes, summaries, copyings, miscellanea of every kind, in a way not to be surpassed for completeness, ingenuity, patience, exactitude, and total and continual absence of fuss."

In spite of this praise, which was accompanied by one gift of £100 and several of £50, Larkin did not emerge quite unscathed from the furnace of Cheyne Row. Working on the maps of battlefields he found a task as repugnant as the indexing had been pleasurable: and to be shut up with Carlyle when he was working the young man declared to be misery. Moreover, Larkin was an earnest Christian: when he sent to Cheyne Row a magazine article he had written on poetry as the embodiment of the Christian ideal, Carlyle returned it "with a serious, almost a grieved look, but without a word of comment", and Jane was equally silent, although she tried afterwards to show him the futility of his ideas. Upon another occasion, when Carlyle first read Mill's *Essay on Liberty*, "he rose angrily from the table with the book in his hand, and gave vent to such a torrent of anathema, glancing at Christianity itself, as filled me with pain and amazement. He addressed himself directly to me, almost as if *I* had written the book, or had sent it to him, or was in some way mixed up with it." Upon the whole, in spite of Carlyle's dignity, "royal graciousness of manner" and richly abundant humour, Larkin preferred Jane as a companion: he noted that Carlyle had very little of that spirit of playfulness which induced Jane one day to bring them both downstairs from work and then hold up before them a piece of paper bearing the words *The First of April*. It should be added, perhaps, that Larkin never heard a harsh word pass between husband and wife.

After some years of working in his spare time for Carlyle Larkin married, and was rash enough to come and live at Number 6, Cheyne Row. Carlyle was delighted to have his assistant so close at hand, and made full use of this fortunate circumstance; he became accustomed to sending across brief notes, which might almost be called commands, inviting

Larkin's attendance. Perhaps Larkin was, upon the whole, pleased when Frederick was done with: but before that time he had moved to Camden Town.

The third of Carlyle's assistants was as raffish as the others were thoroughly respectable. He called himself Frederick Martin, although he had been born in Berlin and was partly Jewish. Like Larkin he wrote to Carlyle, describing his wretched position as a providential schoolteacher with wife and child, and asking encouragement in his purpose of making a living in London. Carlyle characteristically advised Martin to carry on with his work in the provinces; nevertheless the cosmopolitan schoolteacher presented himself at Cheyne Row, received the warm welcome that had been given to many exiles before him, and was engaged on a sparetime copying job at a pound a week. Martin's personal appearance was not prepossessing, and Carlyle may have been disturbed by the drop that depended, it seemed permanently, from his nose: he was allowed to take papers home to copy, and stole a great deal of the original manuscript of the Frederick book, together with much other material later recovered and published (including *The Romance of Wotton Reinfred*) and some hundreds of letters. Carlyle was careless in such matters, and although he missed some papers, never suspected Martin of theft.

With such a considerable volume of assistance it is plain that descriptions given by Carlyle of his agonized burrowing through masses of dead wood had an imaginative rather than a literal truth: he suffered agonies, no doubt, but the root of them lay in his own nature and not in the tedium of research, wherein he very rightly played a largely selective part. He did some research, certainly, and a not intolerable amount of reading; and his eagerness to see genuine portraits of Frederick and others carried him to Windsor Castle, where Lady Harriet had arranged for him to look at the Print Rooms. There he was visited by Prince Albert, "very jolly and handsome in his loose greyish clothes, standing in the door; not advancing till I bowed." They talked for some time about portraits and other things, until "a *domestic* glided in upon us, murmured something, of which I heard 'gone out to the Terrace!' (Queen out, wants you,—he had been in Town all morning)—whereupon, in a minute or two, our Dialogue winding itself up in some tolerable way, Prince Albert (prince of courtesy) bowed himself out, back foremost and with some indistinct mention of 'your *Works*', which did not much affect me; and so ended our interview." Research of such a kind was not unpleasant; and when Carlyle went again to Germany in 1858 after the first two volumes of his history had been published, it was not to undertake research as that word is generally understood, but to look at Frederick's battlefields so that he could gather impressions for some of those extraordinarily vivid and dramatic pictures of battle scenes in which he described with masterly imaginative power the ripe forbidden fruit of action.

*   *   *   *   *

About the relationship of the Carlyles and the Ashburtons as it continued through the years, unchanged and yet always threatening some classical catastrophe, there is something ambiguous and unsatisfactory. The climax of this strange quadrangular relationship was Jane's effort in 1846 to break off relations. She failed: and after the failure there was no drama but, for both Carlyle and Jane, the mere flickering of unsatisfied, and often unacknowledged, hopes and jealousies. Carlyle, who had at least the relief of being able to write his secret letters to Lady Harriet (were they, one wonders, seen by her invariably amiable and complaisant husband?), and who transferred much of his frustration to his book on Frederick, kept his emotions more tightly throttled than Jane: her anger and jealousy and tormented contempt for her own weakness, burst more than once into quickly-quenched flame.

It had become customary for the Carlyles to spend Christmas at the Grange, in the midst of an Ashburton house party. They were never easy guests, for Carlyle either talked himself at immense length or kept (and preferred that others should keep) the gospel of silence; Jane was always on the lookout for slights to her dignity and also told stories which were far too long to be amusing outside her own circle. Not every Christmas went as smoothly as the one when Jane had helped Lady Harriet in dressing dolls; and the party of 1855, which was the last Christmas party given by Lady Harriet, proved particularly unhappy. It began by Jane's declaration that she was being insulted when given a silk dress from the Christmas tree (did she think of her miserable dress allowance?); Lady Harriet, who had chosen this present on the advice of a friend, had to seek out Jane in her room and assure her, to the accompaniment of tears, that no insult had been intended. Then Carlyle, although he had promised to be on his best behaviour, soon showed signs of unrest. In bad moods he was given to making lugubrious philosophical comments about the moon and stars, and it was an unhappy omen when he replied to a remark made on Christmas night that there was a fine moon with the words: "Ay, poor old girl. She's been hanging about this planet off and on for a good number of months now." Any forebodings that may have been felt at this remark were justified when he refused to listen one morning to Tennyson reading his new poem, *Maud*; he was accustomed to go for a walk in the morning, and also to walk accompanied. While the other visitors placed themselves in chairs preparatory to hearing the poet, Carlyle stood in the hall ready for his walk, awaiting a companion. At last two volunteers gallantly rose and joined him. Perhaps they had expected some philosophical instruction: if so they were disappointed, for Carlyle firmly observed his gospel of silence.

A couple of days later Carlyle asked in a loud whisper the name of another guest, and was told that it was Zincke. "Oh, Zincke's the name of him. Well, God give Zincke a good night and may the like of him never cross my path again on this planet for evermore," he said. It was on this visit also that Tyndall, now 35 years old and marked as a coming scientist, sat next to Carlyle at luncheon and tried to convince him of the merits of homeopathic medicine. Tyndall remembered that he would "listen to neither defence nor explanation. He deemed homeopathy a delusion, and those who practised it professionally impostors." His voice was raised to drown all remonstrance, until Jane quieted him with a "Tsh". Carlyle tried more or less successfully, on this occasion as upon others, to restore his spirits by riding: he galloped furiously about the countryside, and recovered so far as to play with much zest the game of Earth, Air and Water, in which he assumed the role of an ass. Nevertheless it was an unhappy party, and when they returned to London he wrote apologetically to Lady Harriet, begging her "with a humble and contrite mind" to "forgive all my sins."

They were forgiven. Within a few days Carlyle was corresponding at length with Lord Ashburton about the science of war as displayed by Frederick, and offering thanks for the Prince Consort's offer, made through Ashburton, to lend Carlyle his copy of Clausewitz's book on the art of war. Over the years the amiable Ashburton was the recipient of many of

Carlyle's ideas, set out on paper at great length and with clear practical intelligence, about such things as the benefit of a National Portrait Gallery: he received them with evident interest, but they were given no effect. The secret correspondence continued without abatement; and in the summer of 1856 the Carlyles were invited to travel up to Scotland in the special railway carriage, called the Queen's Saloon, hired by Ashburton for his wife, who, like Jane, was often mysteriously unwell.

The offer was accepted, but it gave fresh cause of offence to Jane. The Carlyles travelled up with Lady Harriet; but not in the same carriage. The Queen's Saloon was occupied by Lady Harriet alone: the Carlyles travelled with the family doctor and the maid in a communicating carriage which had merely the customary six seats in it. On the journey Lady Harriet opened the door only once, to call out "Here is Hinchingbrooke", as they passed her family seat. Carlyle, who had a happy imperviousness to such social niceties, accepted this separation without question, noting only that the rear axle of the Saloon caught fire, so that it had to be abandoned at Newcastle. Jane, however, was angry: and her impotent fury —for she knew that nothing she could say or do would influence Carlyle's attitude to the family who had become so much part of his life—was not the less felt because it seems to have remained for the moment unexpressed.

When they reached Scotland Lady Harriet went to the Highlands, Carlyle to his sister's farm on the Solway, and Jane to stay with her cousins in Fife. Any visit to Scotland roused the Carlyles' capacity for brooding on the past: Carlyle, between bathing, walking, and working at Frederick, found time to pay a gloomy visit to Scotsbrig where Doctor John had installed his three stepsons; while Jane wept through a variety of sentimental scenes as friends and relations reminded her of her own youth, and of her father and mother. All might have been well, and the Queen's Saloon forgotten, had not Carlyle determined to go and stay for a few days with the Ashburtons at Loch Luichart. Here his spirits dropped still lower, and he wrote to Jane complaining that no fire was permitted in the drawing-room, that Lady Harriet was "capable of being driven to extremities by your setting up a peat from its flat posture", that there was "nothing earthly to be done, nothing good to be read, to be said, or thought." Jane was not sympathetic.

"In spite of all objections, 'for the occasion got up', I daresay you are pretty comfortable. Why not? When you go to any house, one knows it is because you choose to go; and when you stay, it is because you choose to stay. You don't, as weakly amiable people do, sacrifice yourself for the pleasure of 'others'. So pray do not think it necessary to be wishing yourself at home, and 'all that sort of thing', on paper."

She positively refused Lady Harriet's offer to take her back in the Queen's Saloon, although if Carlyle was returning with them "it would be different, as then I should be going merely as part of your luggage, without self-responsibility." This seems to have been the first time that Carlyle understood anything was wrong: and with unusual tact he gave way to Jane. The Carlyles came back to London independently of the Queen's Saloon; although Jane complained that he had made her sit in a violent draught during the journey.

Lady Harriet returned alone: and soon she went abroad to the South of France for her health. She stayed there for Christmas, but her health did not noticeably improve. Her letters to Carlyle became languid, his to her increasingly anxious. She was better, then she was worse. Carlyle was told that she was suffering from an internal growth, and that it was incurable. He refused to believe it, and cursed the doctor who had made the diagnosis as an incompetent fool. And then one day in May, 1857, Monckton Milnes brought the news to Cheyne Row that Harriet Lady Ashburton had died in Paris. The long platonic love affair was over.

Carlyle's feeling for her had been, at its best, part of that pathetic yearning to find his own honoured place amongst an aristocracy of birth and intellect, bound in joint endeavour for human well-being with such a seer as himself. His last letter to her repeats this dream in a wild form, utterly removed from Lady Harriet's real life or character. The Grange was to be turned into a practical school for boys and girls; the lord and lady would be usefully occupied, with no time for wild Highland journeyings; "somewhere in a still glade of the Woods" the prophet would be living quietly in a little brick cottage, and he would ask no more than a sight of the lady once every day, when work was done. . . .

Such dreams—in which Jane, one observes, had no part—were over for Carlyle as he stood beside her grave at the Grange. "Adieu! adieu!" he wrote in his journal. "Her work—

call it her grand and noble endurance of want of work—is all done!" And Jane? The funeral, she wrote to her friend in Scotland Mrs. Russell, "was conducted with a kind of royal state; and all the men, who used to compose a sort of *Court* for her, were there, *in tears!*" When, however, two months later Lord Ashburton gave her some mementoes of his wife she was unable to thank him, because she was so close to tears herself.

CHAPTER EIGHTEEN

THE LAST OF JANE

> This is your birthday. God grant us only many of them!
> I think now and then I could dispense with all other bless-
> ings. Our years have been well laden with sorrows, a quite
> sufficient *ballast* allowed us; but while we are here together
> there is always a world left. I am not to send you any gifts
> other than this scrap of paper; but I might give you
> California and not mean more than perhaps I do. And so
> may there be many years, and (as poor Irving used to say)
> the worst of them over.
>
> THOMAS CARLYLE to Jane Welsh Carlyle, July 1857.

IT SEEMED AT FIRST that the death of Lady Harriet had
come too late to change the domestic habits of Cheyne Row.
Carlyle was fixed as far as possible in imperception of what
went on around him: he worked at his book, rode almost every
day on Fritz, played the part of explosive prophet to disciples,
and ignored as much as possible the ill-health and ill-temper of
his wife. In this he was not by any means heartless. It is difficult
to be tenderly sympathetic through days and months and years
with somebody who is perpetually unwell and yet capable of
rousing herself to talk with apparent ease and gaiety in
company. In Carlyle's letters to his family he mentions almost
always Jane's ill health, and always with much concern: yet,
after all, what could be done about it? His suggestions that
they should keep another servant were decisively refused; he
had learned long ago that holidays were better taken apart
than together; none of the many doctors she consulted was able
to effect any improvement in a constitution ruined by unsuitable food and the constant use of drugs. The harshest word that
can be said of Carlyle's treatment of Jane after Lady Harriet's
death is that, faced by the insoluble problem of making a sick
woman healthy, he tried to pretend that the problem did not
exist.

In the late summer of 1857 Jane went to Scotland, and there
Carlyle wrote her the tenderest letters: telling her that he was
looking after Nero, that he had given chickweed to her canaries,
that he was tending her nettle and gooseberry bush, that tea

I

was a sad meal without her. These letters Jane received, she told him, with such agitation that she had to catch at a chair and sit down trembling before she could open and read them. She was delighted by the first two volumes of Frederick (out of what proved to be six) which she received in proof. "Oh, my dear! What a magnificent book this is going to be! The best of all your books", she wrote in a letter which he remembered as "the last (and perhaps the first, and pretty much the one) bit of pure sunshine that visited my dark and lonesome, and in the end quite dismal and inexpressible, enterprise of Frederick."

She returned to Chelsea a little better in health, but was ill throughout the winter with "*one* influenza lasting all the year round", instead of the eight influenzas annually ascribed to her by Harriet Martineau. She recovered slowly: when the friend of her youth Bess Aitken, formerly Bess Stodart, paid a visit to Cheyne Row her recognition of Jane was hardly complimentary. "She absolutely staggered, screaming out, 'God preserve me, Jane? That you?' " Gaunt, sallow and hollow-cheeked, and very thin, Jane had the appearance of dragging herself about in a world from which she would be glad to depart. Yet through these years of ill health she lost nothing of epistolary wit and skill. Typically caustic and artful is the phrase in a letter written in 1857 to her friend Mrs. Russell, whose husband was himself a doctor: "It is seventeen years now, since a Doctor Morrah, who attended me here, in another such illness, told me I 'should never *live through another Winter* in England!!' He was a man of high reputation, whom I shouldn't have disliked having again, but he died soon after." She was capable still of investing commonplace incidents with extraordinary dramatic art, as shown in the comic and terrifying story of the day when her servant Ann ran in crying wildly that a black beetle had run into her ear. Jane sprang forward and pulled the girl's finger away from her ear, which was full of blood. She called for Carlyle, who took the incident calmly. "Syringe it", he said. "Syringing will bring out any amount of black beetles." He refused to go with Ann to an apothecary, saying, "What good could it do *my* seeing the beetle taken out of her ear?" The girl went alone, but after ten minutes Jane rushed after her, and Carlyle after Jane. In the apothecary's surgery she found that the black beetle had been extracted with a probe. The apothecary said that there might be a leg or so left, which he would take out in the morning; but in fact the beetle had come out legs and all.

*   *   *   *   *

In the summer of 1858 Carlyle made his second tour of Germany, again with the assistance of Neuberg. The tour lasted a month, and Carlyle carried it out with remarkable vigour and enthusiasm for a man of his age. Shortly after coming back from Germany he entered again into the valley of the shadow of Frederick; he paid very little attention to the almost unanimous praise accorded to the first two volumes on their publication. The impress made upon the Victorian world by his personality was reflected in critical views of the work: his style, his conversation, his attitude, had all become legendary. The critics came not to criticize but to express homage which left its object singularly little moved.

This changed attitude of the intelligentsia towards Carlyle, this appreciation of him as a prophetic symbol, is evident in the hum of worship of Chelsea. Sculptors and painters came eagerly to produce their likenesses of the prophet and his wife; men of letters and men of action crowded about him; the setting for the teatime and evening conversations was very different from that of fifteen, or even ten years ago. The prophet exploded sometimes like a volcano, scattering ashes and burning lava; uncheckable by any visitor, yet quelled sometimes by a word from his wife as she rested on a sofa or sat in a corner of the room.

What had the prophet to say? Nothing that he had not said many times before: but some of the listeners were new, and the others were spellbound by that fervent and fiery eloquence. The most interesting of the new faces was that of John Ruskin, who like Neuberg called Carlyle "the Master". Carlyle regarded Ruskin as a gifted man with impractical ideas, and told Lord Ashburton that "he flies out like a soda-water bottle; gets into the *eyes* of various people (being incautiously *drawn*), and these of course complain dreadfully!" Froude, of whose capacity Carlyle thought highly, was a welcome visitor; so too were such various figures as Woolner and Espinasse, Monckton Milnes and Neuberg. Alexander Gilchrist, who was to write the standard life of Blake, came; Tennyson and Dickens came, or were met in polite society. Carlyle's opinion of Dickens rose with the publication of *Little Dorrit* and *A Tale of Two Cities*, which echoed many of his own ideas in the form of fiction. Jane put down in her notebook a little conundrum after Dickens's separation from his wife: "When does a man really ill-use his wife? Ans.—When he plays the Dickens with her."

Many of the visitors, however, were not men of letters but young men of action, eager for advice on their proper conduct as God-fearing British Imperialists, anxious to extend the sovereignty of their country. Such young men found peculiarly sympathetic the ideas they were able to extract from Carlyle's writings: and in their presence the frustrated man of action inveighed against the great froth ocean of literature. Sometimes he scandalized his hearers, when he professed to believe that his own literary activities were merely regrettable inconsistencies; although it is not recorded that anybody ever ventured to agree with him. Generally, however, he was happy when instructing a cavalry officer in the proper handling of his troop, or analysing in the company of a military tactician one of Frederick's campaigns.

Less welcome, upon the whole, than the men of action, were the high-thinking Americans, some of them sent by Emerson, others moved by their own reverence or curiosity. For Emerson himself, now that he was safely ensconced in the United States with no further visit in prospect, Carlyle felt much affection. An article written by the American seemed to him "the only thing that is *speech* at all among my fellow-creatures in this time", and he was much pleased by Emerson's appreciation of Frederick. Disciples of Emerson in the flesh were another thing; and Carlyle learned to avoid them, with a few exceptions. One of these exceptions was the elder Henry James, the amiable Swedenborgian who fathered such a strange brood of Jamesians. The elder Henry was easily shocked, and one gathers an impression that Carlyle was delighted to shock him. On one occasion the flowery speech of James's friend McKay for the help given him by Carlyle's writings received the short answer that the philosopher did not believe a word of it; upon another a former Unitarian clergyman from Massachusetts named Henry Woodman was incautious enough to indicate his laboriously-achieved disbelief in the existence of a personal devil, and brought down upon his head rhetorical thunderings which seem to have been generally enjoyed. On a third visit James, Woodman and Doctor Carlyle were present when an Englishman named Bull praised Daniel O'Connell in

Carlyle's presence, and a furious verbal battle ensued for an hour. Tea was served, but the conflict went on until Jane pressed Bull's foot to implore peace; then he turned upon her savagely and asked why she did not touch her husband's toe. Peace had been restored when the Americans left, but at about eleven o'clock Bull said, "Let us return a moment to O'Connell." The talk then became, according to Jane, "altogether unbearable" and when Carlyle held out his hand to the departing visitor it was rejected with the words, "Never again shall I set foot in this house!"

On these occasions Jane was generally silent, interposing only at times a soft or an ironic word. When she did speak at length on any subject of importance it was to echo her husband's views. Herbert Spencer regretted that her mind had been warped by her husband, and the notes of William Knighton among others record remarks of Jane's in company which are a faithful echo of Carlyle, but seem oddly uncharacteristic of her. She said little, but she thought much: and in her thoughts, as they found a way into her letters, there was often an ungenerous sharp pettiness towards the man who, for all his emotional obtuseness had always loved her, as she well knew, far beyond anyone or anything else on earth. She resented, at the same time that she was proud of, the homage paid him; and she tried often to make him look foolish, although we may believe that she would have been sorry had she succeeded. One must remember that she was a sick woman; and yet when all allowances have been made there is truth in the remark that Geraldine Jewsbury made in one of her bright intelligent flashes: "His was the soft heart and hers the hard one." Or his, at least, was the truly generous spirit and hers the narrow. Carlyle was aware of the existence of the pins so often and deliberately stuck into him. There is a story that, in his last years, a group of people were discussing in his presence the silliness and the blind adulation by which great men's wives often made their husbands look foolish. "In that respect", he said, "I have been most mercifully spared."

*   *   *   *   *

Out of the years spent in the valley of the shadow of Frederick the Great ("I wonder how we shall live, what we shall do, where we shall go, when that terrible task is ended", Jane wrote), a few spots of colour emerge from the prevailing grey background of work and ill health: the death of Nero, servant trouble, Lord Ashburton's second marriage, Jane's accident.

Late in 1859 a butcher's cart passed over Nero's throat. The maid, Charlotte, brought him home, "all crumpled together like a crushed spider, and his poor little eyes protruding, and fixedly staring in his head." Put into a warm bath by Jane, wrapped up and laid on a pillow, he seemed to show no worse after-effects than a tendency to asthma; but within a month or two it became plain that he was not long for this world. Carlyle said more than once that "a little prussic acid" was the only thing for him: but Jane overheard him saying to Nero in the garden, "Poor little fellow! I declare I am heartily sorry for you! If I *could* make you young again, upon my soul I *would!*" At last it became evident, even to Jane, that Nero's continued existence was a burden; and a local doctor named Barnes, who lived nearby in the King's Road, gave the dog strychnine. He was buried at the top of the Cheyne Row garden, with a tablet to mark the place. Carlyle remembered afterwards, typically "the last nocturnal walk he took with me, his dim white little figure in the universe of dreary black"; at the time he was, if Jane is to be believed, in tears, and confessed himself "unexpectedly and distractedly torn in pieces." Jane in her grief gave full vent to the emotional side of her nature. Carlyle, she observed, became soon enough composed; Charlotte, who went about weeping for three days, recovered on the fourth; only she mourned continually her "inseparable companion for eleven years", and reminded herself of the last terrible moment when she kissed Nero's head before Charlotte took him away, and "*he kissed my cheek.*" The occasion moved her to some curious speculations:

> What *is* become of that little, beautiful, graceful *Life*, so full of love and loyalty and sense of duty, up to the last moment that it animated the body of that little dog? Is *it* to be extinguished, abolished, annihilated in an instant, while the brutalized, two-legged, so-called human creatures who dies in a ditch, after having outraged all duties, and caused nothing but pain and disgust to all concerned with him,—is he to live forever?

At the end of the letter containing this question she wrote: "I grieve for him as if he had been my little human child."

The surname of the Charlotte whose misadventure led to the death of Nero was Southern. She was a brisk little girl, who amused both the Carlyles by her remarks. When Robert Tait's picture of the Carlyles at home, "An Interior at Chelsea", was on view at the Royal Academy, Jane took Charlotte to the Exhibition, without telling her what she might see there. Charlotte went off on her own to look at the pictures, and came back to Jane crying: "Oh mum, Mr. Carlyle and you and Nero are in the other room. Come and see them."

Such a story is an indication of Jane's inability to deal with servants on the usual Victorian terms of mistress and maid. Almost every servant she had, after the twelve years' residence of the drunken Helen, was at first petted and made a confidante, only to be revealed after a few weeks or months in the blackest colours. In Jane's letters the servant problem bulks very large after 1860, when she accepted at last Carlyle's suggestion that she should have two servants. Charlotte, after having delighted her mistress by her good sense, her high spirits and her radiant kindliness, suddenly proved to be altogether too slack. She was replaced by a "so called Treasure" in her early seventies, with a young girl named Sarah to assist her. Alas, the treasure was a liar, unable to cook, and stole eight bottles of ale. She was replaced by another Charlotte, "the new tall Charlotte", who at first seemed more satisfactory: but Jane, unable to manage one servant, was altogether lost with two. She felt as if she had lodgers downstairs; she dreaded the solemn conversations about *your* dinner and *our* dinner; with only little Charlotte in the house they had been, she said, moving into an almost mystical flight, "*one* family in the House; *one* interest and *one* Power!"

The new tall Charlotte did not last very long, and the "treasure of a cook" who replaced her, and was to be "the comfort of my remaining years" departed suddenly with strangulated hernia. One disaster succeeded another. Another treasure named Elizabeth turned abruptly into an "emotional young lady . . . capering about me, and kissing my hands and shawl", while inwardly full of arrogance and self-conceit. "Her dinners blackened to cinders! her constant crashes of glass and china! her brutal manners! her lumpish insensibility and ingratitude!" And Elizabeth was not the worst: there was also an "incomparable small housemaid" who was secretly an "incomparable small demon". The small demon, whose name was Flo, told an incoming cook named Mary that Jane was a she-devil and had to be strapped into a chair in fits of madness. Jane, who had dismissed Mary because of her sullenness, rescinded this dismissal and got rid of Flo. Mary, slow, stupid but apparently devoted, stayed for two years: at the end of that time Jane was about to dismiss a big, beautiful goosish house-maid for petty pilfering when she discovered by accident the guilt of Mary, who had kept the other girl silent by threats of cutting her throat. "For two years I have been cheated and made a fool of, and laughed at for my softness, by this half-idiotic looking woman; and while she was crying up in my bedroom—moaning out, 'What would become of her if I died' . . . she was giving suppers to men and women down-stairs; laughing and swearing—oh, it is too disgusting." More, almost incredibly more, and worse: Mary had been delivered of an illegitimate child in the house during Jane's absence. "While she was in labour in the small room at the end of the dining-room, Mr. Carlyle was taking tea in the dining-room with Miss Jewsbury talking to him!!! Just a thin small door between!" It is not surprising that Carlyle in his writings gave vivid treatment sometimes to "the servant problem".

We owe this very particular knowledge of the Carlyles' domestic affairs to Jane's correspondence with her feminine confidantes, who changed over the years, though less often than her servants. Jeannie Welsh, the once adored Babbie, lost favour soon after her marriage in the late eighteen forties: the last glimpse we catch is of her arrival when Jane was on a visit to her cousins at Auchtertool, preceded by five packing cases and accompanied by a baby "about three finger-lengths long" and two nurses "nearly six foot each." Not merely was Jeannie no longer loved: she could hardly be endured. "Such an affected, bedizened, caricature of a *fine-lady* I never came across. I could hardly keep my hands off her. My Mother always predicted what she would grow to." Nobody ever quite filled Jeannie's place, for none of Jane's later friends had all those qualities—youth, high spirits, docility, a modicum of wit, and a provincial readiness to be impressed by descriptions of life in London—that especially attracted Jane in a woman. Miss Barnes, daughter of the doctor who had given the dose of strychnine to Nero, was perhaps the most likely substitute: but an early marriage prevented her from qualifying for the role in any serious sense. "Will you think me mad if I tell you that when I read your words, 'I am going to be married', I all but screamed?" Jane wrote to her in a very odd letter of congratulation. In the eighteen sixties Jane addressed her long letters about the triumphs and miseries of Cheyne Row to three people in particular. Two lived in Scotland: Mary Austin, Carlyle's second sister, the wife of a farmer in Annandale, and Mrs. Russell, married to a doctor with whom Jane was to have something to do, who lived near her mother's old home at Thornhill. The third of these particular friends by correspondence was—Lady Ashburton.

At the end of 1858 Carlyle noted in his journal: "Lord Ashburton has wedded again—a Miss Stuart Mackenzie—and they are off to Egypt about a fortnight ago. 'The changes of this age', as minstrel Burns has it, 'which fleeting Time procureth!' Ah me! ah me!" The Carlyles went to the Grange again, neither of them, perhaps, inclined to think favourably of the new Lady Ashburton: but any resistance they may have felt to her was conquered on this first visit. The second Lady Ashburton was only 34 years old: it was possible for the Carlyles to feel a parental affection for her upon which the image of Lady Harriet, venerated by the one and jealously feared by the other, never intruded. Handsome and intelligent, Louisa had a tenderness and docility of character that made her adaptable to the role of the Carlyles' favoured child—a child, however, distinguished from any possible actual offspring by the aristocratic origin which gave to their relations with her a touch of delighted deference. Jane, by her own account, "stood out for five days" against liking Louisa; it was not until she came up to Jane's room on that fifth day and talked freely and unguardedly "like an unaffected Highland girl" that Jane's heart was won. Like her husband Jane was subject in social matters to a very complex snobbery. To conquer her Lady Ashburton had to behave like an unaffected Highland girl—to acknowledge, that is, her equality with, and almost deference to, Mrs. Carlyle. Such equality once recognized, the aristocratic birth and connections of Louisa could, in their turn, receive a meed of deference. Lady Ashburton was, Jane said, a really amiable and lovable woman, who was "much more intent on making her visitors at their ease and happy, than on shewing off *herself*, and attracting admiration."

She became very soon a good deal more than that. "Oh my Darling! my Darling! who that comes near to you, and is cared for by you can help loving you with a whole heartful of love?" Jane asked: and few things in her life are more remarkable than the reduction of this high spirit into a strange schoolgirlish adoration of Lord Ashburton's second wife. Jane's attitude to Louisa is curiously similar to Geraldine Jewsbury's attitude to Jane herself in the early days of their friendship: but its basis was markedly different. Geraldine's adoration was given to what she took for a masculine and decided spirit some years older than herself; Jane's to a woman young enough to be her daughter, whose particular attractions were her docile nature and her social position. In her letters to Louisa the sentimental side of Jane is uppermost: the witty and acidulous commentator on life and Mr. Carlyle stays in the background. When her beloved Louisa was pregnant Jane dreamt about the coming baby, heard it crying and felt it her duty to go and feed it; after its birth she declared that this was "the first human child that has ever . . . awakened what is called the *maternal instinct* in me, whose lines have always been cast in babyless places." The baby, however, was valued principally as the product of this particular mother, who was "more like an angel than a grand lady", and whose friendship, delicately free from the least hint of condescension, had become indispensable. "If you were to tire of me now, and if you were to die before me! If you were anyhow taken out of my life! Why, I should fall into as great a trouble as I ever was in, when young and excitable about 'a lost love'."

Lady Ashburton seems to have accepted this affection without discomfort, and to have returned it with the generosity of a naturally warm-hearted woman. On her side there were no social ambiguities, although it would not be quite true to say that there was no snobbery. Where, except upon a desert island, can that be truly said? Jane was by now almost a famous woman, as well as the wife of a famous man, and the adoration of such a woman carries its own delicate flattery. At any rate, we may believe that the second Lady Ashburton was not one of those who regarded Jane's stories as too long, but thought with Edward Irving's biographer Mrs. Oliphant that she was a greater story-teller than Scheherazade, because her stories had no need of fantasy to make them interesting, but were rooted in the realities of the life of a woman married to a man of genius. "When one has married a man of genius one must take the consequences", Jane once wrote: and one of the pleasanter by-products of such a marriage was the dozens of stories of which Jane, a comical and not unwilling martyr, was the heroine. The Grange, under its new mistress, was a house that Jane was always happy to visit: she was treated there with a careful solicitude for her social and intellectual position, as well as for her physical well-being, that afforded a delightful contrast to the real or imagined slights offered her in the past.

Such, with the addition of the ever-faithful Geraldine—Miss Gooseberry, as Jane maliciously called her—who was still falling in and out of love, were Jane's friends. She was separated from them all suddenly by a barrier of pain when, in September 1863, she suffered a street accident, slipping on a kerbstone and injuring her thigh. She arrived home in great pain, but did not wish to disturb Carlyle: she sent next door for Larkin. Carlyle, however, came down and saw her, and "looking terribly shocked", helped Larkin to carry her upstairs. For a few days the invalid was cheerful: her left arm, in which she had suffered neuralgic pains a few months before, was now almost useless, and she had an arrangement of cords and pulleys made so that she could sit up, while at a little table by her side a bottle of champagne was arranged so that she could take a spoonful of it when she wished. Carlyle thought she was on the way to recovery when one evening she got up and "came gliding in" to him in the drawing-room, "all radiant in graceful evening dress, followed by a maid with new lights." Within three or four weeks of this date, however, she was back in bed, and did not move from it for months. During this time she was seen by several doctors, including the local Barnes, and Doctor (later Sir) Richard Quain, a fashionable physician of the day. Doctor Quain had recommended for Jane's neuralgic arm quinine pills, an embrocation of opium, aconite, camphor and chloroform and castor oil every two or three days. He now attended her very willingly, refused to accept payment, and prescribed a variety of drugs, which had no beneficial effect. Doctor Barnes declared quite frankly that nothing could be done: and Jane was distressed to find that he appeared to regard her leg as his patient and her arm as Doctor Quain's. In the meantime she was conscious of hardly anything but pain "indescribable, unaidable pain", as Carlyle put it, so great that she asked Doctor Quain for poison to end her life. She rarely spoke of what she suffered, but when she did "it was in terms as if there were no language for it." Carlyle dealt with her correspondence himself, sending to Lady Ashburton almost daily bulletins of the patient's condition.

For months the long misery continued. Almost unable to sleep, and reduced to inaudible expressions of misery, Jane ate little but slops, drank nothing but lemonade, soda-water and milk with bits of ice. Her cousin Maggie Welsh came down from Liverpool and helped to nurse her. At the winter's end she seemed a little better: able to endure transport to St. Leonards in a sick carriage which reminded her of a hearse, with a window for putting in the coffin.

At St. Leonards she stayed at the house of a doctor named Blackiston, who had married Bessie, the very first of their maids at Cheyne Row. The Blackistons and Maggie Welsh nursed her devotedly: but the torments she suffered from the mysterious illness which was thought by some to be a displacement of the womb, and by others to be hysterical mania, were greater than ever. The notes that she scrawled to her husband with her left hand are like shrieks of agony. "I have been wretched—perfectly wretched day and night with that horrible malady", she wrote on April 8, and a few days later said that she endured "a positive physical torment day and night . . . How be in good spirits or have any hope but to die." In most of these letters she spoke of death: and as the idea of it became fixed in her mind she felt a desire to live, and a love for her husband, more intense than she had known in years. "Oh, my Dear, my Dear! shall I ever make fun for you again? Or is our life together indeed past and gone? I want so much to *live*,— to be to you more than I have ever been; but I fear, I fear!" In April Lord Ashburton died after a long illness, and left Carlyle £2,000 in his will. (Carlyle gave away all the money, in sums varying from ten shillings to fifty pounds, noting each payment carefully in an account book, and telling the recipients that it came from a fund for which he was trustee.) Despite her sufferings Jane managed to scrawl a note of condolence to Louisa.

In early May a house was hired at St. Leonards. Jane moved there from Doctor Blackiston's, and Carlyle came to stay there with Doctor John. All his wife's sufferings, all the grief, anxiety and loving-kindness shown in his own letters, could not make him abandon the work on Frederick, which extended unendingly year after year; with the fifth large volume completed, he had discovered that a sixth was necessary. He brought

down a great box of books to St. Leonards, and "in a small
back closet, window opposite to door, and both always open",
was able to work reasonably well, although feeling "as if tied
up in a rack." Jane went out for long drives with Doctor John:
Carlyle went on some of these drives, when she talked to him
with evident effort, swam in the morning with John, and took
long rides on horseback. Visitors came down, Forster and
Woolner among them, but Jane was too unwell to see them.

Early in July, after a dozen sleepless nights, she suddenly
decided to go to Scotland; and John accompanied her on a
journey up to Mary Austin's farmhouse The Gill, broken only
by the stay of a night at the Forsters' house in London. There
seems to have been no suggestion on anybody's part that Carlyle
should accompany his wife on this northern flight: the almost
religious regard felt by everybody concerned that Carlyle's
work should continue undisturbed is one of the most notable
aspects of this period. And in Scotland, staying first for a few
days at The Gill and then for more than two months at the
home of her friends the Russells, she slowly recovered health.
Doctor John, with that indifference to his own idleness which
has its magnificence (or perhaps he regarded the translation of
the *Inferno* as work enough for one man's lifetime) told her that
if she had ever done anything in her life she would not have
been ill: but at Doctor Russell's house she was treated with a
gentleness that had perhaps been lacking at St. Leonards, and
given a milk diet that caused her to put on a pound and a half
in ten days. She became lively enough to note her first laugh
for months, to say a few sharp things about Geraldine, to ask if
the maid was shaking her furs to keep the moths out. She
showed a pathetic reliance on Carlyle: his constant, and
brilliantly entertaining, letters did much to raise her spirits.
These letters are, indeed, more like those of a young husband
to his recent bride than like those written by a man sixty-eight
years old to a querulous and sick woman only a few years
younger. He called her his own Schatz, his Goody, his poor
little Eurydice; he spoke of her as the helm and intellect of the
house and said that he longed for her to be by his side; he told
her of the work that had been done in the house, because she
felt unable to come back without seeing new paper on the walls.
To John, who was to bring Jane home, he wrote a carefully
tactful note saying that "I need not advise you (what will
double and treble the kindness, and is perhaps really the

difficult part) to be gentle, *patient,* and *soft* and yielding in all respects, as towards a creature *without skin.*'' On the 1st October, 1864, Jane returned to Cheyne Row after more than six months' absence, upon her face no despair but a faint and timid smile.

Her reception surprised and touched her. Doctor John had mistaken the time of arrival, so that Carlyle had been expecting them for nearly two hours. He rushed into the street in his dressing gown, to kiss and weep over her: behind him the maids, one of them the treacherous Mary, appeared almost equally moved. Friend after friend came and wept over her recovery: Monckton Milnes (now Lord Houghton), Woolner ("especially trying, for he dropped on his knees beside my sofa, and kissed me over and over again, with a most stupendous beard! and a face wet with tears!''), Forster, several others. Lady Ashburton came on three evenings in the first week Jane was home, and sent two dozen bottles of champagne, and a regular hamper from the country. Jane thought that the remark made by a German girl must be true: "I think, Mrs. Carlyle, a many many peoples must love you very dear!" And Carlyle? "I cannot tell you how gentle and good Mr. Carlyle is! He is busy as ever, but he studies my comfort and peace as he never did before.''

*   *   *   *   *

She had another eighteen months to live: and perhaps they were, as it seemed to Carlyle afterwards, the happiest of her whole married life. She had, at last, the brougham of which Carlyle had often spoken; and Lady Ashburton who had already given Carlyle a horse to replace Fritz, when that faithful animal after many years' service fell down and broke his knees, presented Jane with a smart grey horse for the brougham. She saw the end of *Frederick*, looking on with a "silent, faint, and pathetic smile" when, on January 5, 1865, Carlyle took out to the post office the last leaf of the manuscript. Would he write anything else? asked Gavan Duffy, now in England on a visit from Australia where as Minister of Lands he had taken the opportunity of naming a township Carlyle and its streets Thomas, Jane, Sterling and Stuart Mill. Carlyle answered that he would probably write no more. "Writing books is a task without proper encouragement in these times.''

Duffy asked about George Eliot, whose sex had been discovered by Carlyle while her identity remained publicly unrevealed, by her description in *Adam Bede* of the making of a door. "George Eliot is a female writer of books, like myself and Lewes" (the man with whom she was living), Carlyle replied. "I got one of her books and tried to read it, but it would not do. Poor Lewes! Poor fellow!" Jane was cutting about the Eliot-Lewes ménage. "When one was first told that the strong woman of the *Westminster Review* had gone off with a man whom we all knew, it was as startling an announcement as if one heard that a woman of your acquaintance had gone off with the strong man at Astleys; but that the partners in this adventure had set up as moralists is a graver surprise."

It was noticeable that, now more than ever, Jane echoed her husband's views: her ironic interruptions and observations decreased with the years, although she could not resist correcting Carlyle's slightly erratic version of Browning's courtship. She seems, however, never to have questioned his view of the American Civil War, which he called the most foolish-looking conflict that had taken place in his time. Again and again in the last thirty years of his life Carlyle was led into ludicrous error through disinterest in discovering the facts about anything except the history of Frederick the Great. It was possible to find good logical reasons for supporting either North or South in the Civil War: but Carlyle's attitude, as shown in his little parable printed in *Macmillan's Magazine*, reflected merely ignorance:

ILIAS (AMERICANA) IN NUCE

Peter of the North (to Paul of the South).—"Paul, you unaccountable scoundrel, I find you hire your servants for life, not by the month or year as I do! You are going straight to Hell, you—!"

Paul.—"Good words, Peter! The risk is my own; I am willing to take the risk. Hire you your servants by the month or the day, and get straight to Heaven; leave me to my own method."

Peter.—"No, I won't. I will beat your brains out first!" (*And is trying dreadfully ever since, but cannot yet manage it.*)

Southern Americans were delighted by this little piece. Emerson thought it "unfortunate, but no more than could be expected". Most Northerners were less resigned. The American clergyman Moncure Conway, who had come to engage English support for the Northern cause, was distressed by Carlyle's opinions, but charmed by the guilelessness of their expression. To Conway Carlyle expressed himself more gently and sensibly, not about the war but about progressive movements generally in America. When Jane offered one of her now rare reproofs, pointing out that Conway, a slave-owner's son, had made sacrifices for his cause, Carlyle said: "You will be patient with me. All the worth you have put into your cause will be returned to you personally; but the America for which you are hoping you will never see; and never see the whites and the blacks in the South dwelling as equals in peace." Within a few months, however, he was speaking of the "self-murder of a million brother Englishmen for the sake of sheer *phantasms*, and totally *false* theories upon the Nigger", in the presence of a young girl who had been living in America. She said to him calmly: "You simply do not know what you are talking about!" Those present waited for her to be felled under an annihilating blow but Carlyle contented himself with remarking, a little inadequately, that she was wanting in reverence. Long after the war was over Carlyle admitted to Froude that perhaps he had not seen far enough into the American Civil War.

As the months of 1865 passed Jane became worried by her failure to recover use of her right arm. Doctor Quain was reassuring: she had, he said, much fever, and he gave her three different prescriptions to cure it. She told him that Doctor Blackiston had declared that she had no organic disease, but a strong predisposition to gout. "Quite right." Then, she said, perhaps she had gout in her arm? Doctor Quain replied that he had not the least doubt of it. Within a day or two he was giving her a bumper of champagne, prescribing quinine and a journey to Scotland, since the previous trip had done her so much good. Jane went to Scotland, where Doctor Russell told her bluntly that she might never recover use of the arm. When she returned to London she told this to Doctor Quain, who was indignant. "How could he know? That is what nobody could say but God Almighty." He approved highly, however, of her new treatment: "taking neither quinine nor anything else."

So, in pleasant idleness, the St. Martin's Summer of her life passed; Carlyle, gentle and considerate always, was also idle, reading Racine and Suetonius. Jane went to stay with a friend at Folkestone, and returned with a pug dog called Tiny. She went with Geraldine to meet the Queen of the Sandwich

Islands, "a charming young woman in spite of the tinge of black—or rather green", who expressed a perfect familiarity with Carlyle's name, and even with his works. She rescued their old laundress from the workhouse and, with the aid of the Rector of Chelsea, established her in a small cottage. She was delighted when, early in November, the figures for the Edinburgh Rectorial contest were announced:

| Thomas Carlyle | 657 |
| Benjamin Disraeli | 310 |

Duffy, who went to Cheyne Row soon afterwards, found her in high spirits. Carlyle said that he had accepted the candidature on condition that he should not have to deliver an address: but "Madame assured me that the address would be delivered, in good time" . . . The rest we know. On the morning of Thursday, March 29, Tyndall called for him. Jane poured some old brown brandy into a tumbler, filling it up from a siphon. Carlyle drank it. They kissed each other goodbye.

CHAPTER NINETEEN

THE PAST RELIVED

A hot-tempered creature, too; few hotter, on momentary provocation: but what a fund of soft affection, hope, and melodious innocence and goodness, to temper all that lightning:—I doubt, candidly, if I ever saw a nobler human soul than this which (alas, alas, never *rightly* valued till now!) accompanied all my steps for forty years. Blind and deaf that we are: oh think, if thou yet love anybody living, wait not till *Death* sweep down the paltry little dust-clouds and idle dissonances of the moment; and all be at last so mournfully clear and beautiful, when it is too late!

THOMAS CARLYLE: *Reminiscences.*

OFTEN AFTER HIS wife's death Carlyle brooded upon the sorrows and boredom he had imposed on her during what might be called the Thirteen Years War with Frederick the Great. During the last placid months of her life she had told him with some humour how she had been lying on the sofa, night after night, convinced of her imminent death; and night after night he had come in, to take a spoonful of brandy and water, sit on the hearthrug by the fire so that the smoke from his pipe went up the chimney, and talk to her about—the battle of Mollwitz. He blamed himself for neglect of her, and for his total concern with Frederick; he believed that for the last seven years of the war he had not written the smallest message to friends nor undertaken any business "except upon plain *compulsion* of necessity." That was far from the truth: but it was true that in this long book, this vast mausoleum called the *History of Friedrich II of Prussia called Frederick the Great*, Carlyle had buried his genius.

Jane thought this the greatest of Carlyle's books: and almost every critic of the time agreed with her. They were awestruck, for one thing, by the size of it: the first two volumes were published in 1858, the last in 1865, and there could not have been an English critic who was unaware of the self-proclaimed torments endured by its author in his search for the Fact and for Truth, his investigation of mental dunghills, his battles with the frightful nightmares of error. This indirect, and of course unintended, attack upon the critics' susceptibilities had its effect: few in England had the scholarship, and fewer still the inclination, to criticize the book in detail or to cross a polemical sword with its author on his interpretation of history. The book was translated at once into German and in that country met, not unnaturally, with warm appreciation; in America too Emerson called it the wittiest book ever written, and Lowell thought that the portrait of Voltaire had no superior in imaginative literature; in England Froude expressed a general view when he said that only two historians, Thucydides and Tacitus, had possessed Carlyle's double gift of accuracy and power of representation.

These tributes must seem extraordinary to anyone who opens the *History of Friedrich II* today. Carlyle's position as a historian was always the peculiar one of a man who was unsatisfied until he had placed every event in a satisfactory relation to a divine will which had no other interpreter than himself. His praiseworthy insistence on the importance of fact and truth were a kind of compensation for the freedom of interpretation in which he habitually indulged: faced by criticism of his interpretation he could comfort himself always with the pain he had taken to ascertain the facts. Facts (he might have agreed with a famous liberal publicist) are sacred: opinions are free. Such a doctrine is dangerous at any time, for the sacred facts, whether in the hands of a journalist or a historian, are always a selection from the great mass of facts available: and the selection is made inevitably through preconceived opinions. For a historian like Carlyle, who regarded himself as divinely inspired, there could be no more fatal doctrine. He turned away from the contemporary world after the failure of *Latter-Day Pamphlets* to effect any practical reforms, and transferred to the past his conviction of the people's need for a hero and a conqueror. With many hesitations he settled on Frederick: and from that time onward the facts he accepted were those which conformed to the heroic view of Frederick. The omissions and reticences into which such a procedure led him have been carefully charted by modern critics; it has been less noticed that he was led also, by the logic of his position, to apply different standards of value to Frederick and to his opponents. Chicanery practised by Frederick is not chicanery but a refusal to adhere to "superstitious veracity"; a treaty broken by Frederick becomes necessarily "a kind of provisional off-and-on Treaty"; Frederick did not show dissimulation prior to his unexpected attack on Silesia, but merely "the art of wearing a polite cloak of darkness." Frederick's resistance to France and Russia for the short period when they combined against him was that of a hero; the refusal of the Elector of Saxony to surrender when Frederick invaded Saxony was, however, ovine obstinacy. The magnificently-written descriptions of battles with which the history is studded take notice only of Frederick's version of historical fact.

Carlyle's preconceptions about Frederick, which he could never relinquish, although they became more and more painful to him with each passing year, necessitated also a change in his attitude towards the writing of history: a shift from the view that historical change is ordered by social and economic forces to the idea that it is imposed simply by superior individuals. The role allowed to the individual in history varies with each historian: but it is safe to say that few have attributed such nearly divine power to rulers, and have shown such little interest in the condition of those they ruled, as Carlyle in writing of Frederick. The man who, in dealing with the French Revolution, had shown with unexampled dramatic skill the movement of masses in revolt now concerned himself with gossip about the personalities and ancestry of a whole range of petty German princes and their courts; the man who had attempted to hold in check his dangerous gift of caricature when dealing with a Robespierre and a St. Just now let it run unrestrained in depicting George the Second's "adoration of pragmatic Sanction" or in the comic but wilfully inaccurate portrait of Voltaire. And throughout the book there runs a furious eagerness for absolute despotism, a determination not to let humanitarian considerations interfere with the divine rights of heroes, which must seem ugly (not in its logic, but in the psychopathic desire for violence which it reveals) to a modern reader.

There is, naturally, something to be said in praise of *The History of Friedrich II*: it is, on whatever terms, the product of a man of genius. Those who may be intimidated by its mere size can be assured that it is surprisingly readable; the battle scenes, whatever their approach to accuracy, are written with remarkable power; many of the individual portraits—though here questionable accuracy becomes often positive distortion —are memorable; and almost every chapter shows Carlyle's power of exaggerative irony. Yet this cannot be anything but a sad book to those who remember the generous aspirations for man as a social animal shown in *The French Revolution*: and perhaps the recollection of those aspirations was one of the things that made it sad for Carlyle himself.

* * * * *

The news of Jane's death stunned him. He had never permitted himself to consider her death even as a possibility, in spite of her long illness and subsequent weakness. He went down to London accompanied by John, and looked at her in the coffin; Forster busied himself in avoiding the trial of a coroner's inquest; the coachman drove Carlyle to the fatal spot, and had to recite in detail everything that had happened. Tyndall called: and in his presence, with Jane's body lying in the next room, Carlyle broke into a storm of vivid recollection, describing the struggles and distresses and delights of the past. Three or four times during the course of this narrative he broke down completely.

The journey to her burial place at Haddington was made in the company of John and Forster; on April 26, 1866, he laid her in her father's grave. Afterwards he returned to Chelsea and stayed there, desolate, with Doctor John as company and Jane's cousin Maggie Welsh to look after them. The echoes of the Edinburgh installation address had been heard all round Britain; and among the many expressions of sympathy was one from the Queen giving him "the assurance of her sorrowful understanding of a grief which she herself, alas! knows too well." In acknowledging his "profound sense of (Her Majesty's) great goodness to me, in this the day of my calamity", Carlyle said that it was best for him to speak and write to nobody. He felt that his whole existence lay in ruins around him. To Froude he appeared haggard, and as if turned to stone. From this state of stupefaction a communication from Geraldine Jewsbury turned him to the strangest literary activity of his life.

A few days after Jane's death Geraldine was asked by their joint friend Lady Lothian to write a memoir of the dead woman. She did so; or rather she put down some anecdotes of Jane's childhood and the days at Craigenputtock, as she had received and interpreted them from Jane; and she sent these stories to Carlyle, who was disturbed by the errors of detail they contained, and what he regarded as a weakness in portraiture.

"On the whole, all tends to the *mythical*; it is very strange how much of mythical there already here is." He asked that Geraldine should consign the memoir to his hands for keeping, and she willingly did so. Within five weeks of Jane's death Carlyle began to correct Geraldine's account, and the corrections gradually expanded into a narrative of her life. Within two months he had written sixty thousand words.

The narrative he put down is remarkable in the conversational freedom of its style, in its halts, digressions and apostrophic ejaculations. "Why do I *write* at all", he asks again and again. "Can *I* ever forget? And is not all this appointed by me rigorously to the *fire*?" The most remarkable aspect of his writing, however, is its astonishing quality as a feat of memory. Writing, without notes or references, of things that had happened, and people they had known, forty and more years ago, Carlyle recalled phrases and incidents exactly as he or Jane had described them in letters long ago. There could be no clearer evidence of his photographic memory for people, things and places than this narrative written, with a nice irony, in the notebook which Jane had used during those miserable eighteen fifties. Through the power of memory he relived the past, searching it for the offences he had committed towards her, giving free rein to his melancholy as he moved more and more deeply into the story. The life at Craigenputtock which, looked back on, appeared to him almost their happiest time; fragmentary notes on old friends and enemies unseen for years; then the move to London, settlement in Cheyne Row and the years of suffering and triumph spent there. In the course of writing he created, and came partly to believe in, another Jane Welsh Carlyle than the tart, witty and frustrated woman whose love for him did not by any means exclude hardness and bitterness. "Thanks, Darling, for your shining words and acts, which were continual in my eyes, and in no other mortal's. Worthless I was your divinity; wrapt in your perpetual love of me and pride in me, in defiance of all men and things. Oh was it not beautiful, all this that I have lost forever!"

Such exclamations are less embarrassing than might be expected; they have, somehow, a veracity and a touching appropriateness to the rambling narrative, which moves back from Chelsea to Jane's parentage and childhood. For five days he stopped writing altogether while he and Maggie Welsh searched for and collected together all the letters of Jane's that they could find: letters which, it seemed to him, "equal and surpass whatever of best I know to exist in that kind; for 'talent' 'genius', or whatever we may call it, what an evidence, if my little woman needed that to me!" But he despaired of ever making them comprehensible to others, so filled were they with the coterie speech gathered from their reading, from Doctor John, Mazzini and others . . . and he broke off his narrative to say: "Enter Froude; almost the only man I care to speak with, in these weeks." At the end of his writing he could not decide whether to burn it. He knew that he would be unwilling ever to do so; perhaps, he reflected, worthy friends should see it; but he solemnly told these future friends that what he had written should not be published without fit editing; he added, a little contradictorily, that "the 'fit editing' of perhaps nine-tenths of it will, after I am gone, have become *impossible*."

It was the end of July by the time Carlyle had done with this absorbing renewal of the past: and the problem then recurred of what was to be done in the present. Doctor John stayed with him through the summer, and would have been willing to stay longer: but even in his grief-stricken isolation Carlyle did not contemplate a permanent establishment with his brother. "It is certain that you and I have given one another considerable annoyance, and have never yet been able to do *together*", he wrote frankly after John had gone back to Scotland. He found an old refuge in the necessity of living according to the facts of their own natures, and warned his brother that "the facts will be very rigid when we try them." The facts, perhaps mercifully, were never tried. Carlyle remained at Cheyne Row with two maids to cook and keep the house in order, until his niece Mary Carlyle Aitken came in 1868 to act as his amanuensis and housekeeper until the end of his life.

In August he went to stay near Walmer with a friend of Jane's named Miss Davenport Bromley, and in the winter he accepted Lady Ashburton's invitation to the house she had taken at Mentone. Tyndall insisted on planning the journey and on accompanying him, although he would have time to stay for only a few hours after depositing Carlyle at Mentone. Tyndall helped with the packing, argued vainly with Carlyle about the proper method of packing the fifty churchwarden pipes he was taking; and, one hopes, refrained from comment when only three of the fifty arrived unbroken. Tyndall, also, attended to a creaking window in Paris, wrapped Carlyle in a sheepskin bag on the train journey south, and gave him a demonstration of the effects of synchronism in periodic motion in the vibrations of the water bottle on the train. At Mentone Carlyle listened patiently while Tyndall explained to him contemporary scientific theories of the blue of the sky, and then asked questions which surprised the scientist by their penetration and perception.

When Tyndall had gone Carlyle returned to writing a memoir of Edward Irving, which he had begun at Cheyne Row. He followed it with a memoir of Jeffrey, and then made notes on his meetings with Southey and Wordsworth. He was much pleased by Mentone, and by the little separate house which Lady Ashburton had provided for him to live in: this was the first time he had spent the winter in a warm climate and his Calvinism surrendered, in old age, to the purity of air and light. In the rich, bright, luxuriant scene he recreated more of his own past in the memoirs of Irving and Jeffrey. These too are extraordinary autobiographical performances, in their vivid rendering of the youth and early manhood through which he had lived so miserably, yet with such firm belief in his own genius. In writing of both these men he was reminded continually of Jane; of that day nearly fifty years ago when Irving had taken him to Haddington, of Jeffrey's delightful visit to Craigenputtock when Jane told him that she had cooked with her own hands the fritters he was eating, of a dozen or a hundred other scenes. But at last these fictions became, not merely painful, but even wearisome to him. He abandoned the piece on Wordsworth with the words: "Why should I continue these melancholy jottings in which I have no interest; in which the one Figure that could interest me is . . . wanting! I will cease." And in his journal he noted: "My poor life seems as good as over. I have no heart or strength of hope or of interest for further work."

CHAPTER TWENTY

A LONG TIME DYING

On the whole, I feel often, as if poor England had really done its very kindest to me, after all.

THOMAS CARLYLE: *Reminiscences*.

"It's no use contradicting Carlyle. He is so great, and so old."

T. H. HUXLEY in conversation.

HIS LIFE WAS over, but he did not die. For nearly fifteen years after Jane's death the old man lived, bodily in remarkably good health, mentally deprived of the driving force, the violent irrational energy, that had informed his earlier years. He accepted with resignation, tinged with mild pleasure, the many honours paid him; his talk was still thought by many to be the most wonderful they had ever heard—and now nobody even attempted to argue with him; he waited for death with a patience he had rarely shown in the full vigour of literary activity. Such activity too was almost over. The last important literary fling of the angry man came in 1867, when the extension of the franchise brought about by Disraeli's Reform Bill moved him to write a furious pamphlet called *Shooting Niagara: and After?* Here he attacked once again the principle on which "Count of Heads" was deemed to be "the Divine Court of Appeal on every question and interest of mankind", and described Disraeli as "a superlative Hebrew Conjuror, spell-binding all the great Lords, great Parties, great Interests of England, to his hand . . . and leading them by the nose, like helpless mesmerised somnambulent cattle." Yet Disraeli was almost preferable to Gladstone, "the People's William", who seemed to him quite perfectly representative of "the multitudinous cants of the age." And he repeated once more his old message that the only hope for Britain lay in the aristocracy, "the noble Few, who we always trust will be born to us, generation after generation; and on whom and whose living of a noble and valiantly cosmic life amidst the worst impediments and hugest anarchies, the whole of our hope depends."

The language was as violent as that of *Latter-Day Pamphlets*: but it did not cause the same storm. By the mysterious transmutation that has taken place in the reputation of more than one British thinker in the last two centuries the general recognition of Carlyle's greatness absolved admirers from the need to take him seriously. "They call me a great man", he said to Froude, "but not one does what I have told them." Now he spoke to them no more. A letter to *The Times* at the time of the Franco-Prussian War, elaborating a verbal comparison of France with Satan and of Prussia with St. Michael, one or two more letters on the occasion of the Russo-Turkish War, some mild historical studies of the Kings of Norway, and his public utterances were at an end.

The silent prophet was not unhonoured. One day in 1869 Dean Stanley drove up to Cheyne Row with his wife Lady Augusta, to tell Carlyle that a very high, indeed the very highest, personage had expressed a wish to meet him; and he understood that he was bidden to an audience with the Queen. Punctually he presented himself at the Deanery door, and at 5 o'clock the Queen "came gliding into the room in a swimming sort of way, no feet visible", attended by the Princess Louise and the Dowager Duchess of Atholl. The geologist Sir Charles Lyell and the historian Grote, with their wives, were at the party, and so too was Browning. The Queen spoke a word or two to each of them: to Browning, who had just published his immensely long poem, *The Ring and the Book*, she said, "Are you writing anything?" The ladies sat down, the men were left standing, and black, muddy coffee was handed round. It was nearly six o'clock when Carlyle, who was unused to standing so long, was called by Lady Augusta Stanley to speak with the Queen. She began by saying that the Scotch were an intelligent people, but Carlyle replied that they were like others, neither much better nor much worse. There was an awkward silence, which was broken by Carlyle's saying: "We will carry on the subject with greater ease if Your Majesty will allow me as an old infirmish man to sit down." To the horror of the company he drew forward a chair, and sat down. It was, the scandalized but admiring Lady Augusta said, certainly the first time such a request had been made of the Queen by a subject. The conversation proceeded, but not smoothly: and when the Queen rose to retire it was discovered that her dress was caught under Carlyle's chair.

The interview, Dean Stanley said afterwards, had not been a great success; and when Gerald Blunt, the Rector of Chelsea, asked Carlyle if the Queen had read his books, he replied: "She may have read many books, but I do not think she has read mine." Five years later, however, the Queen readily concurred when Disraeli suggested that Carlyle should be offered a pension and the Grand Cross of the Bath, at the same time that a baronetcy was offered to Tennyson. The offer showed high personal generosity on Disraeli's part, in view of Carlyle's persistent vilification of him; and this was the aspect of the affair which upon the whole most impressed Carlyle. "I do . . . truly admire the magnanimity of Dizzy in regard to me", he wrote to Doctor John. "He is the only man I almost never spoke of except with contempt, and if there is anything of scurrility anywhere chargeable against me, I am sorry to own he is the subject of it; and yet see, here he comes with a pan of hot coals for my guilty head!" The offer itself he refused, without further thought than to wait until Tennyson had decided against accepting the baronetcy. "Except the feeling of your fine and noble conduct on this occasion, which is a real and permanent possession, there cannot be anything to be done that would not now be a sorrow rather than a pleasure", he wrote to Disraeli. He had recently accepted, it was true, the Prussian Order of Merit: but that, he said to Froude, was a reality, given for merit only, while the Grand Cross would be like a cap and bells to him. Disraeli's and Carlyle's letters were published, and it was felt that much credit was due to both of them. The philosopher was now a known and highly respected figure in Chelsea. "Fine old gentleman that who got in along with you", a bus conductor said to Froude, "we thinks a deal of him down in Chelsea, we does."

Froude in these days was his chief companion on walks or in conversation. Himself a historian with a strong dramatic sense, Froude submitted much of his work to Carlyle, who made comments that were both acute and tolerant. The picture that Froude shows us of Carlyle differs from most others in stressing his compassion in practice for the vagabonds with whom in theory he had no sympathy. The man who in the past had been accustomed to leave two guineas on his mantelpiece when Leigh Hunt came to call, so that the essayist could take them without the pain of asking, gave money to all whom he saw in distress. "We should give for our own sakes", he said to Froude, after they had given money to a blind beggar whose dog led him straight to a public house. "It is very low water with the wretched beings, one can easily see that." He gave lectures, accompanied by sixpences, to ragged children who shot off down dubious alleys with the coins. Once in Kensington Gardens, when Carlyle was walking with Froude and the American Thomas Wentworth Higginson, a ragged child passed over the two respectably dressed figures, and, fastening on Carlyle in his old felt hat, faded frock coat, check waistcoat and coarse grey trousers, asked: "I say, mister, may we roll on this here grass?" The sage, leaning on his stick, replied: "Yes, my little fellow, roll at discretion."

Next to Froude one of the most frequent, and certainly one of the most persistent, visitors at Cheyne Row was the Irish poet William Allingham. Carlyle had tried for many years to set this sensitive and delicate minor poet on the wholly uncongenial task of writing a history of Ireland. "You may do a very nice book in ten years", he said, and added casually that "Whatever poetic faculty you may have would be shown in this form." Allingham, who was a customs officer during most of his life, "without", he noted sadly, "the least turn for it", dutifully devoted much time to gathering materials, but the history was never written. He was much more interested in making notes which might be used for a biography of Carlyle. "People say Mr. Allingham is to be your Boswell", Mary Aitken said to Carlyle, who replied: "Well, let him try it. He's very accurate." The particular kind of sensibility possessed by Allingham, however, was something Carlyle could not respect; and the poet had to endure a series of knock-down blows upon his most admired writers, and most closely-held beliefs. When Allingham expressed his admiration for Milnes's life of Keats, Carlyle retorted: "That shows you to be a soft-horn"; when Allingham talked about the technique of poetry, Carlyle expressed his contempt for it; when Allingham spoke of Shelley as "a star in his sky", Carlyle calmly said that Shelley had no poetic faculty. It seems, indeed, that Allingham had hardly to express an opinion before Carlyle demolished it: but neither these demolishments nor an unhappy occasion when Carlyle, mistaking Allingham for a chance visitor, called out: "Go away, sir! I can do nothing with you", checked the poet from calling his son Gerald Carlyle Allingham; and his wife Helen was accorded the privilege of painting Carlyle.

Her portraits were as unsuccessful as those of better painters. In 1868 G. F. Watts produced a portrait of Carlyle which the subject described as portraying "a delirious-looking mountebank, full of violence, awkwardness, atrocity, and stupidity, without recognisable likeness to anything I have ever known in any feature of mine." Nine years later Millais produced a portrait which pleased Carlyle, but which the painter abandoned unfinished. By far the best painting of the old man—appreciation of which, however, was obstructed by Carlyle's distaste for the painter—was Whistler's picture of a worn, resigned and somehow Biblical figure, voluminously coated, with felt hat on knee.

In setting down casual conversations Allingham, like Froude, shows us a Carlyle much mellowed and returning in some things to the Radicalism of his youth. To Allingham's surprise and distress Carlyle supported a strike of agricultural labourers in 1872; he expressed himself against the idea of compulsion; he said that on reading *The Rights of Man* he found himself in agreement with Tom Paine. Privately, the old man put down questions in his journal about "American Anarchy". It was huge, loud and ugly, but was it not necessary? Could even a heroic Frederick have done as well by strict government, as this anarchic America "with its gasconadings, vulgarities, stupidities", was now doing? He answered himself: "No; not by any means."

Other friends came often to visit him—Ruskin, Tyndall, Forster, Moncure Conway, Leslie Stephen, Browning. Carlyle read the four volumes of *The Ring and the Book* through from beginning to end without omitting a word. Soon afterwards he met Browning in Piccadilly and told him, with some pride, of this achievement. "Well! Well?" said Browning, and Carlyle told him that it was a book of prodigious talent and unparalleled ingenuity. "Then, I suppose trusting to the sincerity of my own thoughts, I went on to say that of all the strange books produced on this distracted earth, by any of the sons of Adam, this one was altogether the strangest and the most preposterous in its construction; and where, said I, do ye think to find the eternal harmonies in it? Browning did not seem to be pleased with my speech, and he bade me good morning." Turgenev came to Chelsea more than once, and was appreciated by Carlyle as an admirable talker, "by far the best I have ever heard who talks so much." The old man maintained a steady correspondence with Lady Ashburton, although the increasing palsy in his right hand made writing difficult, and at last impossible, so that all of his letters had to be dictated to Mary Aitken. There were many letters to write: to young ladies wanting information about translations of Goethe, young ladies in low spirits who had to be told that the grand remedy was practical work, and of course to literary aspirants, with whom he had little patience. "Mr. Carlyle bids me say that he has never in his life heard a madder proposal than the one you have just made to him", Mary Aitken wrote to one of them. "He would advise you by no means to quit your present employment. He thinks it would be only a degree less foolish than to throw yourself from the top of the Monument in the hope of flying."

He did not lack visitors nor, if he had cared for it, occupation: but for the most part his mind was set firmly in the past, among the life and the people that had passed away. Every year thinned the numbers of those who could revive with him the memories of the past and of Jane. Neuberg died in 1867 and so did John Chorley, who had run so busily up and down ladders superintending the building of the soundproof room; in 1870 Dickens died, and Carlyle said that no death since Jane's had fallen on him with such a stroke; in 1872 passed Mazzini and a year later Mill, leaving for the old man memories agonizing in their clarity, of the flashing-eyed handsome Italian who sat on the sofa at Cheyne Row and talked of the solidarity of peoples, and of the earnestly-smiling modest young Mill from whom he had somehow become utterly estranged. "Carlyle turned against all his friends", Mill said to Moncure Conway, but in a personal sense it was Mill who had turned against Carlyle. Talking to the American Charles Eliot Norton, the old man spoke ramblingly of Mill's merits, his tenderness, his generosity, his modesty, his willing help with *The French Revolution*; and writing to his brother John he said that "A great black sheet of mournful more or less tragic memories . . . rushed down upon me: Poor Mill, he too has worked out his Life Drama in sight of me; and that scene, too, has closed before my old eyes." On his eightieth birthday a hundred and nineteen admirers (the list of names included Allingham, Browning, the two Darwins, George Eliot, Forster, Huxley, Harriet Martineau, Richard Quain, Tennyson, Anthony Trollope and Tyndall) presented him with a gold medallion portrait and an address which said that he had sustained in his own life the dignity of the Hero as Man of Letters. A letter came from Bismarck, praising the biography of Frederick, and also referring to the Hero as Author. Lady Ashburton and some other friends presented him with a clock. "Eh, what have I got to do with Time any more?" he said.

*   *   *   *   *

Hé had little, indeed, to do with anything any more. The last six years of his life show a gradual, and in general quiet and calm, progress down the road to desired death. Walking for more than a few hundred yards became impossible for him; he lost almost completely the power of his right hand; with the knowledge that death was approaching him more nearly came a calm acceptance of the duties and obligations in this world which he had once found unbearably tedious. He attended within a few weeks the funeral of Forster and the wedding of Tyndall, now in his fifties. Such attendance he would scarcely have considered, as his friend Edward Fitzgerald said, when a younger and stronger man. He went also to the funeral of Lady Augusta Stanley at Westminster Abbey, when he sat next to the Archbishop of Canterbury. Froude raised the question of his own burial in the Abbey, but Carlyle emphatically refused to consider it, saying: "There will be a general gaol delivery in that place one of these days." He told his brother John that his burial place had been chosen years ago. "It is marked in my Will that I am to rest in the Kirkyard of Ecclefechan, as near as possible to my Father and Mother." In 1876 he had news of the death in Canada of his brother Alick who, with his mind wandering at the last, had asked: "Is Tom coming from Edinburgh the morn?"

So many had been taken, and yet he was left: generally very melancholy, and yet still capable of being stirred to interest and excitement when the journalist W. T. Stead, introduced by the unofficial propagandist for Russia Madame Novikoff, told him that Disraeli, now Lord Beaconsfield, was plotting to embroil Britain in the Russo-Turkish War. Carlyle found himself, in company with the People's William, on the side of the Russians; he had already written a famous letter to *The Times* castigating the Unspeakable Turk, and now his language about Disraeli was as violent as it had ever been. At Stead's revelation, or invention, of the Disraelian plot, he was appalled into considering some further literary activity: but although he looked venerably healthy, and his white hair was as thick as it had been forty years ago, he had, as he told Stead, no more work to do. He was unable to write, and found dictation impossible. "I use twice as many words and don't make my meaning half as clear. I must just wait and suffer until I ám called hence." To Helen Allingham he said one day, on taking leave of her: "Well, ma'am, I wish you all prosperity, and that you may not live to be eightytwo." He spent much time in re-reading Shakespeare, Goethe and Gibbon.

Gradually he grew weaker, unable even to dictate letters or to drive out. Ruskin came to see him, and kissed the hands of the man whom he still called the Master. When Froude said that Carlyle must not catch cold, he answered that he wished to catch cold and die and be well out of it. But he did not catch cold, he did not die; he recovered, went up to Scotsbrig to see Doctor John, who was very ill and had had a doctor to examine him: "but you know he has no belief in medical skill", Carlyle said. During the summer the brothers met almost daily: but soon after his return to Chelsea Carlyle had news of John's death. No doubt he felt the loss deeply; but he was no longer able to put down his sorrows in a journal.

Now he became very weak. His part in conversation—he who had been accustomed to beat down interrupters with his raised voice—was limited to answering questions as briefly as possible. When Sir Bartle Frere wrote to ask for an interview on behalf of the Prince of Wales Carlyle refused it. "I am too old. He might as well come and see my poor old dead body", he said. He found it increasingly difficult to take food, could hardly rise to his feet, and spoke so quietly that those who were with him had to bend close to catch his words. In these last months —it was not for weeks, but for months, that he lingered— he pondered the possibility of the existence of hell fire. His father, after all, had believed quite literally in the reality of Hell: and he had known no wiser man than his father. But neither this nor any other speculation much occupied him. When Froude came and told him of new troubles in Ireland, he listened indifferently. "These things do not interest you?" Froude asked, and he answered: "Not in the least." Tyndall brought brandy and a cigar, which the old man puffed with pleasure. Soon after his eightyfifth birthday his bed was moved to the drawing-room. He became unable to assimilate any food, and lived on brandy and water and ether. In this state he survived for three weeks, attended by his niece and her husband, visited by friends to whom he could hardly speak. Bulletins were pinned up outside the house to discourage visitors. At last, on Thursday February 2nd he fell into a deep sleep unbroken except for a moment, when his niece heard him say, "So this is Death—well . . ." He lay in a coma for nearly two days; and then on Saturday morning, between 8 and 9 o'clock, his long journey ended.

THE PROPHET'S FATE

Just then we passed along Church Lane, where Swift used to live, and Carlyle began to talk about him with much feeling. He declared Swift a man of the finest force of every kind, and spoke bitterly of the way in which he had been swamped under "the pressure of an evil time"; then added with a sigh, "but his case is not that of one alone."

MONCURE CONWAY: *Autobiography*.

HE WAS BURIED THEN, as he had wished, at Ecclefechan, with snow gently powdering the grave: the news of his death brought tributes from the whole civilized world. They were tributes to the thinker, the moralist, the seer; but also to the man whose life was believed to exemplify so many nineteenth century virtues—thrift, manliness and perfect honesty high among them—which were the basis, axiomatically, of a contented mind and a clear conscience. Within a few weeks of his death these ideas were upset by the publication of his *Reminiscences* under the editorship of Froude: that is, of the notes on Wordsworth and Southey, the essays on his father, Jeffrey and Irving, and the lengthy semi-autobiographical biography of Jane. Literary men were annoyed by the sharp comments on their trade and its practitioners; but interest was focused particularly on the account of Jane, and the remorse evidently felt by Carlyle for his treatment of her.

How was it that these *Reminiscences* were published when Carlyle in 1866 placed an interdict upon their publication "without fit editing"? In the course of years he had come to rely more and more on the judgement of Froude. He made Froude one of his three executors, together with Forster and his brother John, and after they had died made him joint executor with Fitzjames Stephen. In 1871 he gave Froude a large parcel of papers, saying that after his death they might be published or destroyed, as his executors thought fit. The papers consisted of the biography of Jane, some other biographical fragments, and a large collection of Jane's letters to which Carlyle had added notes, comments and explanations. "The perusal was infinitely affecting", Froude said, and he regarded the attempted construction of these fragments into an ordered whole as a gallant attempt by Carlyle to "remove the shadow between himself and her memory." He told Carlyle that letters and memoir should both be published posthumously; and to this the old man agreed.

So runs Froude's story, which there is no reason to disbelieve: but he was moved also, in urging the publication, and later in writing the biography upon which Carlyle knew him to be working, by a personal zest for the expiation of guilt. The childhood of Froude, like that of many notable Victorians, had been deeply unhappy. His mother died before he was three years old; and the weak, sickly child was beaten whenever he was naughty, and ducked every morning in ice-cold water to harden him. His father, the Archdeacon of Totnes, immersed in grief, ignored him; his harsh, brilliant elder brother Hurrell, played a part in the hardening process by throwing him out of a boat into deep water, and by holding him upside down with his head in mud; he was subjected to savage torments at his public school. From all this Froude emerged, much scathed in spirit, accepting and assimilating into his nature all that had been done to him. His mind was drawn naturally, like Carlyle's, to the blessings of despotic rule; and his *History of England to the Armada*, which made Froude the most popular living historian, enthusiastically advocated the subjection of Church to State.

There was, however, another side to Froude beside the Puritan harshness and disregard for pain that made Carlyle's ideas attractive to him. Gentle, compassionate, and highly sympathetic to women, he had a capacity for sharp and severe treatment of his own friends, hidden behind a deceptive blandness of manner. Allingham was unpleasantly surprised by a notice of his poems in *Fraser's Magazine*, of which Froude was then editor. "What does Froude mean, after all his private cream and sugar?" he asked his diary. Such a man, in writing of Carlyle, would be especially careful that hero-worship should not stand in the way of a conscientiously accurate portrait.

It was thus that when the first two volumes of Froude's eagerly-awaited biography appeared in 1882, Carlyle's admirers were distressed, and the whole reading world astonished. For Froude, the most faithful and next to Ruskin by far the most distinguished of the sage's disciples, had portrayed a self-pitying, cantankerous and egotistical figure; a man preoccupied by furious inner convictions, who often made life miserable for those closely associated with him. All this was put down, in the four volumes of Froude's biography (for the last two volumes, which appeared in 1884, upon the whole darkened the picture's colours), with a frankness shocking and surprising to the age in which he lived. Froude made no attempt to conceal Jane's unhappiness; he excerpted from letters opinions of Carlyle's about his contemporaries expressed, generally, in even stronger terms than those in the *Reminiscences*. And in 1883 the publication of Jane's *Letters and Memorials* intensified the impression that her life had been a peculiarly hard one.

The subsequent controversy continued for years. It centred particularly upon the propriety of publishing such intimate letters and materials at all, and upon the accuracy of Froude's interpretation of the Carlyles' life together. Carlyle's niece Mary and her husband Alexander (son of the Alick Carlyle who had emigrated to Canada) were particularly indignant. They made a determined, but unsuccessful, attempt to stop Froude from completing his biography by getting back the materials which Carlyle had entrusted to him; they obtained the copyright of the *Reminiscences* and sponsored a new edition edited by Charles Eliot Norton, in which many trivial errors made by Froude were corrected; and Alexander Carlyle occupied himself for many years with editing new volumes of Carlyleana, designed to show the untruth of Froude's picture. David Alec Wilson, in a vast six volume biography of Carlyle published at intervals between 1923 and 1934, was even more emphatic about Froude's errors of fact and interpretation: the Carlyles' married life, he said, had been little else than a long honeymoon.

The sound and the fury have died away; the indiscretions of which Froude was accused must seem to us ludicrous, the minor factual errors of which he was convicted are of little importance; but the whole controversy has had its effect upon the general, unformed and uninformed view of Carlyle which is held at the present day. The effect of Froude's brilliant but over-dramatic biography, together with the *Reminiscences* and several collections of letters, has been to shift interest from the work to the man, and to create a picture, which has only a limited truth, of a half-mad figure with some unpleasant racial theories, whose genius lay chiefly in making other people unhappy. Such, at present, is the prophet's fate: one ironic enough

for a man who was anxious that no biography of him should be
written, and said that he would as soon think of cutting his
throat with a penknife as of writing his own autobiography.

*   *   *   *   *

The most obvious, and the most peculiarly modern, approach
to Carlyle is through a consideration of his temperament, which
ignores as far as possible his writings. The psychological influences which acted on him, from childhood onwards, have
been charted very generally in this book; the effects of his
various frustrations on his attitude towards life, politics and
other human beings, has been suggested. Yet the analysis
which reduces Carlyle merely to the level of a psycho-pathological case is unsatisfactory: he was a psycho-pathological case
undoubtedly, but he was a great deal more than that. He was as
much a victim of his period as of his temperament. It must
always appear extraordinary to laymen that psychiatry, in
endeavouring to heal the mentally sick, shows little appreciation of the fact that the society of which they are a part has its
springs in neurosis. Is it not, then, ridiculous to attempt to
produce healthy individuals within it? Has not the character of
Western European society enforced, for a hundred years and
more, neurosis in its artists?

The influence of nineteenth century society in shaping
Carlyle was certainly great: although it is true that there was an
interaction, by which he appeared to play a part in shaping
society. Carlyle spoke to Moncure Conway of "the pressure of
an evil time" upon Swift, and there is of course a sense in which
any society exerts pressure on its artists: but it is, roughly, after
the first thirty years of the nineteenth century that popular art
becomes less an expression of popular feeling and more an
article manufactured deliberately for mass consumption, and
that "art" begins to become the prerogative of a caste. The
process moved slowly in mid-Victorian England, but it was at
work nevertheless; both social and personal pressures operated
to make Carlyle's extraordinary style, the symbol at once of a
confused mind and a divided society. Such pressures worked to
induce this man, who desperately believed that he had a
message of prophetic importance to deliver, to issue it in a
language sometimes resembling that of those Irvingites who
were granted the gift of tongues.

The reasons for reading Carlyle today—distinct, as far as they can be, from the interest of his life story—rest in his social message: not, however, as the kind of divinely-inspired prophecy that he imagined it, but as an explanation of social action far nearer to reality than that produced by his contemporaries. Taken upon his own terms Carlyle's approach to the problems of society and history was exceedingly odd. He was indignant always when it was said that he believed that right was might: his opinion, he answered angrily, was that right is "the eternal symbol of might". Such was the principle upon which he found a meaning in history. Right must triumph in the end, since the world had been made by God; evildoers would in the end be punished, the power of the wicked give way to the power of the virtuous: but what, after all, was "the end"? The divinely-inspired Carlyle alone could make a correct distinction between virtuous Frederick and his obtuse opponents, virtuous Cromwell and the society he helped to overthrow. Carlyle was rarely attacked upon such a ground, for the Victorian age had great respect for the self-proclaimed seer: but upon those rare occasions he fell back on rhetoric, or on his relation with God.

This relation he was never able to put down to his own satisfaction, or to that of anybody else. Nobody was ever able to answer that question of Erasmus Darwin's: "What the deuce is Carlyle's religion, or has he any?" Carlyle said repeatedly to the end of his life that Gibbon had taught him the untruth of Christianity; he disbelieved in a resurrection; except for a brief faltering when near to death, he thought it was a great gain to have abolished the idea of hell. He had not attended a place of worship for many years. And yet: "I find lying deep in me withal some confused but ineradicable flicker of belief that there is a 'particular providence.' Sincerely I do, as it were, believe this, to my own surprise." That is a mild enough expression of belief: much more strongly he thought that belief in a supreme being was vitally important to human welfare. Reversing Bakunin's heresy, he might have said that if God did not exist, it would be necessary to invent him.

This, in effect, was what he did: the conclusions he arrived at about the nature and proper ordering of society are those which might have been reached by an atheist. Once the answers had been found, he gave them the seal of divine approval. His intellect was slow in comprehension, but extraordinarily wide in range; his learning was immense; by their aid, and through the circumstances of his early life, he gained an insight into the nature of society with which his religious beliefs or hopes had nothing to do. In a time when most thinkers believed that the world could be changed by goodwill he understood the basis of force upon which all modern societies rest. In a time when political economists thought that the industrial revolution must bring automatically an increase in prosperity, he realized that it would involve the overturn of established society. In a time of continual abstract arguments about the amount of liberty that might reasonably be allowed to human beings, he saw that liberties are obtained by one social class at the expense of another and that they are not abstract ideas but concrete realities. And in spite of his formal belief in God, he had no liking for any existing religion.

Such were the insights of Thomas Carlyle into the nature of the future: insights which were reached through intellectual power and logical thinking. Such insights can be variously used. In Carlyle's case they were turned from respect for the mass of people into contempt for them; from hatred of a game-shooting aristocracy into hope that from such an aristocracy might come the saviour of Britain; from a generous view of human potentialities into the vicarious sadistic lust for power of a disappointed man. These are sad things to record; but they do not render invalid the special and peculiar insights of Carlyle. He rubbed the wrong lamps: but he was a great magician.

THE END

SELECT BIBLIOGRAPHY

(Note: This Bibliography includes only a selection from works of particular biographical interest in relation to the Carlyles. Critical or general books used have not been included.)

ALLINGHAM, WILLIAM. *William Allingham, A Diary.* Edited by H. Allingham and D. Radford. (Macmillan, 1907.)

ARCHIBALD, R. C. *Carlyle's First Love, Margaret Gordon Lady Bannerman.* (John Lane The Bodley Head, 1910.)

BROOKFIELD, CHARLES AND FRANCES. *Mrs. Brookfield and Her Circle.* 2 vols. (Pitman, 1905.)

CARLYLE, JANE WELSH. *Letters and Memorials.* Prepared for publication by Thomas Carlyle and edited by James Anthony Froude. 3 vols. (Longmans, Green, 1883.)

—— *New Letters and Memorials.* Edited by Alexander Carlyle, with an introduction by Sir James Crichton-Browne. 2 vols. (John Lane The Bodley Head, 1903.)

—— *Early Letters of Jane Welsh Carlyle.* Edited by G. D. Ritchie. (Swan Sonnenschein, 1899.)

—— *Letters to her Family, 1839-1863.* Edited by Leonard Huxley. (John Murray, 1924.)

—— *Letters of Jane Welsh Carlyle to Joseph Neuberg, 1848-1862.* Edited by Townsend Scudder. (O.U.P., 1931.)

CARLYLE, THOMAS. *Reminiscences.* Edited by James Anthony Froude. 2 vols. (Longmans, Green, 1881.)

—— *Reminiscences.* Edited by Charles Eliot Norton. 2 vols. (Macmillan, 1887)

—— *Early Letters of Thomas Carlyle, 1814-1826.* Edited by Charles Eliot Norton. 2 vols. (Macmillan, 1886.)

—— *Letters of Thomas Carlyle, 1826-1836.* Edited by Charles Eliot Norton. 2 vols. (Macmillan, 1888.)

—— *New Letters of Thomas Carlyle.* Edited and annotated by Alexander Carlyle. 2 vols. (John Lane The Bodley Head, 1904.)

—— *Love Letters of Thomas Carlyle and Jane Welsh.* Edited by Alexander Carlyle. 2 vols. (John Lane The Bodley Head, 1909.)

CARLYLE, THOMAS. *Letters of Thomas Carlyle to his Youngest Sister.* Edited by Charles Townsend Copeland. (Chapman and Hall, 1899.)

—— *Correspondence between Goethe and Carlyle.* Edited by Charles Eliot Norton. (Macmillan, 1887.)

—— *Correspondence of Thomas Carlyle and R. W. Emerson.* 2 vols. (Chatto and Windus, 1883.)

—— *Letters to John Stuart Mill, John Sterling and Robert Browning.* Edited by Alexander Carlyle. (Fisher Unwin, 1923.)

—— *Letters of Thomas Carlyle to William Graham.* Edited by John Graham, Jr. (Princeton U.P., 1950.)

—— *Last Words of Thomas Carlyle.* (Longmans, Green, 1892.)

CONWAY MONCURE D. *Thomas Carlyle.* (Chatto and Windus, 1881.)

—— *Autobiography* (Cassell, 1904.)

DUFFY, SIR CHARLES GAVAN. *Conversations with Carlyle.* (Sampson, Low, Marston, 1892.)

ESPINASSE, FRANCIS. *Literary Recollections and Sketches* (Hodder and Stoughton, 1893.)

FROUDE, JAMES ANTHONY. *Thomas Carlyle, 1795-1835.* 2 vols. (Longmans, Green, 1882.)

—— *Thomas Carlyle, 1834-1881.* 2 vols. (Longmans, Green, 1884.)

—— *My Relations with Carlyle.* (Longmans, Green, 1903.)

HOUGHTON, LORD. *Monographs, Personal and Social.* (John Murray, 1873.)

HOWE, SUSANNA. *Geraldine Jewsbury.* (Allen and Unwin, 1935.)

IRELAND, MRS. ALEXANDER. *Life of Jane Welsh Carlyle.* (Chatto and Windus, 1891.)

JEWSBURY, GERALDINE. *Selections from the Letters of Geraldine Endsor Jewsbury to Jane Welsh Carlyle.* Edited by Mrs. Alexander Ireland. (Longmans, Green, 1892.)

LARKIN, HENRY. *Carlyle and The Open Secret of His Life.* (Kegan Paul, 1886.)

MASSON, DAVID. *Carlyle Personally and in His Writings.* (Macmillan, 1885.)

NICHOL, JOHN. *Thomas Carlyle.* (Macmillan, 1902.)

ORIGO, IRIS. *The Carlyles and the Ashburtons.* (The Cornhill, Autumn, 1950.)

SHEPHERD, RICHARD HERNE. *Memoirs of The Life and Writings of Thomas Carlyle.* 2 vols. (W. H. Allen, 1881.)

SYMINGTON, ANDREW JAMES. *Some Personal Reminiscences of Carlyle.* (Alex. Gardner, 1886.)

TYNDALL, JOHN. *New Fragments.* (Longmans, Green, 1892.)

WILSON, DAVID ALEC. *The Truth about Carlyle.* (Alston Rivers, 1913.)

—— *Carlyle till Marriage, 1795-1826.* (Kegan Paul, Trench, Trubner, 1923.)

—— *Carlyle to the French Revolution, 1826-1837.* (Kegan Paul, Trench, Trubner, 1924.)

—— *Carlyle on Cromwell and Others, 1837-1848.* (Kegan Paul, Trench, Trubner, 1925.)

—— *Carlyle at his Zenith, 1848-1853.* (Kegan Paul, Trench, Trubner, 1927.)

—— *Carlyle to Threescore-and-Ten, 1853-1865.* (Kegan Paul, Trench, Trubner, 1929.)

—— (with DAVID WILSON MACARTHUR). *Carlyle in Old Age, 1865-1881.* (Kegan Paul, Trench, Trubner, 1934.)

INDEX

ADAM BEDE, 270
Aesop's *Fables*, 136
Aitken, James, 62
Aitken, Mrs. James (Carlyle's sister Jane), 111, 218
Aitken, Mrs. James. *See* Bess Stodart.
Aitken, Margaret. *See* Margaret Carlyle.
Aitken, Mary Carlyle. *See* Mrs. Alexander Carlyle.
Albert, Prince Consort meets Carlyle, 251-2. Mentioned, 253
Alcott, Bronson, 175
Allingham, G. C., 284
Allingham, Helen, 284-5, 288
Allingham, William, at Cheyne Row, 241; friendship with C., 284-5. Mentioned, 286, 291
Ambrosianae Noctes, 107
America and Her Resources, 50
Amours des Voyages, 216
Analysis of the Human Mind, 136
Angus, Robby, 62
Annan Academy, 27-8, 33-4
Arabian Nights, 136
Aristotle, 136
Arnold, Doctor, admires *French Revolution*, 181. Mentioned, 201
Ashburton, Lady (Lady Harriet Baring), character, 193; first meeting with C., 194, and with Jane, 194; appearance, 195; attitude to Jane, 195-6; relationship with C., 204-9; treats Jane as hypochondriac, 235; tactful at a Christmas party, 236; less tactful at another, 252-3; journey to Scotland with C.s, 254; death, 255. Mentioned, 211, 217, 224, 245, 246, 249, 251, 257
Ashburton, Lady (the second Lady Ashburton), marriage, 265; friendship with Cs., 265-7; visits Jane after illness, 270; C.'s hostess at Mentone, 279-80. Mentioned, 286, 287
Ashburton, Lord (Bingham Baring's father), 193, 196
Ashburton, Lord (Hon. W. B. Baring), 193, 205, 207, 209, 211, 217, 224, 228, 235, 243, 252-4, 259, 262, 265, 268
Atholl, Dowager Duchess of, 282
Austin, Mrs. James (Carlyle's sister Mary), 20, 265, 269

Badams, John, 87, 134
Baird, James, 62
Bakunin, 294
Ballantyne, Thomas, 205
Bannerman, Alexander, 54
Baring, Lady Harriet. *See* Lady Ashburton.
Barnes, Dr., 262, 267
Barnes, Miss, 264-5

Barnet, Bessy, 146, 268
Biographie Universelle, 153
Bismarck, 287
Blackiston, Dr., 268, 272
Blackwood's, Carlyle on, 143. Mentioned, 107
Blake, William, 225, 259
Blunt, Gerald, 273, 283
Boehme, 225
Bonn University, 233
Bossuet, 35
Boswell, James, 224, 285
Bowring, John, 135
Brewster, Sir David, gives C. work, 49, 55, 70; visits Cs. at Comley Bank, 106. Mentioned, 14, 48, 109
Brienne, Loménie de, 159
Bright, John, 18, 211
Bromley, Miss Davenport, 279
Brougham, Viscount, 107, 129, 156, 163
Brown, Professor, 33
Browning, Robert, admirer of C., 165; sends him poems, 166; resents remarks about *Ring and the Book*, 285. Mentioned, 133, 175, 223, 237, 271, 282
Buchanan, Craig, 62
Buckle, 223, 224
Bull, Mr., 260-1
Buller, Arthur, 69
Buller, Charles, taught by C., 69, 82, 84; visits Cheyne Row, 149; recommends C. to read *Pickwick*, 165; brings Milnes to Chelsea, 167; at Radical meeting, 178; death, 217. Mentioned, 136, 138, 150, 194, 205, 231
Buller, Mrs., engages C. as tutor, 69; introduces Jane to Lady Harriet, 194; death, 218. Mentioned, 79-80, 81, 84, 89, 210
Buller, Mr., 79, 84, 109, 218
Buller, Reginald, 198
Bunsen, 163
Buonaparte, Napoleon, 157, 162
Burns, Robert, 123, 162, 265
Butler, Mrs. Pierce, 156
Butler, Samuel, 103
Byron, Lord, 36, 62, 71, 123, 170

Cagliostro, C.'s essay on, 141
Campbell, Mary, 138
Campbell, Thomas, 55, 81, 82-3
Canning, 76
Canterbury, Archbishop of, 287
Cardale, John, 150
Carlyle, Alick (C.'s brother), farming Craigenputtock, 110, 111, 118; lack of success, 128; opens shop in Ecclefechan, 184; emigrates to Canada, 206; death, 287. Mentioned, 55, 63, 76, 86, 90, 93, 96, 106, 117, 292